SNAPSHOTS FROM MEMORY

THE AUTOBIOGRAPHY OF A GREENOCK ACADEMY SCHOOLBOY

JO JOHNSON

Rosebine Press

Published by Rosebine Press
www.rosebinepress.com

A catalogue record for this book is available from the
British Library.

ISBN 978-0-9536238-8-4

Cover by Jo Johnson
Large Print Hardback First Edition

CONTENTS

PREFACE

even when I am old and grayheaded, O God, for-
sake me not; until I have declared your
strength unto the next generation, your might
to every one that is to come.

PSALM 71:18

The chapter headings in this book are the pegs on which
I've hung this collection of personal memories. Inevitably,
there is some overlap and, like my cover photograph,
which a curious child once experimented on to find out if
Dad's paper punch actually worked, it's an uneven picture and there are a few holes in it. For example, my de-
scriptions of the important people in my life can only ever
be like a series of snapshots or sketches for a painting.
What's left out is often just as important as what's left in.
The sum of their lives, character, personalities and
achievements is beyond mere words. Memory is notori-
ously subjective. As Queen Elizabeth said recently, "Recollections may vary." But perhaps my scattered musings

will give readers some insights into the people and events that shaped the course of my life and contributed to the formation of the convictions and beliefs I hold.

However, it's easy to view the past through rose-tinted spectacles. I know my parents gave me the best start in life. Even so, 'not everything in the garden was rosy'. I have presented the facts about certain incidents with minimal analysis or comment, and I'm reminded of Ecclesiastes 7:10 "Do not say, "Why were the former days better than these?" For you do not inquire wisely concerning this." With that proviso, I have two primary intentions in writing this book. First, to reflect on my life's experiences and learn from them myself, or give readers food for thought when they encounter similar situations. Second, to leave a written legacy for my children and grandchildren. My opinions are just that. Others are at liberty to form their own.

This book comes with a 'don't try this at home' warning. Some things we got up to as children went beyond normal childish pranks. We deserved—and got—severe punishment when we were found out. I debated with myself whether to put these in or leave them out. I left them in because they show that even at a young age, the propensity for sin is latent in the human heart and only needs circumstance and opportunity to be given action. To me, God's grace is even more wonderful when I think of His mercy and love for a sinner like me.

> The 'Notes' section at the end of this book explains some 'common parlance' words used by brethren and sisters[1] in the Churches of God. I've also used the notes section to amplify a miscellany of other details.

1 EARLIEST MEMORIES

A gentle light diffused my parents' bedroom. Perhaps it was the day I was born. I just remember feeling peaceful, secure, and contented.

~

MY NAME IS JO JOHNSON. Full name, Peter Joseph Johnson, after my two grandfathers, but I've always been called Jo.

I was born in the front bedroom of the ground-floor flat at 19 Bentinck Street, Greenock, on 25th February 1957.

19 Bentinck Street, Greenock.

I was the first of five children, four boys and a girl, born to Mum and Dad between 1957 and 1963. In order of birth, my siblings are James, William, John and Elisabeth. Mercifully, perhaps, most of my earliest memories have disappeared into the mists of time. Only a few snapshots remain—some are actual photographs taken by Mum or Dad, others are memories, imprinted with greater or lesser detail on my mind.

∾

Dad and Mum on Octavia Terrace. I'm in the driving seat, James facing Dad and Mum, baby William inside pram.

MUM'S FATHER, Peter Christison, came to live with us for two or three years before he died. Until he retired, he was the Head Gardener at Milton Lockhart estate in the Clyde Valley. We called him Grandad. I remember him sitting on the sandstone wall outside the house, dabbing the end of a dandelion stalk on his tongue. He liked the bitter taste and used it as an herbal aid to health. Another time, he was eating an apple. When I imitated the way he munched it, he laughed and exaggerated the munching for my entertainment. Mum told me he wanted to see me going to school before he died. He got his wish.

Mum and Dad also brought Grandad's sister (Mum's Aunt Mary), to stay with us when she could no longer look after herself. I only ever remember her lying in bed—but she was always pleased to see us children when we ventured into her room.

Dad was teaching Maths at the Mount School at the time but had rented a shop in Cathcart Street, which he stocked with drapery goods and children's clothes. He employed a girl to work in it during the day. Grandad was so keen to see Dad's new venture, he walked all the way from Bentinck Street to the shop and back again. Mum said it was too much for him. She thought the extra effort had damaged his heart. He became ill and was confined to bed. Whenever he wanted anything, he took his knobbly brown walking stick, whacked the end of the bed

Grandad, keeping an eye on me and James in the pram

and shouted "Jean!—Jean!" Eventually it was too much for Mum to look after him. An ambulance arrived and took him to Larkfield Hospital where he died of heart failure some weeks later. He told Mum his heart was 'done'. She visited him a day or two before he died and said, "If it's the Lord's will Dad, you'll get better." He knew different and said sharply, "Jean! Speak the truth!"

As a Christian, Grandad was a conscientious objector during the first World War. When he stood before the tribunal, the judge said, "What would you do if the Germans came and started killing your family?" He answered: "It would be a quick despatch to glory." The judge gave him work of National Importance in Forestry.

At one of our Bible conferences, some young people were sitting in front of Grandad, giggling and laughing. He leaned forward and said, "There'll be nae laughin' in hell."

Harry King told me that Grandad had some memorable turns of phrase when he prayed, such as "We lift our hearts to Thee as a flower lifts its face to the sun."

Dad related a story Grandad told him, about a carter pulling a heavy load of hay up the Lanark Brae—a steep hill between the Clyde Valley and Lanark. His horse was making heavy weather of it despite the carter's not so gentle efforts to 'encourage' her up the hill. All of a sudden the poor nag collapsed and died. Her master ran to the cart, pulled out a handful of hay, stuck it in the horse's mouth and said, "Well, they cannae say ye deeid 'o hung'ur![1]"

Mum told us her father used to get up before dawn and read his Bible by candlelight.

Grandad with me, James and William

When I was three or four, Mum and Dad sent me to the local nursery school. We called it "Miss Francis". James and William also went there. Miss Francis was both owner and teacher at 'Beltrees Private Kindergarten'—a house on The Esplanade, just around the corner from Bentinck Street. To reach the school, you entered a gate and walked up a long narrow lane with a hedge on one side and a wall on the other. The basement rooms were the schoolrooms and Miss Francis' living quarters were upstairs. She was a diminutive woman with brown hair, intelligent eyes, a gravelly voice and a friendly, smiling face. Her fingers were stained brownish yellow with nicotine. Occasionally she took a coughing fit—a full-blown, rattling smoker's cough.

The day at 'Miss Francis', began in the playroom, which had French windows opening onto the lawn. Then we went through to the schoolroom where we sat at little wooden desks. Each desk had a lid. Inside was a tin of coloured chalk crayons, a small, lined writing jotter and a drawing notebook with pastel papers interleaved with tissue, so that the chalk didn't rub off on the facing page. After morning lessons, there was a milk break. The milk came in a crate of half-pint bottles and had silver foil tops. Patricia Rice, one of the older girls, poked a hole in each foil top with Miss Francis' penknife and pushed a paper straw into each bottle. We 'sooked' our milk with gusto and had a short free-play session. During one play time, I sneaked along the corridor between the schoolroom and the back kitchen and helped myself to some biscuits from Miss Francis' biscuit tin.

After break we sat on the playroom floor around the blackboard, which was mounted on a wooden easel. Every day, Miss Francis told a story, illustrating it with coloured chalk as she went along. I was enthralled. It was the highlight of my day. The stories usually ended when Miss Francis said with a smile, "And they all lived, happily, ever, after." An ending that never failed to satisfy my simple little mind.

At home, we often played in 'the hall', (the entrance hallway of the flat), from which all the other rooms opened. Mum's brother, Uncle John worked at Hairmyres Hospital in Lanarkshire. He was in charge of the engineering workshop attached to the hospital, where they made prosthetic limbs and mobility aids. He had contracted polio himself when in his late teens, and walked with a pronounced limp, using a calliper on his bad leg as well as a walking stick to enable him to get about. His car was specially adapted with apparatus coming up from the footwell to allow him to operate the clutch and gear lever by hand. Uncle John made a set of three wooden lorries for me and my brothers, with our names painted on the front. We used to sit on the lorries and ride them up and down the hall. For Christmas one year, Dad got two red Triang pedal cars for James and me, which we loved.

On Christmas Eve, Dad and Mum gave each of us a pillowcase to hang over the end of our bed. We were so excited we stayed awake for ages. Before he went to bed, Dad crept into our room wearing a red dressing gown and wellington boots, and a cotton-wool beard on his face. He quietly filled our pillowcases with presents. We pretended to be asleep, but all the time enjoying the thrill of seeing 'Santa' arrive. We knew fine it was Dad, but willingly suspended belief to enjoy those magical moments of make-believe. Even though Mum and Dad told us there was really no such person as Santa, they weren't so rigid in their thinking that they couldn't see it from a child's point of view and allow us a bit of harmless fun.

One day I was playing in the kitchen with a sewing pin I'd found lying about. I'm guessing Mum didn't know I had it or she'd have confiscated it. I inserted it into the space behind the control knob on the washing machine. Suddenly, an electric shock shot through my fingers and arm. I cried out in alarm and Mum said, "Oh, you silly boy!

What did you do that for?" It was a valuable learning experience.

During those early years, Dad used to sit James and me, one on each knee, and tell us Bible stories. Jacob and Esau, Gideon and his three hundred men, David and Goliath, were some of our favourites. But the one we asked for more than any, was Samson and the lion! Dad built the suspense to a crescendo by telling it in real time: "I'm going to see my girlfriend, tum te tum… Grrrrr! The lion growled in the long grass… la la la" (Samson humming a tune) "….Grrrr! GRRR!" Then—"RAAAAAHH! The lion jumped out at Samson and the Spirit of God came mightily upon him, he took it by the jaws and tore it apart." Dad acted it all out, leaning forward with the two of us still on his knees—what excitement! I think Dad enjoyed telling the story just as much as we enjoyed hearing it—which is why it was so memorable.

Mum and Dad wanted the best for their children. They arranged an interview for me at Greenock Academy (the Scottish equivalent of an English Grammar school). There was a small but affordable fee to pay for the privilege, but Dad and Mum thought we were worth it. Mum took me for an interview with Mr Chadwin the Rector[2], a diminutive, florid faced man with a brylcreemed wave of black hair swept back over his head. Like all the teachers in those days, he wore a black teacher's gown. He looked very grand. When he appeared, I whipped off my cap and saluted. Mum had instructed me beforehand. Mr Chadwin took me by the hand with a smile, and led me into his office with Mum. There he showed me a little book with pictures of carrots and other interesting items. I had to draw lines between one thing and another and match them up. Easy! That was the entrance exam. The old Greenock Academy was an austere, Gothic revival Victorian building which was demolished to make way for the James Watt College building (now renamed as 'West College Scotland').

Across the road from the old Academy was Ardgowan Primary school. Because the Academy intake was later, I was sent to Ardgowan Primary for the first couple of terms, until old enough to join the Academy. I don't re-member the Ardgowan school teacher, but I remember a girl called Elspeth Edgar who sat at the next desk to mine. She was a happy girl with a big friendly smile. The infant classrooms at Ardgowan were upstairs, as was the school gym. Every week, we trooped along to the gym for 'Music and Movement'. We did all sorts of creative poses with our bodies to the music. One song we sang as we went round and round in a line behind each other, was, "tipper ipper arper on my shoulder, "tipper ipper arper on my shoulder, "tipper ipper arper on my shoulder, I am the master." We drummed our hands on the shoul-ders of the person in front as we sang. What it meant I had no idea, but I enjoyed it immensely!

The boys toilets at Ardgowan were in an un-roofed, open toilet block outside, in a corner of the playground. Ce-ramic urinals lined the wall. Whenever I went near the toilet block, the overpowering stink of stale urine assailed my nostrils.

I used to prance around the playground as if riding a horse. I had a little song which I sang in the saddle, which went: "one more river and that's the river of Jor-dan, one more river, there's one more river to cross." It was my own little world and a satisfying way of spending playtime.

My first teacher in the old Academy 'Annexe' building, was Miss McAusland. She was probably nearing retirement age by the time I arrived in her class, but she was an excellent teacher. Gentle but firm. She and her sister lived in the top flat of a house on the corner of Newark Street and Madeira Street, not far from Bentinck Street. In my Primary One class photograph taken at the old Greenock Academy, I'm sitting cross-legged, second from the right in the front row. You can just make out a paper lifeboat badge pinned on the lapel of my blazer.

Primary 1 class photograph at the old Greenock Academy, 1963 or 64 - I'm second from the right in the front row

Here are the names of the classmates in the photograph —as many as my faulty memory can recall—from left to right, starting at the back row and working down:

Back Row (left to right): Donald Mcintyre, Michael Wright, Robin Pollock, Graham McFarlane, William Taggart, Christopher McLean
Second row: Hunter Bowie, Eric Cuthil, Rodger Davies, Kenneth Cochrane, Colin Galbreath, Robin Grant (Titch), Findlay McFee, Stuart McDonald

Third row: Siobhan Kennedy, Helen Osborne, Allison Brown, Moira Taylor, Janice McLaren, Judith Hawkins, Elspeth Edgar
Fourth Row: Christine Hutchieson, Anne McAdam, Morven Lambie, Jennifer Baird, Jacqueline Talent, Lesley Carrick, Jean Carroll, Catriona Stewart, Margaret Henderson, Christine Dunwoody
Front Row: Michael Hall, Brian Hendry, Janice Kennedy, Jo Johnson, Billy Kilpatrick

∾

I CAN'T REMEMBER if it was in Miss Mcausland's class or later on in Mrs Russel's class, but whenever the sun came out, we stopped whatever we were doing and sang:

"Good morning Mr Sun,
Our day has just begun,
We love to see your smiling face,
It fills our hearts with warmth and grace,
Good morning Mr Sun!"

We chanted the last line in unison at the tops of our voices: "GOOD MORNING MR SUN!"

∾

THE JANITOR at the old Academy, was a fierce-looking man with a Hitler moustache. He lived in 'the Janny's house' next to the school, the garden of which was separated from the playground by a wooden fence. Known universally as 'the Janny', he kept hens in his garden and I often used to look over the wooden fence and watch them clucking and scratching around. I can still smell them in my mind! One boy in my class was Stuart Mac-Donald. He had glasses and very thin legs. I remember asking him, "How can you run so fast when you have such skinny legs?" William Taggart's teeth were rotten and his breath smelled like a drain. I stood well back when I spoke with him. I remember him singing the song that was on everyone's lips in the playground that year, The Beatles song: "She loves you, Yeah, Yeah, Yeah, you know you should be glad…" That must have been 1963 or '64.

~

2 GREENOCK ACADEMY PRIMARY

The new Academy[1] was a modern, red brick building which included both Primary and Secondary departments and filled the whole of one side of Madeira Street, on a hill between Newark Street and Finnart Street. The school motto, in Latin, was written in raised letters underneath the Greenock Academy logo on the painted metal plaques on the school gates. It read: "Hinc Vera Virtus" (From this place comes true worth).

I don't remember anything about the move to the new Academy. I just remember being there. In the lower Primary Department building, there was a child sized cloakroom area with wooden rails and coat hooks fitted at child height. The classroom door handles were lower down than normal, to accommodate us little people. It was a bright, airy building.

The teacher I remember best from my days in lower Primary was Mrs Russell. She was a good natured, older lady with laugh lines around her eyes and white hair. She had such a winsome way that everyone liked her. I don't recall that she ever gave anyone a telling off. One morning at playtime, I was walking in the playground with Graham McFarlane, one of my classmates, when Mrs Russell came to open one of the classroom windows which opened out onto the playground. She saw us watching her and smiled. Graham said to me, "Isn't she a dear?" to which I mumbled a half-hearted agreement. Calling someone a 'dear' was not a word that featured in my vocabulary

Greenock Academy Motto (courtesy of Greenock photographer, Kenny Ramsay)

and I felt distinctly uncomfortable—especially since the window was open and we were within earshot of its subject. Mrs Russell set up a Nature Table in the classroom. On it she displayed various items such as leaves and wild flowers. In the autumn, she brought in samples of cereal crops, wheat, barley and oats, to show us what they looked like. One of the wild flowers was Colt's Foot, which I recently found growing near our home in Fife. Once seen, never forgotten.

It was Mrs Russell who introduced us to Enid Blyton's stories about 'Brer Rabbit'. Friday afternoons were always devoted to painting. After we had put our paintings over to dry, washed the paint palettes and brushes, and removed our painting 'smocks', she read a chapter from the book before we went home. One of the most memorable was, "Brer Rabbit and the Tar Baby"—a story about a doll made of tar by Brer Fox, to try and catch Brer Rabbit. Another was about Brer Rabbit pleading with Brer Fox not to throw him into the bramble patch—Brer Rabbit cunningly kept repeating:

"Whatever you do, please don't throw me into the bramble patch"—which temptation became too much for Brer Fox, and allowed Brer Rabbit to make good his escape!

It was Mrs Russell who taught us 'The Galin Paris Chevé Sight Singing System'—a system of rhythmic syllables, equivalent to the length of each note in music. We had to repeat after her: "ta-a, tat-ti, ta; Ta-fe-te-fe, Ta-fe-te-fe, ta-ti ta!" Or: "Ta-fe-te-fe, Ta-fe-te-fe, Ta-teh-ta; Ta-fe-te-fe, Ta-fe-te-fe, ta-a!" I suppose it made us more aware of the variety of rhythmic values.

My Primary Three teacher was Mrs Caldwell, a very large lady with a correspondingly fat voice who used to take a wooden ruler in her podgy hand and rap the back of our knuckles if we stepped out of line. One day, one of the girls brought in a goldfish bowl with frogspawn in it. Mrs Caldwell was delighted, as we all were. It lent an added interest to the routine tasks of learning our tables. We huddled around the bowl, watching with interest as the little black dots gave a wriggle now and then. Over the weeks they grew and developed until they turned into fully fledged tadpoles. One Monday morning after the bell went to call us to class at the start of the day, Mrs Caldwell puffed up the stairs while we waited obediently in line in the corridor. When she opened the classroom door, we filed in and immediately saw lots of tiny brown froglets jumping over the classroom floor. Christine Dunwoody was sent to fetch a plastic basin from the cleaner's cupboard and we gathered up the little darlings and kept them safe until their release to the wild could be arranged.

I don't remember much about Miss McDonald and Miss McFarlane, my Primary four and five teachers, or about anything that happened while I was in their classes.

Mrs Scott, my Primary six teacher, was a sharp-witted lady with a curly black perm and a rather dry sense of humour. She wore glasses and lived in Gourock. Her daughter, Jacqueline was in my class.

Toward the end of that school year, we staged a classroom cabaret show. The only bit I remember was a girl called Ann dressed as a glamorous dilettante. She waltzed in with the memorable line: "Sock it to me, babe!"—at which point someone threw a sock at her.

Primary School portrait photo, aged eleven or twelve, looking as if butter wouldn't melt in my mouth!

Miss Lindsay was my Primary seven teacher. She wore her glasses on a gold chain round her neck, which allowed her to rest them on her chest when not in use. About ten minutes before lunch every day, she took a little round folding mirror out of her handbag, held it up to her face, reapplied her lipstick and powdered her nose and cheeks. She had a rather ugly shaped mouth with quite prominent teeth, which the red lipstick only accentuated. She was one of the 'old school' and stood for no nonsense, although she occasionally relaxed and was actually quite a good soul.

At playtime, the boys often played British Bulldog. We all stood round in a circle. One boy held a tennis ball between his fists and threw it to someone. They had to catch and hold it with clenched fists and throw it to someone else. The first person to drop the ball had to run to one of the walls at either end of the playground, which were the safe areas. The exact rules of the game have disappeared from memory, but the main element of the game involved us all running madly around the playground trying to avoid someone throwing the ball at you. If you were hit before you reached the safety of the wall, you were out. It was a fast-paced, exciting game which allowed us to run off excess energy. One day, I must have done something against the rules. Eric Cuthill, a freckle faced, fair-haired boy, took exception to whatever it was I had done and punched me in the face. Until then, I'd been friendly with Eric and had even been to his house on several occasions. The pain of being treated with such unexpected violence by a friend hurt me more than the punch.

Bentinck Street was only a quarter of a mile from the Academy, so we walked to school every day. The lollipop man stood at the corner of Madeira Street and Newark Street to help us cross safely. I seem to remember, one of us kicked his lollipop. (James? William? Me? John? Who knows.) The lollipop man complained and we were pulled up before Miss Kirkwood, the Primary Headmistress. She gave us a fearful row but stopped short at belting us. (In those days, every teacher kept a leather 'belt' or 'strap' [2]in their desk. They used this to whack or 'belt' misbehaving pupils on their outstretched hand. It didn't happen often and was usually deserved.)

After thanking the lollipop man for helping us cross the road safely, there was usually quite a clump of pupils walking up the steep hill of Madeira Street. For several weeks, some of us had great fun teasing a boy who had extremely fat legs. They were almost tubular. In those days all the boys wore shorts, so his chubby pink calves were difficult to miss. The words "Piggle Iggle!" "Piggle Iggle!" were accompanied by an unkind prodding and plucking at his fleshy calves. Every now and then he turned round and said "Stop it!" in a distressed tone of voice. This continued until it reduced him to tears. It was only right that Miss Kirkwood severely reprimanded our nasty behaviour when it inevitably came to light. As has often been observed, children can be very cruel.

3 GREENOCK ACADEMY SECONDARY

After Primary seven, we graduated to the Secondary department. It was connected to the Primary department building by a set of stairs and a corridor which went through the dining hall, past the assembly hall, and Rector's office, and on into the Secondary building.

Greenock Academy, from the corner at the bottom of Madeira Street, where the Lollipop man stood (Photo by Dave Sousa)

Being built on a hill, there were always lots of stairs to climb or run down. There were several floors and the stairs at the end of the main secondary block led down to the PE and Technical Wing at the bottom of the hill.

First year boys were permitted to wear long trousers. Except for a few die-hards, who preferred shorts or had parents who either refused to buy them or couldn't afford them, we couldn't wait to get into them. Long trousers marked the transition from childhood to adulthood.

The school day began with 'Assembly'. The whole of the lower school from first year to third year assembled in the assembly hall to listen to Mr Campbell, the rector (otherwise known as 'the Heedie'). After his general remarks and announcements, he always read the prayer of Ignatious Loyola, the founder of the Jesuits. This cued us in to repeat the Lord's prayer together before we were dismissed and went off to morning classes. Here is that remarkable prayer, with its lofty ideals:

> Teach us, good Lord, to serve thee as thou deservest; to give and not to count the cost; to fight and not to heed the wounds; to toil and not to seek for rest; to labour and not to ask for any reward, save that of knowing that we do thy will; through Jesus Christ our Lord. Amen

Even though we lived nearby and could have gone home for lunch, we usually stayed in school and had a school dinner. I liked school dinners, especially the custard! One boy from Gourock always asked for seconds of cabbage. Maybe that's where he got his rosy cheeks. In the dining hall, the teachers had a long table at the far end.

One day, I sat at the same table as Dougie Learie. Rice pudding was the dessert. Dougie went up to the hatch and asked for seconds. It was so good, he went back to ask for a third helping. Naturally, I joined him, holding out my plate alongside his. A Maths teacher, (I think his name was Mr Thompson), was on duty that day. When he spied Dougie going up to the hatch for a third helping, he said, "You like rice pudding, do you? Right, you're not leaving this table until you finish that between you." And he brought the huge serving bowl of rice pudding from the service hatch to our table and stood over us while we ate spoonful after painful spoonful 'til our stomachs were bursting. Tough guy Dougie began to cry. "Let that be a lesson to you," said Thompson. If I'd known which car he drove, I'd have let his tyres down.

The school library was a favourite lunchtime haunt. I enjoyed reading and spent many enjoyable hours there. However, one incident led to trouble. Not long after we entered S1, some of my friends and I were found huddled round a thick, hard-backed Oxford Dictionary, looking up all the naughty words. Gary, an athletic third year boy with slick black hair and a wicked smile, caught us laughing like hyenas at the definition of the word 'fart' — 'an explosion between the two legs', and said in a most disdainful voice: "You dirty little men!" We quickly made our escape from such embarrassment, hoping he wouldn't 'tell on us.'

Talking of third-year boys reminds me of the fifteen-year-old thug from Port Glasgow who bullied me in the lunch queue every day for several weeks. He had a mop of curly red hair and a rash of matching pimples on his face. Nearly every day he grabbed my wrists and gave me a 'Chinese burn' — he gripped my wrist with two bony hands then twisted fiercely in opposite directions, causing an extremely painful friction burn. Eventually, I decided enough was enough. We had a steel can opener in the house—essentially a flat piece of shiny metal about four inches long, with a bottle opener on one end and a sharp 'V' shaped can opener on the other. I put it in my pocket and went to school, knowing exactly what I would do. Sure enough, my red-haired tormentor made a bee-line for me in the queue at lunchtime. I waited till he got both hands on my wrist, then whipped out the can opener and scored the sharpened 'V' as hard as I could across the top of his wrist. He let go and stepped back, rubbing his injured wrist and giving me a baleful look. I stared him out, ready to use the can opener again if need be. He never came near me after that!

Mr Love, the Depute Rector, introduced us to the joys of Latin. He was a dapper, efficient man with wavy black hair brylcreemed flat against his square head. "Amo, Amas, Amat, Amamus, Amatis, Amant". (I love, you love, he loves, we love, you love, they love). This was our intro-duction to Latin verb conjugations, and we had to chant it after him until we could repeat it without thinking. I was glad not to have to take Latin after first year.

More interesting to our impressionable young minds were the inscriptions on the old wooden desks in the Latin classroom. Originally from from the Old Academy, they were covered in graffiti, which generations of former pupils had carved or scribbled over the years. One snippet of doggerel verse inside one desk lid which I read with interest, went something like: "I used to stand up straight and tall… but now I just hang down and…." (I can't remember the rest). I was dimly aware of its meaning at the time and found it strangely fascinating.

My first English teacher was Mrs MacDougall. Like all secondary teachers in those days, she wore a black gown which amplified her air of authority. 'MacDougall' was a formidable lady. Her gimlet eyes matched her beaky nose and unsmiling mouth. Like many teachers at the Academy, she spoke with an Anglified Scottish accent, common among the 'old school' teaching staff of that era. Instead of 'that' they said, 'thet'. 'Bag' was 'beg' and so on; for example: "Put thet beg down, boy". I got on fine with MacDougall because being an avid reader, I was good at English and along with my classmates in Primary, endured many hours of 'parsing' sentences (identifying their parts, such as: 'a subordinate clause of reason' etc.) Mrs MacDougall approvingly said to me on one occasion "You hev a very good vocebulery". Coming from her, that *was* a compliment. However, MacDougall didn't suffer fools gladly. Alistair Still, one of my pals, sat in the row beside me in 'English'. He was my polar opposite in terms of his love for the subject, so he was never at ease in MacDougall's class. I've never forgotten the day she turned her guns on him. Alistair, as usual was daydreaming about becoming a pop-star and failed to follow the passage we were reading. When MacDougall pounced on him, he had no idea which page we were on, never mind which paragraph. In her most scathing tone, she said "Still, you're just a cebbage". Alistair went redder than a red cabbage and looked as if he wished the ground would open up and swallow him. MacDougall went down in my estimation from that day forward.

I was in Greenock recently, taking some photos for this book. Driving past the house where Alistair used to live, by chance, I saw him getting into a smart looking German marque. I looked him up later on Facebook and discovered he's done very well for himself, running a successful business in Greenock. He'd been taking his mum out for a run in his Tesla. So the 'MacDougalls' of this world can 'stick that in their pipe and smoke it.'

> The race is not to the swift, Nor the battle to the strong, Nor bread to the wise, Nor riches to men of understanding, Nor favour to men of skill; But time and chance happen to them all.
>
> ECCLESIASTES 9:11 NKJV

On the top floor, at the farthest end of the Academy building (the Newark Street end), was the Art Department. Mr Brown was the Principal Teacher of Art. His daughter Alison, a friendly girl, had been in my class all the way through Primary. Her father was one of those people who pronounced the letters 'r' and 'l' as 'w'. So unfortunately, he said 'bwown' instead of 'brown' or 'wook' instead of 'look'. The boys in my class fastened on this immediately and took every opportunity to imitate him behind his back. "Wook here boy, pick up that wubbewr off the fwoowr immediatewey" (Look here boy, pick up that rubber off the floor immediately.) One day, Mr Brown tasked us with designing an army 'wecwuitment' poster. We set to work. I drew a group of gun toting soldiers piling off a landing craft onto a beach with the caption in bold letters: "Join the Merchant Navy and see the world!" When Mr Brown saw it he said: "that's not an army wecwuitment poster Johnson! You don't get Sowldiers in the Mewchant Navy!" Paul Whiteford, (an Academy recruit from England) fell about laughing, as did the others. It's just possible that I did it deliberately to provoke a laugh. The boys in that class never missed a chance to have fun at a teacher's expense.

Mr McFarlane, the French teacher, was a tall, straw-haired man with glasses and a diffident smile. His fingers were nicotine yellow and his full-blown smoker's cough punctuated every lesson. The rank and file knew him as 'Pa Biscuit.' He had the reputation of being 'soft' and, unsurprisingly, 'strap happy'—always calling someone out to the front of the class to belt them. Regrettably for him, he never drew the belt hard enough to cause anything more than a mild slap. The boys in my second-year class vied with each other to see who could get the most of the belt from 'Pa Biscuit.' It's still a bit of a puzzle that I learned any French from the 'Whitmarsh' textbooks that we were working through with him.

Pa Biscuit's wife, Mrs Macfarlane, also taught at the school. She was my Maths teacher. Unsurprisingly, her nickname was '*Ma* Biscuit'. She was a motherly woman, and I liked her even though I was hopeless at Maths. I never saw the point of Algebra—all those formulas with letters inside multiple brackets made no sense and I quickly 'tuned out'. I also had a long-standing mental block with arithmetic. In one of my Primary classes, the teacher gave each pupil a set of 'Cuisenaire Rods'—coloured wooden rods which were supposed to represent hundreds, tens and units. I think my difficulty with mathematical thinking may have begun at that point. The abstract meaning of those little sticks was a mystery to my young mind. Perhaps the teacher didn't use them correctly, or perhaps I needed a fresh approach. I don't know. As a result, I gravitated towards subjects that didn't involve the use of Maths, at least not formally. However, I think I developed an intuitive understanding of certain mathematical concepts because, when computers came on the scene, I immediately saw their potential, first as devices to produce graphic art and later in my career, I took like a duck to water to a brilliant spreadsheet-based programme created by a Finnish PhD student which helped me unravel the horrendous 'Gordian Knot' that was the annual school timetable at Kingspark School in Dundee. The teacher who took over the timetabling remit from me when I retired was a Maths teacher. So perhaps Dad's valiant attempts to tutor me, Ma Biscuit's patience, and the cryptic symbolism of Cuisenaire Rods, finally got through my thick skull and made sense after all.

~

4 RUGGER, TECHIE DRAWING, GILBERT & SULLIVAN

Greenock Academy had a proud reputation in the West of Scotland schools Rugby League. In the P.E. department, boys did Rugger training from first year onwards while the girls got Hockey training. James was far better at sports than I was. He got a broken nose, playing in the first year "A" team. I was only ever good enough to make the 'B' team. Ian Lobban was the 'Gym' teacher. Some boys called him "heid the ba" but at home we only ever called him "Lobban." He showed us how to pass the oval leather rugby ball along the wing with a flick of the wrists. I also remember him demonstrating a proper Rugby tackle. First, he wrapped his arms around a sturdy boy's thighs and told him to run on—the boy dragged him along the ground. Then the correct method—he threw himself down low, pulling the boy's ankles in close to his neck (to avoid a kick on the head), and brought him down in short order. Lobban used to say: "Football is a gentleman's game played by hooligans, and Rugby is a hooligan's game played by gentlemen!"

As a family, we had an inbuilt bias against Lobban because of an incident Dad told us about when Lobban and
Uncle Joe were training together to become P.E. teachers
at Jordanhill College of Education in Glasgow. Lobban
had put his foot on Uncle Joe's tracksuit top. Uncle Joe,
who was normally one of the most easy-going of men,
asked him to take his foot off. Lobban refused, so Uncle
Joe punched him on the chin. Perhaps Lobban har-
boured a bit of a grudge against us 'Johnsons' I don't
know. Anyhow, I usually played on the wing, not having
the muscle or weight of the forwards, but at one of our
practice games, Lobban said: "Right Johnson, you go in
here." He put me in the middle of the front row of the
scrum. As we locked on to the opposing team's forwards, I felt the colossal weight of sixteen bodies bearing
down on my back. It felt as if it was about to snap. I was
extremely glad to come out unhurt and even more
thankful I never had to do that again.

We played home games on Saturday mornings on the
Rugby pitches at Greenock Wanderers playing fields at
the end of Octavia Terrace, where the school held its annual summer sports day. After every inter-school match,
the home side formed two lines outside the clubhouse
and clapped as the visiting team clopped into the clubhouse in steel studded boots to have a shower. Before
the visitors got back on their coach to go home, they
were treated to a sit down 'meal' comprising of a hot pie,
buns and a cup of tea.

Away games were something else. There was great excitement and camaraderie as we boarded the 'Rugby
Bus' taking us to the other team's playing fields. I always
went onto the top deck, where we sang Rugby Songs
with great gusto, amidst much laughter, foot stamping,

and general 'carry-on'. Most of the songs were politically incorrect or obsessed with sex. One, the meaning of which I was only dimly aware, was a fast-paced ditty in which the last line of every verse was progressively shortened before the chorus was hammered out at the top of our voices. The last line of the first verse went: "And this is what she said: Oh, Sir Jasper, do not touch me!" At the end of the second verse, it became: "Oh Sir Jasper, do not touch!" the third: "Oh Sir Jasper do not!" the fourth: "Oh Sir Jasper!" and the fifth: "Oh Sir!" and last of all, a big gasping, "OH!" The chorus, drummed out after each verse, went: "As she lay between the lily-white sheets with nothing on at all!" In one way, it was harmless fun, in another, not so much. The peer pressure to be 'one of the boys' in that macho culture was very strong and certainly not conducive to my moral or spiritual health. Perhaps it was just as well we moved away from Greenock.

I remember an away game at Marr College in Troon. During the game, two of the Marr College team were injured. At half time, to even up the sides, Lobban said "Johnson, you play for them." I couldn't believe he considered my value to the team to be so low that they could do without me. To myself I said, "Right, I'll show you." To begin with, the Marr boys did all they could to stop me getting my hands on the ball. Unsurprisingly, they suspected I would do everything in my power to aid my team. Suddenly, I got the ball in my hands. I started running as hard as I could for the Academy side goal posts. To my amazement and the consternation of my Academy teammates, I scored a try! Lobban was not at all happy but couldn't say anything! It didn't endear me to my teammates, but I felt vindicated. I was a player of some standing after all.

During that era, there was a stricter delineation between subjects considered suitable for boys and girls. Girls got Cookery while the boys got Woodwork, Metalwork and Technical Drawing.

The head of Metalwork and Woodwork was Mr Carson. In contrast to the Woodwork teacher—a benign pipe-smoking old chap with a moustache and tweed jacket— Carson was a white-haired, stern individual. He wore a dusty grey suit and fastened his unsmiling eyes on us as we walked along the corridor. His son Kenneth was in the year above me. For some long-forgotten reason, I took issue with something Kenny Carson said or did. I swung my leather schoolbag and landed a bruising direct hit on his leg. The next day as I stood in line in the corridor out-side the Woodwork workshop, sour-faced Carson sud-denly appeared from his office. "Come with me," he said. A great sense of foreboding engulfed me. On his desk, laid out full length, lay his brown, quarter-inch-thick, Lochgelly leather strap. Without further ado, he belted me for bullying his son. Six of the best from Carson was pretty high on the pain threshold. My damaged hands buzzed for at least half an hour afterwards. If only I'd done a quick cost/benefit analysis before assaulting the Techie teacher's son!

The 'Techie Drawing' room had rows of large sloping desks with high stools, standard furniture in a drawing office. Our Technical teacher was a younger man with a debonair wave of dark hair and glasses. While he com-manded our respect and drew the belt as hard as any, he had a sardonic sense of humour and was well liked by the boys. Unfortunately, his name escapes me, but he in-troduced us to top, front and side elevations and taught us how to run a wooden T-Square up and down the side of the desk with set-squares and protractors to produce the plan drawings required for making three-dimensional items from wood or metal. This teacher was a film buff. He ran the school film club. Toward the end of term, he set up the 35mm projector at the back of the room, pulled down the blackout blinds, and treated us to a film-show. Some of his favourites were black and white films of the early days of motor racing, which we also enjoyed. Some of the crashes were spectacular!

The Techie Drawing room doubled as our Religious Education classroom. Religious Education (R.E. for short) was the only compulsory subject on the timetable, but there was only one R.E. teacher for the entire school. Teachers of other subjects were therefore co-opted to teach the required one period of R.E. per week. Our R.E. teacher was a young P.E. teacher. He was an excellent gymnast and could hold a rock steady handstand for minutes before a controlled return to his feet. Understandably, he was more shaky on the R.E. front, so he mostly used the time to promote discussion of moral questions. When he discovered one of the girls was a Spiritualist and had a Ouija Board, he invited her to bring it in the following week, to find out if it really worked. When I reported this to Dad and Mum, they were very concerned. Dad contacted the Rector, Mr Campbell, to express his concern. Campbell gave me permission to study in the school library instead of going to R.E. that week. According to my pals, nothing much happened during the 'seance' but I was glad my father had intervened on my behalf. I preferred to abide by the wise counsel of Paul to the Church of God in Rome:

"I would have you wise unto that which is good,

and simple unto that which is evil." (Rom. 16:19)

The Secondary playground was an undulating tarmac slope. There was a grassy area next to the part of the playground where the teachers parked their cars. Mr Stenhouse, a friendly Geography teacher who had horn-rimmed glasses and was nearing retirement age, had a beautiful big Humber Hawk Series 1 or 2 which he parked there. Or, it may have been an early Super Snipe with the single headlights, I'm not sure. I often admired it. It was two-tone grey and green with whitewall tyres and had lovely leather bench seats. In contrast to the Primary playground where the children ran around exuberantly every playtime and lunchtime, most of the senior pupils spent the time walking back and forth across the play-ground, talking with each other. This was a feature unique to the Academy. I never saw this in any other school I attended. The bottom half of the Secondary playground, being more level, was used for playing a game of 'footie' (soccer).

Every year the senior pupils performed a Gilbert and Sul-livan Opera. The school staged these polished produc-tions at the Greenock Arts Guild and the lower school usually attended the dress rehearsals in the Guild theatre in Campbell Street. The Art department, in collaboration with the Technical department, made amazing sets and the Music staff excelled themselves, coaching the chorus and the stars of the show. Many pupils were part of the school orchestra and the whole thing came together when the lights dimmed and the curtain went up. Every year the female lead captivated me. I loved the witty repartee, the attractive melodies and the rousing songs of The Pirates of Penzance, The Mikado, Ruddigore and Iolanthe. I still sometimes break out into the stirring lines of "I am a Pirate King! It is a glorious thing to be, to be a pirate King!"- or, "when the foeman bares his steel, tarantara…" etc., and ending with: "tarantara, tarantara, tarantara, tarantara, taranta ra ra ra tarantara!" - or, "Bow, bow, ye lower middle classes! Bow, bow, ye tradesmen, bow, ye masses! Blow the trumpets, bang the brasses! Tantantara! Tzing! Boom!" Complete rubbish but very enjoyable, great fun, and very accessible to lesser mortals not trained in the appreciation of the finer points of Italian opera. In 'Ruddigore' there is a scene in which the paintings on the wall turn into real people—they did that scene so convincingly that we really believed it was happening before our eyes—the music and the lighting all created the eerie atmosphere and we sat enthralled as the ancient paintings of eighteenth-century lords came to life and sang the ghostly dirge: "The dead of the night's high-noon! High Nooooon, Ha-Ha! The dead of the night's high-noon!" Scary stuff. But, even at that early age, I realised that when the froth and bubble of this world's entertainment is over, there is nothing of substance to it. It left an unsatisfied void in one's heart.

The annual sports day was a grand occasion, attended by a large crowd of parents, extended family, staff and stallholders who sold ice-cream, etc. I can still hear the announcements on the loudspeakers and feel the general air of excitement as the various races were run.

Dad's Uncle Willie always came to watch us run our races. A tall, spare, well-dressed bachelor, he had served his time as a joiner before starting his own business. He wore a flat cap, suit and tie and had a laid-back air about him that belied an astute business mind. For us, the best thing about Uncle Willie, was the manilla envelopes with money in them that he handed out after the races. We would run over to where he was sitting at the side of the track with Dad and Mum and hang about expectantly, while Uncle Willie exchanged a few words with us about our perfor-mance, then with a smile, said "Well I think that deserves something…" His hand went to his waistcoat pocket and he drew out three or four folded over envelopes with our names on them. Inside was usually a couple of half crowns. Off we skipped to the ice-cream van! Simple pleasures, never forgotten.

Mum and James, Dad and me with Dad's Uncle Willie

5 BENTINCK STREET, OCTAVIA TERRACE, BATTERY PARK

Bentinck Street links Newark Street to Octavia Terrace, then curves off steeply down the hill and crosses Eldon Street to the Esplanade at the bottom. Wellbeck Street is off to the left as you go down the hill between Octavia Terrace and Eldon Street.

Bentinck Street, looking up the hill from Welbeck Street (No 19 partially hidden behind tree)

We lived about halfway up the hill on the left-hand side, in the ground-floor flat of number 19. The frontages of the flats were grey granite, and the backs were sandstone. Our flat had a basement, which originally housed the coal cellar and a storage room. Dad eventually had them converted into two bedrooms for James and me. There was a door at the bottom of the bare wooden internal stairs which led to the basement. This door had a big old-fashioned steel key and a metal latch. It opened into a dark stone floored passageway which led out to the back green. There were a couple of cellars on the other side of this passageway, belonging to the flats above us. This was where they stored their supplies of wood and coal for their fires. There were three flats in our 'close'[1], one above the other, spanning the entire width of the building. "The Bruces" lived in the middle flat above us and "The Hammonds" had the top flat.

The residents of the flats next door (number 18) were the two "Miss Kerrs" in the bottom flat, above them Dad's cousin Hugh Black, his wife and girls (they were young women when we were children) and above them, Mr and Mrs More and their son Stewart.

19 Bentinck Street

'The back green' was the shared back garden area. You reached it from the flagstone'd basement part of the close via some stone steps. Each flat had its own garden section for cultivation around the shared 'green'—the grassy area in the middle, bounded by iron poles for washing lines at each corner. At the far-left corner of the green was a grassy mound, which was all that remained of a wartime bomb shelter.

One of my earliest memories of the back green was being pushed around the back green in our Triang pedal cars at great speed by the McCowan boys, the family who lived in the top flat prior to the Hammond's taking up residence there.

Learner drivers, Jo, William and James

Next door to us up the hill, lived a man called Mr Haughton. He used to shake his apple tree so that we could get the apples which fell on our side of the garden. Dr Snow and his wife and family moved into his house when he left. Further up, at the top of the hill on Bentinck Street, was Dr Martin's house and at the very top, on the corner of Newark Street and Bentinck Street opposite St Paul's Church, lived Dr Baxter, a genial man with a moustache who smoked a pipe. He had a dark green Ford Corsair (or possibly, a 305 Vauxhall Victor), which he used to leave running outside his house before he drove to work. We passed his gate every morning on our way to school. At the beginning of Octavia Terrace was the house belonging to Dr Ramage. It had a nice driveway leading up to it. So we had four Doctors living nearby.

One day James was whacking a spade into the trunk of the tree which stood just down from Dr Martin's house when he suddenly appeared and said in a stern voice: "Do you want the tree to die?" That put paid to James's destructive diversion.

When it rained, the water gushed down the gutter to the drain at the bottom of Bentinck Street. This was the ideal opportunity to make dams with stones and bits of stick and gravel that accumulated at the side of the road.

Mr White lived in the last granite flat at the bottom of the hill. He had white hair, a white moustache, a white face, drove a white car and his front door was painted white. Mr White was never in a good mood and often displayed his annoyance and disapproval of our activities—especially when he had to walk round the giant dam we had made, to get to his car. He wasn't a nice man like his neighbour, Mr Ferguson. His car was a beauty though, a two-door Ford Consul Capri. It had stylish wings at the back with a double set of circular red lights on each side, set into chrome surrounds at the back. Did I mention its colour? It was white.

At the bottom of the hill, after Mr White's house, were several large sandstone houses, divided into flats. Mr Ferguson was a well-spoken, friendly old man who lived in the top flat of the first of these. He was always well dressed with a smart hat, white shirt and tie. He used to go for a walk down to the esplanade every day. He spoke with a slight lisp and his fingers were nicotine orange from smoking cigarettes. For some strange reason, Douglas Hammond always tried to break his walking stick by whacking it on the ground. Mr Ferguson was a retired engineer and explained how, when he was a boy, he had a crystal set radio which worked with a pin, a crystal and an earpiece. No batteries. You can still buy them as antiques on eBay.

There was a large tree outside our house. When I was about seven or eight, I used to climb up and sit high up in the tree watching for Dad arriving home from Glasgow University where he studied for an M.A. Degree when we were young. He got off the bus at the bottom of the road and walked up the hill. Just before he reached the entrance to number 19, I cried, "Hello Dad!", and scrambled down from my 'crows nest' to go into the house with him in time for tea.

In those days there wasn't so much traffic as there is now and I rode my bike everywhere. One day, I was cycling very fast along Octavia Terrace and cut the corner of the blind hairpin bend that swings round and down into Eldon Place. As I leaned into the curve, to my horror, a car met me, coming up the hill. It was too late for brakes. I hit the front of the car, sailed over the handlebars and landed on the road. The driver got out to see if I was okay. He looked quite shaken. Thankfully, I was fine, apart from a scrape or two. But my bike wasn't. I lifted the buckled front wheel and hauled the damaged thing home. A salutary lesson.

James, William, John, and I, slept in bunk beds in the same room. At night, before we went to sleep, we told each other stories. I enjoyed making them up, and my brothers enjoyed listening to them. One of their favourites came to be known as 'Asez Woman.' I loosely based this character on Mrs Cootie, the lady who came once a week to scrub the stone stairway in our close. She started at the top landing outside the Hammond's and worked her way down to the bottom. We used to hear her industrious scrubbing: "Shhhh! Shh! Shhhh! Shh! Shhhh!—"Shhhh! Shh! Shhhh! Shh! Shhhh!—"Shhhh! Shh! Shhhh! Shh! Shhhh!" as her sturdy arms went flying back and forth along each step. The close smelled of disinfectant afterwards. When she finished, Mrs Cootie came and sat down in our kitchen, where she had a cup of tea with Mum before going on to her next assignment. She smoked a cigarette and drank her tea while chatting with Mum. Mrs Cootie came from the East end of Greenock, had a gravelly smoker's voice and spoke in what we might call 'the Greenock vernacular'. One of her favourite expressions was "Ah says to him…. Ah says,…" So, I made up stories that went along the lines of "Ah sez to him, away doon 'ae th' shoaps and buy me a pun o carrots. Two oors la'er, he comes back and says, Ah couldnae get carrots, so ah got a leh'uss (lettuce) instead. Ah sez tae him 'You got leh'uss instead o' carrots?' Ah sez tae him, ah sez, 'Aw fur goodness' sake, ye styoopit? Ah sez tae ye — buy me a pun o carrots, an you come back wi a leh'uss?" Ah sez tae 'im: "D'ye think wur gonnae hiv leh'uss wi oor tatties 'n mince? Eh?" Ah sez, "'ah've a good mind tae gie ye it fur yur tea th'night." And so forth. When Mrs Cootie was in the toilet one day, I stole a couple of 'Embassy Regals'[2] from her handbag which she'd left in the kitchen. But that's another story.

Another favourite bedtime story I made up for my brothers was 'Dirty John'—a fictitious rascal who got up to mischief, playing pranks or doing outrageous things to officious adults, but always getting away with it. For example, Mr Plod, the policeman, stepped on one of Dirty

John's 'jobbies' (we called them 'messes', as in "I need to go to the toilet and make a mess"). I'm not sure, but I think we got that name from Dad talking about a dog's mess. Dirty John got up to lots of stuff. He threw rotten eggs at authoritarian figures and ran away laughing when they slipped on the broken egg or a banana skin as they tried to catch him.

Octavia Terrace was an interesting street. Lined on one side with large, detached mansion houses, some had been divided into upper and lower flats. Mature hedges fronted most of them and they had fine driveways leading to the front doors. On the other side of the terrace, wooden fences, garages and walls bounded the back gardens, which sloped up from the houses below, in Wellbeck Street. Farther along, the houses gave way to the playing fields belonging to Greenock Wanderers RFC (Rugby Football Club).

One day James, John, and Martin Hammond, were playing on Octavia Terrace. The story is best related in James' own words: "John, me and Martin Hammond were amusing ourselves by disturbing a hedge which was on Octavia Terrace. I think we were making a hidie-hole, when suddenly, this Singer Chamois car drew up and the woman driver emerged swiftly and said, "What are you doing spoiling my hedge?" Us three boys were by this time standing on the pavement as she continued to scold. Then she said, "Right! Get into the car. I'm taking you to the police station!" My instincts kicked in and I shouted "Run!" (Martin insisted later that John was already getting into the car). The three of us sprinted away from that dangerous situation back to Bentinck Street. I think Martin added to the story something about

John getting into the car and coming out the other side, but Martin always liked a tall story!"

I looked up 'Singer Chamois' on Google and discovered it was a posh Hillman Imp—but, being a two-door car, it's more likely John stepped back out of it, rather than going out the door on the other side.

Walking along Octavia Terrace brought you to Fort Matilda railway station and past that, the road joined Eldon Street, which you crossed over to get to the Battery Park, a large green space where you could play football, fly a kite or walk along the seashore at Cardwell Bay, on the Clyde estuary. Cardwell Bay forms a natural boundary point between Gourock and Greenock. We spent many a summer afternoon at the Battery Park. When the tide was out, there were plenty of crabs and other interesting creatures to be found in the pools and under the boulders along the shoreline.

∾

6 GROWING UP IN GREENOCK

"COAL!.... COAL!" This was the familiar distant shout we used to hear all over Greenock when we were young. Usually, Dad ordered coal for a pre-arranged delivery date, but the coal merchant's lorries also plied their trade up and down the streets in much the same way as ice-cream vans go around touting for business today. Nearly every house had coal fires and many, including ours, had a coal cellar, or a coal bunker in an outhouse next to the building. When the coal lorry arrived, the coal men jumped out of the cab and carried the sacks of coal through the close and down the stairs to the cellar door, in the basement. They stood with their leather-clad back against the side of the lorry, put one grimy hand over their shoulder, grabbed the sack full of coal, humphed it onto their back, then walked into the close and down the stairs where they emptied the coal-bags into the cellar with a crash. Their faces were filthy black with coal dust.

~

WE ALWAYS WENT for a haircut to Paterson the Barbers in Kelly Street just around the corner from the shops on Union Street. We sat on a wooden bench and read a comic from the pile in the corner until it was our turn. Paterson, the owner, was a stout faced, white-coated man with neatly combed brown hair. His partner in the shop was a rosy-cheeked, smiling, black-haired man with a bulbous nose who also wore a white coat. The apprentice boy, a gangly red-haired youth of about eighteen, wore a grey coat, presumably to differentiate him from his time-served colleagues. He had a pointed nose and whenever someone vacated a barber's chair, intoned with a nasal accent, "Next please!" When you climbed onto the barbers chair, he draped a grey nylon gown over you and tucked it in at the back of your neck with his bony, cold hands. Among ourselves, we used to imitate his "Next please!"After Ginger-heid had prepared you for the maestro, Paterson or his partner took over and asked what you wanted done. We always said "square back and leave the sides." In our minds, that was a more 'with it' look than the old-fashioned short back and sides, which in those days, was the only other alternative apart from a crew cut. Those old school barbers would turn in their graves if they knew about the freakish hairstyles that pass for a haircut these days.

～

OCCASIONALLY, a deaf and dumb man came to visit us. Dad invited him to the house for tea and gave him some clothes. The deaf and dumb man wore a heavy cloth overcoat and smelled as if he hadn't washed for a long time. We watched him sitting at the kitchen table, where he enjoyed interacting with us children. He communicated by a combination of gesture, writing things down on paper, and by making a noise that sounded to us like "Nying nying!" "Nying nying!" His drawings of trains, ships, and cars fascinated us as much as the laborious sound of his breathing, while he carefully sketched them on bits of paper.

~

MUM'S SECOND COUSIN, Jock Bell from Walkerburn in the Scottish Borders, came to stay with us for a few days one summer. The son of one of Grandad's cousins, Jock was an outgoing character who spoke with a broad Borders accent. At night, he slept in a single bed in the bedroom that James and I shared. We doubled up in the other bed during his visit. One day, he took me for a walk from Bentinck Street to the Farm to visit Betty MacDonald. She lived at Auchenfoyle and rose early every day to milk the cows. We called her Aunt Betty because she always gave Mum presents for us at Christmas. It was a scorching hot day and as we climbed the hill going up the Kilmacolm Road out of Greenock, Jock was sweating profusely. Every so often he stopped, turned round, and with one leg forward, he leaned back on the other and launched forth into a discourse on whatever subject was on his mind. He frequently mopped his brow with a large white handkerchief. Eventually, we reached the farm and spent some time there before walking home again. Perhaps he overdid the exercise, or ate something which didn't agree with him, but that night, he constantly tossed and turned in his bed. I heard him saying under his breath, "Oh Lord, Lord." Suddenly he passed wind. When James started giggling under the covers, Jock said, 'Stop the pumping James!'—which made James laugh all the more. Another day, Jock took me to a second-hand bookshop near Greenock Fire Station and bought me a hard-backed Revised Version Bible. It had a red leatherette cover and red-edged pages. I used that Bible for several years before the binding came loose and it became unusable. Before Jock left, someone took a photograph of him standing beside me in the back-green. My pet white mouse was on my arm.

Jock Bell, with me and my white mouse, in the back-green at 19 Bentinck Street.

Dad later told us with some amusement that both Jock and his brother William Bell had been deserters during the war. Jock had joined the army. As soon as the troopship docked at Cape Town, South Africa, Jock ran off into the bush. He hated the strictures of army discipline. His brother William joined the Navy and did the very same thing! When his ship called for provisions in Newfoundland, Canada, he high-tailed it into the Canadian backwoods, where he hid out for some weeks before they eventually caught him. Dad said they were free spirits who just couldn't cope with military discipline.

~

WHEN JAMES and I were about twelve or thirteen, we saved up enough pocket money between us to buy a Charles Atlas course. This came as a series of printed pages stapled together with a smart blue card cover which arrived in the post every two or three weeks. We performed the 'dynamic tension' exercises each day, and worked our way through the course. We chewed our milk to digest it properly as Charles Atlas recommended, imagining we were going to develop the magnificent muscular body promised in the magazine adverts: "You too can have a body like mine!" We did plenty of press-ups—but skipped the bit in the course that advocated taking an 'air bath' in the nude with friends. That was a step too far! I kept up the morning exercise routine even after I went to Art College and and worked up to fifty press-ups without stopping. I still haven't got a Charles Atlas body!

~

I HAD a fishing rod and used to fish from the Esplanade along with other anglers who often fished there. I remember fishing off Princess Pier one summer, catching Mackerel and Saith by the dozen. In contrast to the bigger, iridescent, lively Mackerel—which you caught with a coloured fly, Saith were small black fish and didn't put up much of a fight. We never ate Saith—the anglers considered them a 'dirty' scavenger fish which would eat anything. I also caught several rock cod from the Esplanade. They were lovely to eat.

~

DAD SENT James and me for piano lessons to a Mr
Sandison who lived in a tenement flat at the top of Kelly
Street. Mr Sandison was a kenspeckle figure around
Greenock. He had a shiny bald pate, wore glasses and
rode his bike with socks pulled over his trouser legs to
stop them getting chain oil on them. He used to sit beside us at the piano with a mug of tea, munching his way
through a packet of rich tea biscuits, while we studied
the notes in the music book and picked out the tune.
Sometimes when we arrived, we had to sit and read a
comic or two from his pile of old 'Beano's', 'Topper's',
and 'Dandy's' while he finished tutoring a girl who was
learning some sort of operatic piece. We sat on the sofa
and listened as he played and sang the various parts with
gusto so that his pupil would hear how it ought to sound.
He was a superb pianist. Sometimes he rattled through
the arpeggios on the piano, going through all the major
and minor keys one by one, right up the scale on the piano. It sounded fantastic! At first, I made good progress.
Mr Sandison helpfully wrote the fingering for each hand
in pencil above the notes on the pieces I was learning to
play. I faithfully practised on our piano at home. One day
though, he said, "Right Jo, you've got the fingering. We
can rub out the numbers." So he took a rubber and
scrubbed out all the pencilled numbers he had written
above the notes to help me remember the fingering. This
was an enormous setback. Unconsciously, I had associated the numbers with the notes. Without the numbers, I
was lost. I stared at the little black hieroglyphs and
couldn't figure them out at all. Each week after that, my
retarded progress became painfully obvious as I hesi-
tantly pecked at the keys. There were long pauses between each note as I tried to decide which key to press
next. Mr Sandison had a long thin stick wrapped round

with sticky brown paper tape. He used this as a pointer to show which note I should play next. During these increasingly monotonous sessions, his pointer gradually faltered across the page as he momentarily nodded off. Who could blame him? Eventually, because I wasn't making much of this 'sight reading' business, we came to a mutual agreement with my father that it wasn't worth continuing. But I'd picked up enough musical knowledge to play tunes by ear in the keys of C, B, F and G. I often wish, though, that I'd learned to read music properly.

James and William fared little better. Dad sent them for piano lessons to a music teacher named Mr Ferguson who lived in Carmichael Street. It soon became obvious that a musical education was low on their list of priorities. James reminded me that Mr Ferguson's form of encouragement took the form of sarcasm, such as, *"a hen could play better than that!"* or, *"My cat could play better than that!"* It wasn't long before things came to a head.

Several months after they'd been attending Mr Ferguson's Saturday morning music lesson, Dad received a letter from him which read:

DEAR MR JOHNSON,

James and William did not turn up for their music lesson on Saturday until 11:30 am, which, of course, was one hour late. When questioned about their late arrival they treated it as a huge joke and ran away laughing. As this is the third time this has happened in the last quarter I feel it would be better if you were to find another music teacher for them. I enclose the account for the two boys up to date and should be pleased to have settlement at your earliest convenience. You will note not I have not charged for the days on which the boys just did not turn up.

Yours faithfully,

S Ferguson

Dad must have seen the funny side, because he filed that letter away in his filing cabinet. We found it recently and had a good laugh at the memory.

∾

THERE WASN'T a lot of traffic on Bentinck Street, but now and then, a car drove up or down the hill. To amuse myself one day, I tore a leaf out of my A3 drawing pad, and in large capital letters, wrote, 'NO ENTRY'. I poked a couple of holes in each corner and threaded some thin string through the two holes. I tied one end round the trunk of the tree outside the house, walked across the road, and tied the other end to the fence on the opposite side. I made sure I positioned the 'No Entry' sign in the middle of the road, then found a vantage point just inside the door of the close where I was out of sight. It wasn't too long before a car came up the hill. It slowed down as it approached the home-made sign, then accelerated through the string and on up the hill.

∾

ONE DAY, James and I were on the bottom deck of a bus on our way into town. On all the buses, the downstairs seats were designated as a 'no smoking' area and the upstairs deck was for smokers. The bus stopped at a bus-stop and a woman got on with a cigarette between her fingers. She sat down in the seat opposite me and continued to puff away, blowing blue smoke into the air. As the bus slowed down to let us off at our stop, I got up, pointed to the 'no smoking' sign along the roof of the bottom deck, and said to the woman, "Can you read what that says?" She looked at me with stunned amazement. She had no words. I suppose she didn't expect that from an eleven-year-old boy.

~

THE LAUNCH of the QE2 ocean-going liner was a big occasion on Clydeside. Built by John Brown's shipyard at Clydebank, they launched her on 20 September 1967. I remember going to the Esplanade to watch the great ship sailing down the River Clyde on her way to the Cunard Line yard at Southampton for finishing touches and sea trials, before her maiden voyage. Gordon McDonald, from the Church of God in Port Glasgow (who taught me some useful techniques on the accordion), was a ship's carpenter and cabinetmaker. He made many of the built-in veneered wooden cabinets in the luxury cabins on the QE2.

~

BIRTHDAYS in our house were special occasions. Mum always baked and iced a cake and put the correct number of candles on it. We usually had one or two school friends for tea. James, whose memory for these things is so much better than mine, reminded me that on my eleventh or twelfth birthday, I had invited Alistair Still to celebrate the occasion. After tea, as a special treat,

Dad said he was taking us on a 'mystery tour'. We piled into the car with anticipation. As we drove off, Alistair said, "Maybe he's taking us to the pictures." Little did he know, that was the last place Dad would have taken us! (Although, he did allow me to go to the pictures for Colin Galbreath's birthday to watch 'The Incredible Journey', a film about some family pets that followed their owners across America.) Anyway, my mystery birthday destination turned out to be Auchenfoyle Farm, which was even more interesting than going to the pictures.

~

ONE YEAR, Dad and Mum decided to cut down on the amount of money they spent on jam. Dad announced they would buy us each a jar of our favourite jam, but we had to make it last a whole month, otherwise we'd have to make do with bread and butter until the next pot arrived. I always asked for Hartleys Pineapple jam but invariably finished it with at least a week to go on bread and butter before the next one arrived. It was just too delicious to spread thinly!

~

COLIN GALBREATH WAS QUITE A CHARACTER. His father and mother had adopted him. They lived in an elegant flat near Brougham Street Post Office on the corner of Forsyth Street and Eldon Street, before they had a new house built for them farther down the street. Colin's father was a quiet man who had a certain 'presence' about him. He drove a cream-coloured Volvo 122 Coupe. He was an RAF pilot during the war and, according to Colin, was a close friend of Douglas Bader, the wartime ace.

Colin's mum was a cultured, well-spoken lady who ran a private chiropody practice. The way she said "Colin" was very particular—she articulated the 'l' with a delicate inflection and laid the stress on the 'in' so that it became "Co-l-in". Colin and I had several escapades. One time, he filled a brown paper bag with whelks. He had prised them off the big stones on the shingle beach beside the Esplanade, so that he could cook and eat them with a pin from their shells. The very thought revolted me, which was just as well because Colin became very sick after eating them. A sewage pipe dumped its contents into the Clyde near that spot, and contaminated the whelks.

One glorious summer's day Colin and I cycled to Kilmacolm, where we bought a giant bottle of Bulman's cider. We had made up a packed lunch and also brought our fishing rods with us, to fish the Gryffe near the Duchal Castle, just behind East Green Farm. I was more interested in exploring the remains of the overgrown ruins of the castle while Colin took his rod and went downstream to try his luck. We had imbibed a fair bit of cider and were feeling quite light-headed. Suddenly I heard Colin shouting excitedly, "Jo! Jo!Come quick! I've caught one! I've caught one!" I hurried down river, jumping from stone to stone. "Too late, I've lost it," said Colin. I strongly suspected he'd been bluffing and just wanted to tell his friends at school about 'the one that got away.'

~

BEFORE MUM DIED, I found an old school jotter in Dad's filing cabinet. The teacher had obviously cut it in half with a blunt guillotine or pair of scissors to make the jotters go further because it had a ragged edge across the top. On the front, in joined up writing, was the inscription, "James Johnson, Free Writing". The entries are dated between January and June 1969. In one of them he had written that he was thinking of going for a cycle ride to Loch Thom. This was the reservoir in the hills above Greenock, which supplied the town with water. There were miles of rough tracks in the surrounding countryside, which were ideal for cycle outings.

James, fixing his bike in the Back Green at Bentinck Street

Another good place to go on a nice day, was the Greenock 'Cut'. This is a four-mile track along an old canal which goes all the way from The Whinhill in Greenock to just above Inverkip and on to Loch Thom. 'The Cut' was an aqueduct made in the 19th century to bring water from Loch Thom to Greenock. Sometimes we also took a picnic lunch and walked along The Cut.

WE LEARNED to swim in the public swimming baths at Port Glasgow. Dad took us every Wednesday night over the course of a couple of years when we were about five or six. Frank McGarvey was our swimming instructor. He was great, and had us swimming lengths of the main pool in no time. There was a plump girl called Sabra, which I thought was a strange name.

We always took the bus to the baths from the bus stop on Eldon Street at the bottom of Bentinck Street. After our swimming lesson, Dad bought us a packet of crisps each, which he called 'a chittering bite'. We always ate our crisps sitting at at the front of the top deck of the bus, enjoying the novelty of the elevated vantage point on the way home.

When we were older, we often walked to the Hector Mc-Neil Swimming Baths in Greenock for a swim on a Saturday morning. Sometimes we went with Graham Hoey, who lived in South Street before he and his family emigrated to Canada. We ran around the sides of the pool and jumped off the springboard into the water. Occasionally, we plucked up the courage to climb onto the high diving boards, which had two platforms. This was where the big 'show-offs' dived into the pool to impress the girls. One fat guy always did a huge 'belly flopper' every time. After our swim, we sometimes went to the high-rise flats nearby and played in the lifts. There was no such thing as security entrances in those days.

~

7 UNCLE JOE

Dad's brother Joe emigrated to Canada. He settled in Vancouver, and worked at the University of British Columbia, where he was Associate Professor in UBC's 'School of Human Kinetics'. He had played professional football with Glasgow Rangers after the war, during the 1940s and '50s.

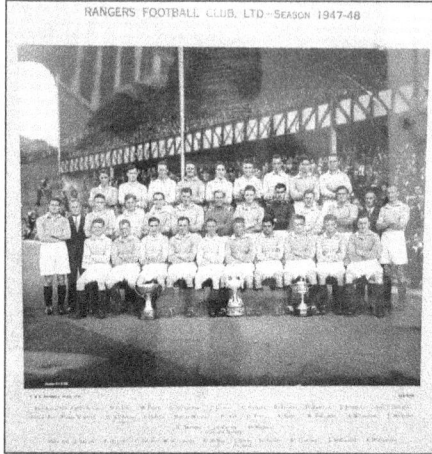

Rangers Team Photo, 1947-48. Uncle Joe, top right. This snap of the original was taken by his grandaughter Lara. The original is owned by his daughter Leah. You can just see Lara's reflection in the glass of the frame! (Photo, courtesy of Leah Butner).

Uncle Joe, Glasgow Rangers team player

In Canada, Uncle Joe became head coach for the famous UBC Thunderbirds soccer team, where he put his skill and knowledge of the game to good use. Under his leadership, 'The Birds' went to the top of the Canadian Soccer league. Every few years, he came back to Scotland and stayed with us for a few days. We loved Uncle Joe—he was so full of fun. Once he took us a run in a Humber Sceptre borrowed from one of his friends who owned a garage in Kilmacolm. We were driving along the Kilmacolm Road, somewhere near Gateside Farm, where his cousin Robin Orr still lives, when two or three girls on horseback came round the corner. As he drove past with the driver's window down, Uncle Joe shouted, "Yoo hoo!" We laughed like anything!

He parked the car near the little stone bridge over the Gryffe near Gateside and took us along to a bend in the river where he waded into the water and started feeling underneath the big stones. Suddenly he said "Oh! Here's one!" He scooped out a small trout and threw it, wriggling and twitching onto the grassy bank. It was too small to keep, so we threw it back. It was great entertainment and we spent a good hour there, messing about in the water before he took us home again.

Uncle Joe married Aunt Eleanor and they had three children: Joel, Leah, and Brent. He used to send Dad photographs of them all at various stages in their lives. He brought Aunt Eleanor to Scotland on their honeymoon, but unfortunately, it rained most of the time and Aunt Eleanor didn't get as good an impression of the country as he would have liked. So, when his family was up a bit, he brought them over for a summer holi-

Uncle Joe and Aunt Eleanor on their honeymoon, outside Auchenfoyle

day. By this time, we were in our teens and had moved away from Greenock to Ayrshire, where Dad had bought a bungalow in John Knox Street, Galston. We didn't have enough bedrooms to accommodate all the Canadian cousins, so Dad constructed a home-made arrangement of bunk beds in the study. This worked well, and it was great to have their company for a few days before they went off up north to visit Uncle Hugh and Aunt Nan in Sutherland.

One day we were all sitting round the dining room table enjoying some good-natured banter with Joel and Leah. (Brent was only four or five at the time and needed a fair bit of attention from his mum and dad). The conversation was going along well when, to my chagrin, my body let me down. As they say in Scotland, I 'let off without letting on'.

Canadian cousins, Leah, Brent and Joel

Any hope that no-one would notice evaporated when cousin Joel exclaimed in his Canadian drawl, "Who cut the cheese?" I looked sheepishly around to deflect attention from myself. I'm still not sure if I got away with it.

Cousin Joel died from a rare form of cancer just a few years ago. He had no inkling of that when he and his wife, Carol, and their three boys visited us in Fife a couple of years before he became ill. Joel was Principal of a Primary School in the Surrey district of Vancouver. He was very popular with staff and students.

Uncle Joe worked out regularly at the gym and kept himself very fit. He wanted to continue working past retirement age but there was some archaic rule at UBC, which forced him to retire, despite his efforts to appeal against it. He resisted the pressure brought to bear on him by the University administrators as long as he could. I sometimes wonder if the stress of all that brought on his diagnosis of liver cancer, which seemed to come out of the blue around that time. He visited Dad and Mum at Dunlop in 1985, the year before he died. If he knew about the diagnosis, he said nothing to us. I took a couple of Polaroids of him with Dad and Mum when I went down to Dunlop to see him from Glasgow. When I showed him the snap, he said with a chuckle: "Aye, the camera doesn't lie." He certainly looks older in those photographs, even though he still had the same energy and sense of humour.

A year later, it became clear he was seriously ill. Dad and Mum flew to Vancouver to be with him. Dad told me later that he got such a shock when Uncle Joe got off the couch and came to the door. The man who'd been so fit and powerfully built only a year before was now thin as a rake and very weak. He died while Dad and Mum were there. Dad paid his own personal tribute to him at the funeral. It was a tough time for Dad—and for us all. In one of his letters to Dad a year or two before he died, Uncle Joe quoted from an old poem:

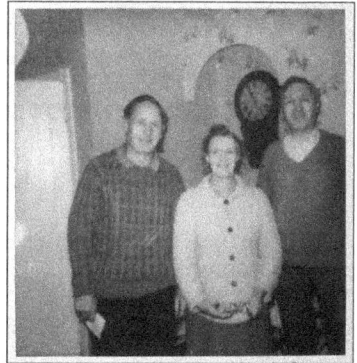

My Polaroid snap of Uncle Joe with Mum and Dad, 1985

"Only one life, 'twill soon be past,
Only what's done for Christ will last."

8 HALLOWEEN AND GUY FAWKES NIGHT

The week between the end of October and the beginning of November was always an exciting time. On Halloween night we always went out 'guising'. One year, Stuart More came to our door dressed as a robot. All he'd done was cut a hole in the bottom of a cardboard box for his head and two holes in the sides to put his arms through. Not the most original idea, but at least he tried. Then there was the time James and I went out with Douglas and Martin. We had done well, with plenty of fruit and nuts and packets of sweets in the carrier bags we'd brought for the purpose. Unfortunately, we agreed to put all the money into the bag that Martin was carrying. We were on the way back home with our stash of cash and sweets, after working our way round the houses of the generous residents on South Street. We took a shortcut through the grounds of a new house that was being built. It was pitch black. The others were some way in front of me when I heard a sudden commotion. By the time I reached them, it was all over. Two thugs from Grieve Road had attacked them and stolen the bag of money from Martin.

We were at the top of Finnart Street, just across from Dr Kennedy's house. His daughter Siobhan was in my class at school. I went and rang their bell. Siobhan came to the door, and I asked her to get her dad. I told him what had happened. To his credit, Dr Kennedy put on his coat and hat and came out with us to see if he could catch the culprits. By this time, they were well on their way up the Lyle Road. There was no use chasing them on foot. Dr Kennedy phoned the police, and we went off home, sorely disappointed at being robbed of the cash we'd collected. The story had a happy end though. Apparently two policemen in a Panda car[1] caught up with the yobboes on the other side of the Lyle Hill, just as they were about to vanish into the housing scheme behind Grieve Road. Best of all, they retrieved our money! They returned the bag of loose change to Martin and Douglas next day. We sat on the top landing outside their door and shared out the cash between us.

James reminded me of another year, when he and I and Graham Hoey went round the doors together. Graham was dressed in a smart suit and hat and had a briefcase with him. I don't remember this, but apparently we were accosted by another two tough guys from the East End of Greenock.

"I'm a city gentleman," said Graham, and he wheeched his briefcase upsides with the two East Enders' faces! James said that I then had the job of pacifying the two hard men. Funny, the things one person remembers, and another forgets!

Halloween was also the time of year we enjoyed 'Dooking for apples'—a traditional game, which we looked forward to every year. Mum poured a bag of apples into a plastic basin and filled it with cold water till the apples were floating around in the water. We pulled out a chair from the kitchen table and placed the basin of apples on the floor behind it.

We took turns to kneel on the chair with our hands behind our backs and a cold metal fork between our teeth. Dad or Mum swirled the apples round the basin and we had to aim our fork at an apple and let it go just at the right moment to spear an apple with the fork. We ate the one we had speared. It was great fun!

Hard on the heels of Halloween, came 'Guy Fawkes Night'. We always had our own mini fireworks display in the back green, with all the families from the three floors of number nineteen coming together for the event. Albert Hammond usually took the leading role. He organised the bonfire with the 'Guy' on top and supervised the lighting of rockets which were placed in a row of empty milk bottles on the ground next to the iron clothes poles. It was a magical time of year, just after the clocks changed and the darker nights came in, giving early promise of the approach of Christmas, always the most exciting time of year for us.

∼

9 CHILDHOOD FRIENDS

Kenneth Cochrane lived in the older part of South Street. His parents were both doctors. We usually played together in the living room. Now and then, his big sister Rosemary looked in to see what we were up to. Kenneth's father, a tall, bald-headed, bespectacled man, had bought Kenneth a static model of a steam engine, made by a company called Mamod. It ran by heating the water in its boiler with methylated spirits, which went into a metal pan underneath the engine. An astringent smell rose from the clear purple liquid as his dad poured the methylated spirit into the firepan. It was fascinating to watch as the water in the metal boiler reached boiling point and developed enough pressure to drive the little piston which made the flywheel spin round and pick up speed until it was birling away good style. That paled into insignificance, though, when Kenneth announced his dad had bought him a motorbike. We spent a fair bit of time in his dad's double garage, cleaning the various parts, inhaling the glorious smell of engine oil and petrol, admiring its rugged beauty and imagining ourselves riding it. Kenneth told me his dad took him to the rough ground on the golf course behind where he lived, to let him ride it. I was envious.

Another of my school pals was Gordon Knight, or 'Knighty' as we all called him. Knighty's dad owned a car showroom where he sold Triumph cars. His parents were rarely at home and Gordon more or less did as he pleased. He had a big sister who was much older than him, but I only ever saw her once or twice. She inhabited a different universe. He lived in the upstairs flat of a large old house in Finnart Street, near the Academy. In his living room was a coffee table with an ornate cigarette box. We used to take one or two now and then and go off somewhere to smoke them undisturbed. One day Alistair Still and I went to Gordon's house. None of the family were home, so we took a bunch of cigarettes and retired to the garden shed at the back of the garden. Each of us stuck two or three cigarettes in our mouths. We lit up, inhaled, and savoured the aromatic smell of tobacco with the added thrill of doing something which would have got us in plenty trouble if we had been found out.

Alistair Still's Dad was a pharmacist and worked in the Chemist shop on the corner of Kelly Street and Union Street, round the corner from Paterson the Barbers. He lived at the top of Madeira Street with his brother and sister. Alistair wasn't academically inclined. He was an easy-going chap who dreamed of becoming a Pop Star. He talked with a slow drawl and while he would never put himself in any situation which involved risk, was quite happy to egg others on to daring acts of mischief. One of those mischievous games was 'Ring, Bang, Scoosh'—one of us went up to someone's door, rang the bell, then ran for it as fast as we could. Sometimes the occupant chased us, but mostly we got away without incident. One time, Alistair said to me, "I dare you to ring Maitland's bell, Jo!". 'Maitland' was Jim Maitland, who lived in a nice old sandstone house on the corner of Madeira Street and Finnart Street. His mother was a teacher at the Academy, which is why we didn't like him all that much. I opened the squeaky iron gate, tiptoed up to the front door, and rang the bell. What I didn't know was, Jim Maitland's Dad had been watching us. He was hiding just behind the storm door. When I rang the bell, he flung open the door and ran after me. Fear and adrenalin lent me speed and I out-ran him. That was more excitement than I'd bargained for, though, and we turned our attentions to other things.

Dougie Learie lived in the top flat of a big sandstone house on Newark Street. He had a shock of black, straight hair which fell over his forehead and ended in a straight fringe atop his black glasses. Dougie was a smart, cocky boy with an opinion on everything and a confidence about him which inspired others to take their lead from him. His Dad regularly took him to Ibrox to watch Glasgow Rangers play, and he regaled us on Monday at school with the highlights of Saturday's match. Dougie's mother became ill, with cancer I suspect, and died. He was not the sort who hid his feelings, and the bitter hurt of his emotions sometimes spilled out when he was with us.

We used to go to the 'SSC' (the Scottish Schoolboys Club) some evenings which was held at the Academy. We played indoor football and other games. One of the Techie teachers ran it. One evening after the club, we were milling around under a tree on the corner of Madeira

Street and Newark Street, chatting with Margaret Henderson and some other girls. The yellow street lamps had come on. I had a metal catapult in my back pocket. Dougie said "I dare you to hit one of those windows up there," nodding at the house across the road, which had several windows made of little squares of leaded glass. Wanting to impress the girls, I said, "watch this". I placed a stone on the leather pad, drew the strong, square sectioned catapult elastic to its full stretch, and let fly. The stone arced through the night air and hit the window with a resounding smash. Margaret gasped, "Oh No!" Before we knew it, the door of the house opened and out came an angry man shouting "Right, who did that?" We didn't wait around to enlighten him. I wasn't proud of what I'd done, but I brushed off the guilt as unavoidable collateral damage, justified by the need to maintain a 'cool' image in front of my mates.

Margaret Henderson was in my class at Primary School. I don't remember how I got friendly with her but I used to go to her house to play with her after school. She lived in Eldon Street, about three quarters of a mile from our house. There were two stone pillars at the entrance of the long narrow driveway, which led up a steep slope to her house. Each pillar had the name 'Glenpark' inscribed on it. At the top of the drive was a large detached house, reminiscent of a French chateau. A symmetrical stone staircase with spindly wrought-iron railings ran steeply up like an inverted 'V' from either side of the facade to meet the front door at the top.

Margaret's Mum was a small, attractive woman, who had one of the kindest and gentlest voices I ever heard. She was always pleased to see you and welcomed you in. The large, stone-flagged kitchen at the back of the house had a door which led to the back garden. There was a good-sized swing in the garden, which we played on. Margaret had several brothers and a younger sister, some of whom were in my brothers and sister's classes and who also became friendly with each other. In fact, Dad and Mum became friendly with Margaret's parents. Her dad, Robert, ran the family accountancy business. Margaret's brothers told me their dad could swing them right over the bar of the swing. He asked me if I'd like to try it. Margaret and her brothers laughed like anything when I said "No Thanks!"

Towards the end of Primary/beginning of Secondary, I started visiting a girl called Moira Oxley, who lived in 14 Cambridge Avenue in Gourock, just above Cardwell Bay. I used to cycle along Octavia Terrace, past Fort Matilda train station and up the Lyle Hill Road, 'till I came to some pedestrian steps which connected with Cambridge Avenue. I lifted the bike up the steps and jumped on again to get to her house. Moira had long blonde hair, spoke softly and had not long moved into the new bungalow in Cambridge Avenue. The house had a smell of new wood and fresh paint and sat at the bottom of a short driveway. Her Dad was a yachtsman and had the weather-beaten, tanned face of a man who spent lots of time on the water. Her Mum was a tall, dark haired lady and a lovely person. Moira and I used to take their beautiful golden retriever for a walk along a stretch of rough ground which started at the end of Cambridge Avenue and opened out into an extensive area of scrubland which sloped down a steep hill towards an old quarry. A girl named Angela, lived in the end house. Moira didn't approve of some things Angela had done (something to do with a party at her house, I think) and confided in me about it. Of course, I agreed with Moira. One balmy summer's evening, we took the dog for a walk before I went home. Moira said, "Lets lie down here." We lay down, side by side, in the grass, looking up at the blue expanse of sky above, content in each other's company. It was a special, never to be repeated moment of childhood innocence which lives in my memory. Who knows, perhaps if Dad hadn't moved our family away from Greenock, our friendship might have blossomed into something more serious.

When I started 'S1' (first year of Secondary school), several pupils joined us who hadn't been with us at Primary school. One of those was an attractive, doe-eyed girl with a shock of dark hair and a nut-brown face. She lived in Kilmacolm and her name was Hazel. I fell in love with her immediately but was too shy to bring myself to talk to her. Her desk was at the front of the class in the row next to mine. Sometimes she furtively turned round and saw me looking at her. I quickly averted my gaze and looked down at my books. I think she knew I was interested, and I cherished the hope that she might also be interested in me—but by this time, male hormones were playing havoc with my previous emotional equilibrium. Girls suddenly became fascinating, unpredictable, slightly dangerous creatures, and always just out of reach. In a moment, especially if you fancied them, they could reduce you to a tongue-tied, stammering idiot. Young love is so complicated! Eventually, I plucked up the courage to pick Hazel at gym when we were practising Scottish Country dancing. But of course, as is the way with such dances, you swap partners every few moments and inevitably end up with someone you wouldn't have chosen in a month of Sundays.

Even after we moved away from Greenock, we still had a connection with the young people in the Churches of God in the West of Scotland. They usually invited us to any parties or get-togethers arranged for the young folks. One of those events was a Christmas or New Year party held in Clune Brae meeting room, an old wooden Hall owned by the Church of God in Port Glasgow. One game involved a kissing session with a girl in a back room. How we got away with this, I don't know. Anyway, neither the girl nor I were very experienced. She stuck her tongue rapidly in and out of my mouth. I was completely unprepared for this and was more than relieved when we had to return to the main hall for the next party game. "Yuck!" I said to myself. That wasn't what I thought kissing was about. Thankfully, I learned otherwise when eventually I met Norma, the girl who became my wife and the love of my life! (No doubt my erstwhile partner's kissing skills also improved in later years!)

~

10 A BAD MAN

Mum always used to warn us about certain men who she said were 'bad men'. On no account should we ever go away with a bad man. Somehow, I imagined 'bad men' would be old men. I never imagined a younger man would want to harm me, so the idea of 'a bad man' was a fairly abstract concept until the following events occurred. Even then, I was much older before I really understood what might have happened if events had not taken a fortuitous turn for the better.

I must have been about nine or ten. I used to play inside the half-built houses on the South Street building site, which sloped up onto 'the rough' at the edge of the golf course. In the unfinished rooms, I jumped from one wooden joist to another. On the upper floor, I stood behind the empty window spaces in the walls and enjoyed the view over the rooftops to the river Clyde and the hills beyond. One of those buildings overlooked a previously built bungalow on the other side of the road, owned by

Eric Sørensen the Danish football player. He played for both Greenock Morton and Glasgow Rangers.

I got friendly with two of the apprentice bricklayers on the building site. One of them had long hair and red-raw knuckles from accidentally hitting his hand as he chipped the ends of the bricks with a hammer. One day, I went to Woolworths with them after their work. The long-haired apprentice grabbed a handful of loose sweets as we walked past. I thought that very daring and was almost tempted to copy him.

The Brickie's apprentices were relatively harmless however, compared to the plumber's apprentice. He was a tall, quiet chap with a pale white face and black hair. One day he and I were alone in that same half-built house. We were standing looking out one of the window openings. He exposed his private parts in front of me. I said nothing to anyone about what he had done to himself but I knew it wasn't right. A few days later, on a blazing hot Friday afternoon, I was playing on the building site again. Friday afternoons were early finish days for most workmen, and the majority had gone home. But the plumber's apprentice was still there. He took me into the temporary toilet block hut, which stood on the street alongside a cement mixer and a pile of sand. In the cubicle he asked me to face the wall and take my shorts down. Suddenly we heard men's voices outside the cubicle. I was aware of the plumber's apprentice behind me hurriedly sorting out his clothing. He opened the door and went out. I followed him and saw two workmen washing their hands at the sink. They gave the plumber's apprentice a penetrating stare as he walked past them.

I didn't realise it at the time, but looking back, I'm sure I came within a hairsbreadth of being violated, possibly even murdered, by a paedophile. I believe God intervened and sent those workmen into the toilet block just in time to prevent him doing something very bad to me.

I only saw the plumber's mate once after that. He was standing outside a house near Madeira Lane at the top of Bentinck Street, waiting for his older workmate to get something out of the plumber's van. I walked past him without a word. He looked at me but gave no hint of recognition. I locked the experience away in my head and told no-one. I knew what he'd done was wrong, but I was too ashamed and confused about what the man had done, to speak about it.

∾

11 PAPER ROUND

Brown's Shop was a small shop on Finnart Street, not far from the top of Madeira Street. Academy pupils frequented it at lunchtimes and it was also the shop where we spent our weekly pocket money. I suppose we'd be about five or six when we discovered that other children got pocket money. Dad started a regular pocket money handout of threepence a week. A threepenny bit—pronounced "thruppenny bit"—was a distinctive, twelve-sided, square edged, yellow metalled coin equivalent to three old pennies. Dad increased this to sixpence a week as we got older, then it became a shilling, two shillings, two and six (or half a crown), five shillings and ultimately, around the age of ten or twelve, it went up to ten shillings, which felt like a substantial amount because it often came as a ten shilling note instead of coins. At Brown's shop you could ask Mrs Brown to bring out the penny tray, on which there were McCowan's Highland toffee caramels with their distinctive green tartan and white wax paper wrappings and other interesting sweets, including one that looked like a miniature white spaceship. You could buy packets of Spangles (square shaped boiled sweets), 'Beech Nut' chewing gum, Sherbet, Liquorice, Black Jacks, circular discs of home-made tablet, or a packet of sweetie cigarettes with a spot of red food colouring on the end, which you licked to make it look brighter, like the glowing end of a real cigarette. We used to 'smoke' them—holding the thin white ciggy stick between first and second fingers and pretend we were taking a drag, the way we saw grown-ups doing! You could also buy a 'lucky bag', which had several sweets in it plus a surprise gift—usually a cheap plastic trinket. I once got a plastic ring with a skull on it, which allowed me to imagine I was a pirate when I wore it.

When I was about eleven or twelve, I got the chance of a paper round at Brown's Shop. The older boy who was finishing up showed me the ropes and took me round for a week before he left. His key piece of advice to me was "always eat something before you come out." Later, James got a paper round there as well, so we both used to get up at six o'clock every morning to do our paper rounds before going home and getting changed for school. We used to walk or cycle to the shop in the early morning through silent streets in the yellow light of the street-lamps. Usually, the bundles of newspapers were lying on the pavement outside the shop where the John Menzies (pronounced "Ming-iss") van driver had dumped them. We cut the string with a penknife (I had a good sharp one with a pearl handle), then counted and sorted the various papers into wide canvas bags, which we then shouldered and set off on our round. The papers had the distinctive smell of printer's ink and by the end of the round, our thumb and fingers were black where the ink had rubbed off. My round took me up to the houses on the Lyle Hill, along South Street, down to Newton Street and back along Finnart Street to the shop. On Saturday mornings, there were extra weekend papers to deliver and my round extended to Margaret Street and Newark Street. Winter mornings when the snow laid a pale yellow blanket of street-lit stillness, were a magical experience. Our footprints were the first to violate its pristine perfection.

Some mornings the John Menzies van was late, and we had to wait outside the shop until it arrived. In a house opposite the shop, there was a young man called 'Walmsley'. We only knew him by his surname. Walmsley was a wee bit simple. He had a bald patch surrounded by a scrunch of sandy hair and lived there with his older brother. Only later did I discover his brother was a policeman. Walmsley used to leave the house around quarter-to-seven each morning, while we were fixing our papers at the shop. I am ashamed to say it, but I hatched a nasty, pre-meditated trick to play on poor unsuspecting Walmsley. I painted a bald-headed caricature of him on a piece of paper and took it with me next morning. It was still dark when we arrived at the shop. While we were waiting for the van to deliver our batch of morning papers, I found some heavy stones and an old bag of cement and carried them across the road. I piled the stones up against the gate, dumped the bag of cement over the gate and onto the path and threw the cartoon sketch of Walmsley on the path outside his front door. We hid in the dark shadows beside the shop to watch what happened when he came out. Sure enough he emerged as usual, clutching his packed lunch. When he saw the stuff lying all over the path, he about turned and went back into the house. When he came out again, instead of trying to open the gate, he took a flying leap over the low wall onto the pavement and off he went. James and I watched the whole drama with suppressed giggles. However, as I set off on my paper round, I'm sure I saw a slight movement behind the curtain of the window in Walmsley's house.

When we got back to the shop, Walmsley's policeman brother emerged very purposefully from his house across the road and made a bee-line for us. He asked if we knew anything about what had happened and made it very clear that we were his prime suspects. I denied any knowledge of the vile deed, but I felt guilty and ashamed of myself for playing such a rotten trick.

Perhaps I got a little taste of what it was to be on the receiving end when I had a run in with the butcher's delivery boy one Saturday morning. Uncle Joe had played for Glasgow Rangers, so naturally we were all Rangers supporters. I'd bought a Rangers cap and football scarf, with the unashamedly partisan red, white and blue colours of the team. I was wearing the cap and scarf that morning. Nearing the end of the paper round at the old sandstone buildings on Union Street between Fox Street and Margaret Street, I noticed the butcher's boy looking at me with a baleful eye as he got off his bike on the other side of the road. He was bigger, broader, and several years older than me, about fifteen or sixteen. He leaned the black-painted butcher-shop bike against a tree and came straight over to me. "Take that aff," he said in a menacing tone. I said "No, why should I?" He grabbed my jacket and said, "Take it fuckin' aff". He whipped the cap off my head, stamped on it, and ground it from side to side with his foot. It began to dawn on me that he wasn't a Rangers fan. To emphasise the point, he grabbed my scarf with both hands and pulled it tight. I choked, gasping for air. The venom in his eyes was lethal. He stalked back across the road to his bike. I escaped into the building beside me to deliver my next paper, thankful he hadn't hit me. It was an old sandstone house divided into an upstairs and downstairs flat. I climbed the internal staircase, which had ornate cast-iron railings and a polished mahogany banister. My customer, Mr Bain, lived in the top flat. As I reached the top landing, I heard the outside door at the bottom of the stairs creak open. I looked over the narrow gap of the banister and glimpsed the butcher's boy slipping inside, where he stood motion-less between the outer and inner doors. My heart thumped and my legs turned to jelly. I rang Mr Bain's doorbell, and to my relief, after a moment or two, he opened the door. I blurted out what had happened and that the butcher's boy was hiding inside the doorway downstairs. Mr Bain came down the stairs with me. As soon as the butcher's boy realised someone was with me, he skedaddled. From then on, I kept a weather eye out for my assailant when I delivered papers along that part of Union Street. Fortunately, I only ever saw him from a distance after that and could easily avoid him. This was my first taste of the intensity of the infamous West of Scotland rivalry between Rangers and Celtic, Protestant and Catholic. I guessed he was a Celtic sup-porter, indoctrinated from birth with hate-filled propa-ganda against Rangers, in the same way that Rangers' fans imbibed the same hatred of Celtic. Completely irra-tional and extremely dangerous up close.

James reminded me of the sequel—and strangely, I have no recollection of this. Apparently, Mr Bain called the po-lice, who questioned the butcher's boy about his intentions. When the baddie (trying to avoid censure) said to the policeman, "I've got to get on with my deliveries"—the policeman said, "And this boy also has papers to deliver!" He wasn't let off the hook so easily.

Another incident, of which I am not proud, happened in the early morning twilight as James and I made our way to the shop to start our paper round. We usually took a shortcut through Madeira Lane, a rough, unsurfaced lane between Bentinck Street and Madeira Street. It had high stone walls on either side, punctuated with several garages and gates which led into the back gardens of the houses on Newark Street, which was parallel to the lane. It so happened that Mr More, our next-door neighbour, rented a garage halfway along the lane. That was where he kept his Rover P4 (that lovely bulbous shaped old Rover—now a classic car). There was a brick lying on the untidy grass verge. I picked it up and said to James "Watch this". I lobbed the brick high onto the pitched roof of Mr More's garage. A crash of shattering glass and the simultaneous clang as the brick bounced off a car roof told us I'd done *more* damage (pun intended) than first imagined. James was aghast. A garden gate squeaked on its hinges. I said "let's get out of here." We thought we'd escaped unseen. However, the scripture says, *"be sure your sin will find you out",* and as I soon discovered, my reckless actions had unpleasant consequences. The squeaky garden gate belonged to Mrs Main, a Primary teacher at the Academy. We think she heard the crash and came to find out what had happened. The next day, as I passed the end of Madeira Lane on my way to school, Mr More was standing waiting for me. "Could I have a word with you Jo?" he said in his Caithness accent. There was no use denying it. The long and short of it was that Mr More paid Dad a visit and Dad had to pay a considerable amount to have Mr More's car roof repaired and resprayed. I gave up my pocket money for the foreseeable future and was obliged to hand over my paper round money for many weeks. As Dad used to say "By these things men learn." I must have been a slow learner.

~

12 FAMILY LIFE

Sunday evenings in our house were very often social events. Dad and Mum regularly invited people home for supper after the Sunday evening Gospel meeting. They loved nothing better than friendly conversation and fellowship with friends. They also loved 'a sing-song'. At some point in the evening, we handed out a pile of hymnbooks—usually the old green, cloth-bound 'Gospel Hymns of Grace and Glory', but we also used the 'PHSS' hymnbook (containing Psalms Hymns and Spiritual Songs). Everyone was free to call out their favourites. To save time and allow as many choices as possible, we usually sang the first and the last verses of each hymn. This rich heritage of song was full of wholesome evangelical doctrine, many written by great men and women of God, including Isaac Watts, William Cowper, Mrs Cousin, Charles Wesley, Horatius Bonar, Fanny Crosby, Ira D. Sankey, Frances Ridley Havergal, P.P. Bliss, as well as some of the early pioneers of the Churches of God such as, Dr Luxmoore, Mrs Hickling, Cecil Belton, and so on.

At the end of the 'sing-song', Mum brought through a selection of sandwiches and home-made cakes or, when we moved to a bigger house, we went into the dining room where the table was laden with goodies. Dad gave thanks for the food and we all tucked in. However, we were well warned only to to take ONE of each item on the plates. We dutifully observed this rule but as soon as Dad and Mum went to get the visitors' coats and hats, we had a great free-for-all, diving into whatever bits of apple tart, sandwiches or biscuits that were left.

Now, a quick pen picture of my four brothers and my sister. (I hate the word 'siblings'. Far too clinical).

James was a natural athlete. He had a strong physique, and unlike me, loved to play football or any team sports. He had (and still has) a great sense of humour. He can easily keep the entertainment going and have us all in stitches. But he also had a stubborn streak. One time we had a fierce argument about the pronunciation of the word 'towel'. It irked me that he pronounced it as "till". He persistently called it 'a till' and I kept correcting him:

Family portrait, taken about 1970, a year or so before we left Greenock. Left to right: William, Mum, James, Elisabeth, Dad, John, me

"It's not a till—it's a towel!"

"No, it's a till," he said, laughing at the mounting indignation in my voice. He knew how to 'press my buttons' and I rose to the bait every time. Another thing that annoyed me was the noises he made at night before he went to sleep. I slept in the top bunk, he on the bottom. Just as I was drifting off, he went: "Eee! Eeck!"

"Be quiet!" I said. Silence. Again, an infuriating couple of squeaks arrested my descent into the land of nod. "Eee!" "Eee!", "Eeck!" "Stop doing that!" And so it went on, until James gave up and we fell asleep. Apart from all that, James and I were very close and often used to talk and share our thoughts. To this day we relish every opportunity to review the topics of the day, or exercise our minds discussing the scriptures.

William was always very tidy. He kept his clothes beautifully folded in his drawer—but he also hoarded them. If he got a new jumper, he kept it in the drawer for months on end before he wore it. He had a friend named Duncan Telfer. Duncan's mother asked William to accompany Duncan to elocution lessons. He entertained us afterwards by his exaggerated imitation of the phrases he learned, such as "How now, brown cow!" William's other friend was Ian Abrahams, the only child of a Jewish couple who lived on the corner of Eldon Street and Madeira Street.

One day, William met David Bruce at the entrance to the close. He said 'Would you like a penny stamp?' David said 'yes' and held out his hand expectantly, whereupon William stamped hard on his foot. David went howling up the stair to his mother. I don't remember if she came down to complain to Mum or not.

William gave us some unexpected entertainment when a plumber came to do some work on a dripping pipe. While the plumber was kneeling down, training his blowtorch on the pipe, we stood around him, watching with interest. Suddenly William did a couple of karate chops in the air behind the plumber's back. The swish of air caused him to turn round suspiciously, only to see William, hands by his side, innocently watching him at work. As soon as he started working on the pipe again—more karate chops. Whenever he looked round, there was William, watching with rapt attention. We barely suppressed our laughter. The man knew something was going on, but William was too fast.

James reminded me about the time I threw a Joiner's jacket down the stairs and poured ink on it. Strangely, I have no recollection of that whatsoever!

Mum befriended a lady called Mrs Edwards, who lived with her son in the downstairs part of a house on Brisbane Street, just off Madeira Street. Her son had two pet mice in a cage in her conservatory. On one of her visits, Mum took William, James, and John with her. While Mum was doing something inside the house, William and James opened the cage and started playing with the mice. When Mum came out, the two white mice were lying dead in the cage. A mouse had bitten William's finger. His instinctive reaction was to fling it back into the cage, where it must have caught a sharp bit of the cage and died. How the other one died, I'm not sure. Can a mouse die of a broken heart? It was an unfortunate accident. Mrs Edwards didn't invite them back.

John went through a phase of smoking 'doubts'—the cigarette butts thrown away by Mr Ferguson. He also had a fascination with matches and fire. In the kitchen one evening a week or two before Christmas, we started writing letters to Santa and sending them up the chimney. There was a fire on in the fireplace which created a good draught of wind to snatch the bits of paper from our hands. After about fifteen minutes of industrious note writing and chimney posting, we heard a muffled roaring in the chimney. Mum went outside to investigate. Flames were shooting out of the chimney-pot on the roof. She phoned the Fire Brigade, and it wasn't long before several big firemen with black jackets and yellow helmets arrived to put out the fire. None of us volunteered the reason for the start of the fire and the firemen didn't ask.

John had a mischievous sense of humour and Mum was probably more lenient with him than his three older brothers. On one occasion, Mum reprimanded him about something and warned him that as a sinner, if he didn't repent and believe on Jesus, he'd end up in the Lake of fire. "Huh," said John, "I'll just make toast!" Mum saw the funny side of his remark but felt obliged to emphasise the vital importance of having his sins forgiven.

John, aged about five, snapped by street photographer, with the photographer's pet monkey on his shoulder.

Elisabeth, being the youngest, had quite a hard time with four brothers who were not at all sympathetic to girlish interests. She was too young to accompany us on most of our adventures, which was probably just as well. Because Elisabeth was the only girl, Mum allowed her to stay up later than we had been allowed when younger, so that when Dad came home from work, he could spend some time with his little girl. In families, petty jealousies can develop based on real or perceived differences. It was only right that Dad and Mum should make special provision for their little girl. And even if they indulged her a little, who could blame them? As boys, though, we saw everything through childish eyes and resented the fact Elisabeth had her own room and certain female privileges, which we construed as 'not fair'. Dad and Mum rightly protected her from our protestations and soon put us in our place if we complained. How true the words of the apostle Paul:

> When I was a child, I spake as a child, I felt as a child, I thought as a child: now that I am become a man, I have put away childish things.
>
> 1ST CORINTHIANS 13:11

One day Dad brought home a record player. The base and lid were covered in a sort of two-tone cream and red plastic which had a fabric-like texture. Uncle Willie had been learning French from a Linguaphone course for several years. He'd reached the point where he didn't need to listen to the lessons anymore. So he gave the record player and the complete set of records and textbooks to Dad, thinking it might be useful for us. Unfortunately, none of us were terribly keen to learn French and Dad didn't insist that we take it seriously. We dipped in and out whenever we took the notion. The small black 45 rpm records were the same size as 'singles' of the latest hits. They each had a brown paper sleeve with details of the subject and section printed on it. We followed along with the native French speakers and imitated them as we read the illustrated text in the books: "Deuxieme Partie."— "Parlez vous Francaise?"—"Oui, je parle Francaise." "Voici le livre. Le livre et dans sur le table". "Voici le pipe." "Parlez lentement si'l vous plez", and so on. I suppose we gained a smattering of words and phrases, although what use "Vwasee leh peep" (Here is the pipe) would ever be, was always rather doubtful.

Every year, Dad used to go down to the furniture trade exhibition at Earl's Court in London. He offered to buy us each a record to listen to on the record player when he next went to the trade fair. He asked each of us which record we'd like. It must have been around 1968, because he suggested I might like a recording of Israeli Army marching songs. The six-day war in June 1967 had sent a thrill through our church community. We saw the overruling hand of God in the Israeli victory, outnumbered as they were by the Arabs by almost ten to one. It sounded like an exciting record to have, so that became my choice. Elisabeth got a record of 'Salvation Army Christmas Carols for children', and Mum asked for a Kathleen Ferrier record. I don't remember what William and John got, but James got one that turned out to be a bit too jazzy, so Dad took him to a music shop in Greenock to change it. He ended up with a tenor singer named Al Bryn (at least he thinks that was the name) who sang 'Count your blessings…' among other hymns in his high pitched male voice. Dad also bought a LP of two of Billy Graham's recorded addresses at one of the mass gospel rallies he'd held in London. We liked the passion-ate, straight-talking way he preached with his American accent. We listened to that record over and over until we could virtually repeat Billy's sermons verbatim. In one of them he said, "Then some say if you're sincere, that's all you need. I saw a man pick up a football once and run forty-five yards with it. He was the sincerest man I ever saw—but he ran the wrong way and lost the game!" The audience roared with laughter. We instinctively under-stood he wasn't talking about football as we knew it, but we enjoyed the way he told the joke even though we hadn't a clue about American Football.

Around this time, Donny Black lent me his little Hohner 48 bass Piano Accordion. He showed me the diagonal arrangement of the bass buttons, and that you only needed to use three rows at a time to accompany any key. By this time, I had my own room in the basement. It used to be the cellar but Dad commissioned Jack Bar-bour to dig out all the hard packed earth and rubble left behind by the builders, until he got the floor down to a level which would allow a proper floor to be installed. There were no windows in the old cellar, but it was my room and I liked it. Dad allowed me to choose the wall-paper and paper the walls myself. I picked a fake wood-panelling pattern, which, to my adolescent brain, looked really cool.

I used to practise the accordion looking in the mirror to ensure I was hitting the correct buttons. I picked out some simple tunes. One of my favourites was a rousing

Israeli marching song called 'Shoshana! Shoshana!' I imagined it meant Hosannah. The Israeli singers sang it with tremendous enthusiasm, but it was all in Hebrew. I pieced together a transliteration so that I could sing along, even though I'd no idea what it meant. The bit I remember was Effi Netzer, the leader of song, singing a solo, which went something like: 'a trici du fah….' then everyone joined in with the rousing chorus: 'Shoshana! Shoshana! Shoshana!'And so on. You can now listen to a version on YouTube—but you'll only find the original if you put the following Hebrew words into the searchbar: אפי נצר - שושנה שושנה - הבה נשירה. (Here's the URL: https://youtu.be/1iW-j2h01iI) It has an orange album cover with a photo of Effi Netzer playing the accordion and the English words 'Sing along with Effi Netzer - live recording'. Scan the QR code below to listen on your phone.

Much later in life, I discovered the story behind the song. Jewish poet Haim Hefer wrote it in 1947. It's all about an old diesel-powered wooden ship named 'Susanna', which was used to take Polish, Romanian and Hungarian survivors of the Holocaust to Israel from Italy. They renamed the ship 'Luzinski' after a Zionist leader who'd been looking after the survivors. Tragically, he died in a car accident in Rome later that year. These Jewish refugees were living in a survivor camp near near Metaponto, at Bari in Southern Italy. In defiance of the British ban on Jewish immigration to Israel, a daring band of sympathisers organised the clandestine transfer of more than eight-hun-

dred Jews from Trento Bay to the ship. They then sailed by a circuitous route to Nitzanim beach in Southern Israel, where they ran the ship onto a sandbar and disembarked their passengers via a long rope stretched from ship to shore. The British military discovered the operation and arrested seven-hundred of them. They took them to Haifa and put on a ship to Cyprus where they were detained. Eventually, most of them returned to Israel. The background to the song only increases my admiration for the resourcefulness and indomitable spirit of these great people, who, although they suffered so much, rose above the injustices and sang with such cheerful gusto and optimism. It's a great tune, and as a young man, I wrote some words to go with the tune which, I fondly imagined, we might teach to the boys at camp. Sadly, that never materialised. For what it's worth, here's my alternative version of the Israeli folk song, 'Shoshana! Shoshana!':

> Hosannah! Hosannah! Sing praise to the Lord,
> Yes, Bless Him and thank Him for his mighty Love;
> He loved us so much that he went to the Cross,
> Hosannah! Hosannah! Praise God!

> Chorus:
> Hosannah! Hosannah! Hosannah!
> We love to sing of our King!
> Give thanks to God forever,
> Hosannah! Hallelujah! Praise God!

> Yes Jesus loves you, and Jesus loves me,
> He bore all our sins when He died on the Tree;
> But He rose from the dead, He's alive evermore,
> So give Him the glory today!

When Jesus returns, He'll rule us in peace,
The desert will bloom and fighting shall cease,
The wolf and the lamb together shall feed,
Hosannah! Hallelujah! Praise God!

13 DAD

Dad and Mum's wedding day, at the Douglas
Hotel, Glasgow, 8th February 1956. Left -
Right: Willie Terrell (who married them), Dad's
mother, Janet Johnson, Ellen Brindle
(bridesmaid), Dad, Mum, Uncle Willie,
Grandad (Peter Christison), Mrs Terrell.

I remember the first time I called my father, 'Dad'. I must
have heard other children addressing their father as
"Dad", and decided that continuing to call him "Daddy"
was too babyish. I was playing in the back green and had
come to the kitchen window, which was half open. Dad

was sitting at the table. I poked my head in the window and when he looked up, I said "Hello Dad!" He laughed and said "hello" back.

Dad was an exceptional man, not just because he was my father. He had force of character coupled with humility and a big-heart. A rare combination. Although serious by nature, he was always quick to see the funny side of things. His own father, Joseph Johnson (my grandfather), died of stomach cancer at fifty, on 29th June 1930. Dad was only twelve years old. His father had migrated from Sutherland in the north of Scotland to find work. He spoke with a Highland accent and started an auctioneering business in Greenock.

Dad's father and mother on their wedding day, 16th July 1914 at the Tontine Hotel, Greenock. They were married by A.J.B. Paterson, minister United Free Church, Kilmalcolm. Seated: Dad's Granny and Grandfather, Marion and William Orr. Standing: Dad's Aunt Mary, Uncle Robert, best man Mr Steele, Bridesmaid Lizzie Holmes, Uncle Willie and his father's sister - Aunt Barbara. Sitting on ground: Jenny and Mirn Black.

He used to make a regular trip with horse and cart to Glasgow, where he bought second-hand furniture to sell in his Greenock saleroom. He became friendly with Isaac Woolfson, a Jewish furniture dealer who later became the founder of Great Universal Stores.

Dad's mother was Janet Orr. Her parents farmed the land on a small farm called Gateside, between Greenock and Kilmacolm. I don't know how she met Grandfather Johnson, but Dad said she once told him her troubles began the night she got married. She was a Christian, and he wasn't, and it became a cause of friction between them. She experienced the bitter reality of the scriptures which say: "How shall two walk together except they be agreed?" and "Be not unequally yoked with unbelievers…what fellowship has light with darkness?" Dad's father was saved[1] on his deathbed, after a visit from a local Christian couple who spoke to him about the Lord Jesus who died on the cross for sinners. Dad's parents were married in the United Free Church. Their first child, William Orr Johnson, was born on 25 June 1915 at 27 Argyle Street Rothesay, on the island of Bute. Tragically, he died in the Spanish flu epidemic of 1918-19. He was just three years old. Dad's mum always remembered how, when 'wee Wullie' as they called him, finished what was on his plate, he said "aw' done!"

Dad was born on 22 May 1918 and his brother Joe, a couple of years later. Their names were John Holmes Johnson and Joseph Robert Johnson.

After his father's death, his mother attended the Church of Scotland but became dissatisfied with some things being taught there. Her sister Mary, who'd married a farmer named John Black and lived at Auchenfoyle Farm in the countryside above Greenock, invited her to come to the Church of God with her. Prior to this, Dad's mother had taken him and his brother Joe to an evangelical mission near Greenock docks, called Barnard's Court Mission. A few years before he died, Dad got in touch with a Mr Dunn, a descendant of the original founding family of Barnard's Court Mission. He enjoyed telling him about his previous connection.

Dad started his working life in the Kilmacolm branch of the Royal Bank of Scotland and would probably have worked his way up to become a Bank Manager if it hadn't been for the Second World War, which disrupted the lives of a whole generation for several years. Although he' was saved, baptised and added to the Church of God in Greenock, rightly or wrongly, Dad joined up to fight the menace that was Hitler and Nazi Germany. He told me on more than one occasion, that he knew he'd made a mistake several days later, when with the other recruits, he was lined up on a parade ground and the sergeant major shouted "Jesus Christ Almighty!" Dad said he felt as if the very building would fall down on them. He knew he should have been a conscientious objector, but it was too late for that. There was no turning back.

Dad served with the 78th Royal Artillery regiment, which saw action in North Africa at El Alamein. He applied for and was accepted for officer training in Palestine, after which he was deployed to Italy as a liaison officer. When the fighting was over, he was sent back to Palestine to protect railways and strategic positions from the Irgun—Jewish paramilitaries who were angry with the British Navy for preventing shiploads of Jewish refugees entering Israel from Europe.

He was stationed at Nazareth for six months and while waiting for demobilisation, visited several Biblical sites. He was repelled, however, by the commercialisation of religious sites, especially in Bethlehem and Jerusalem.

After the war he got a job at Glasgow University. He attended various social events, dances, and dinners, but enjoyable as these things were, they couldn't satisfy the spiritual part of his being. His mother invited him to special meetings being held by evangelist Joe Lindsay at Caledonia Hall. Night after night, Joe spoke on the Deity of Christ. On the last night he was so deeply moved by Joe Lindsay's preaching, that the tears ran down his face. After the meeting, Joe spoke to him and encouraged him to come back to the church. Dad said he went home and threw his packet of cigarettes on the fire. He never smoked another. He asked the Lord for a second chance 'to stand up for Jesus, to testify to the grace of Christ.' In his autobiography, he wrote: "Within one month my prayer was answered." Two letters arrived, one from the War Office, instructing him to report for duty at his local Territorial Army office and the other from the Colonel, welcoming him. He replied to both, saying that as a believer in Christ, he'd been wrong to engage in combatant service and wished to conscientiously object. He also wrote letters to many of his army acquaintances, urging them to trust in Jesus as their Saviour.

In 1950, Dad accepted an invitation to join Uncle Willie in his furniture business but then decided to change tack and study for an M.A. Degree at Glasgow University. He went on to Jordanhill College and trained as a Maths Teacher. He taught Maths at The Mount School, Greenock—which John Bradley euphemistically called "a finishing school for young gentlemen". ('Brad' as we all called him, was a pupil at 'The Mount' when Dad taught there. He was one of the young men in the Church of God in Greenock when we were growing up.)

At Greenock Academy, my teachers wrongly assumed because Dad was a Maths teacher, that I was also good with figures. He tried his best to help me with my maths homework. I would follow his reasoning so far, then became hopelessly lost. Dad would go back over his working again, briskly writing out the figures in pencil as he explained how to reach the solution. I became increasingly wooden headed until eventually he gave up in despair and left me to try and figure it out for myself.

Dad and Mum, James, Jo, William, John

Dad sometimes reflected on his career, switching from one thing to another—leaving teaching to work for Uncle Willie, back to teaching again, retraining as an R.E.

Teacher, then back to work as a Maths teacher again (latterly, at Greenock High School until he retired). As a result, he ended up with a smaller teacher's pension than he would have had if he hadn't chopped and changed so often. He advised me and the rest of us not to do what he did, but to find something we enjoyed doing and stick at it. His advice has served me well and I recommend it to my own family.

Dad was an avid Bible Student. He told me that when he first began to study the Bible, a brother told him he was spending an hour a day studying the scriptures. Dad wasn't impressed, because he was spending several hours in his Bible each evening! He deliberately chose Biblical Hebrew as one of his options on the M.A. course at Glasgow University so that he'd be able to read the Old Testament in its original language. He was in the same Hebrew class as Eric Archibald from the Church of God in Glasgow. Dad had a great admiration for Eric's ability in Hebrew and other languages. Dad got second prize for Hebrew, but Eric thought he deserved the first prize, which went to a Jewish girl in their class. The Hebrew letters and the right-to-left direction of words on the page fascinated me. I used to ask Dad to read aloud from his Hebrew Bible:

בְּרֵאשִׁית בָּרָא אֱלֹהִים אֵת הַשָּׁמַיִם וְאֵת הָאָרֶץ
As Dad enunciated it: 'birishith bara Elohim ayth hashamayim v'ayth ha-aretz' — In the beginning, God created the heavens and the earth.

It amazed me that he could extract meaning from those curious, hieroglyphic letters. He was very organised and kept meticulous records. I have his handwritten notes on

Bible subjects, which he kept filed in alphabetical order in several filing cabinet drawers in his study, as well as the notes of nearly every gospel or ministry address he gave. A lifetime's work which I am loath to throw away. I would like to digitise and preserve them for future generations. As Dad used to say: "If I'm spared."

Dad's Austin A40, Jo, William, Dad, James

Dad owned a succession of cars over the years, some more memorable than others. The first one I remember was an Austin A40. When James, William, and I were very young, Dad took us on holiday to Sutherland. Dad and Mum sang hymns and Sunday school choruses as we drove along. I remember how happy I was, standing up with my hands on the back of Dad's seat, singing with them as we sped along the road. William was just a toddler, but James and I were old enough to take a keen interest in driving. We watched Dad's every move as he changed gear, steered the car and worked the foot pedals. When he was managing director at 'Orrs', he got a maroon Vauxhall Victor. It had bench seats and was roomy enough for four boys in the back and Elisabeth in between Mum and Dad in the front. For a short time, he had an old Humber Hawk, which broke down one afternoon at Wemyss Bay, where Dad took us for a run. We left it parked in the old quarry and took the bus home. Another time, Dad bought a big blue vintage car (possibly a Humber 12) which had running boards and elegant rounded mudguards which swept down on either side of the long bonnet, with big round headlights mounted on them. The back doors opened like a mirror image of the front doors. The mingled smell of old leather, oil and petrol was something to be savoured. Eventually, Dad got rid of it because the cost of repair and maintenance was just too much. As we grew older and bigger, we needed a roomier vehicle, so Dad bought a Volkswagen Caravanette into which we were all able to fit with ease. I remember feeling sick on a Sunday morning journey between Greenock and Galston, where Dad had been invited for the day by Jimmy and Elsie Barr. I was in a backward-facing seat going up and down all the hills, and the twists and turns on the road between Kilmacolm and Lochwinnoch. It was at the part of the road between the West Knockbartnock Farm entrance (where Dad's cousin Ruby and her husband Bobby Laird lived) and the road that goes off to the Muirshiel Estate, that the queasiness really kicked in. I said "I'm going to be sick!" Dad stopped the van. I got out, couldn't be sick, got back in and swapped places with one of my brothers so that I could sit in a forward facing seat (which we all preferred) for the rest of the journey.

One year we were sitting in the Caravanette, ready to set off for a summer holiday at Uncle Hugh and Aunt Nan's in Sutherland, when we overheard Mr More saying to Dad "D'you think you'll make it?" We laughed our heads off at the stupidity of this comment. Of course Dad would make it! He could do anything!

Dad had a strong connection with Sutherland because his father had come from there. He kept in touch with his cousin Hugh Mackintosh and Hugh's wife, Nan. We called them Uncle Hugh and Aunt Nan. Uncle Hugh was a Ghillie on the river Oykell, a salmon river. He showed wealthy clients where and how to catch those amazing fish with a fly rod. I'd been given a little grey plastic Brownie 127 camera for my birthday and

Dad and Mum with Uncle Hugh and Aunt Nan, outside 'Badfluich', Altass, Sutherland.

had high hopes of snapping a salmon as it leapt up the famous Shin Falls. Uncle Hugh took his pipe out of his mouth in his slow and measured way. "I don't think you'll be able to it with that", he said. Next day, undeterred by Uncle Hugh's pessimism, I got myself into position on the rocks at the bottom of the falls, squinted through the viewfinder and waited until one of the seething mass of salmon in the pool below, attempted another leap.

I pressed the button at the first streak of flashing silver. When the prints eventually came back from being developed at the Chemist, to my great satisfaction, one of my snaps had captured a salmon, frozen in mid-air above the rushing torrent of the Shin Falls.

Uncle Willie's business was expanding. He told Dad it "needed a young man's push", so he asked Dad to come

Salmon leaping, Shin Falls. Kodak Brownie 127 Third Model, f/14, 50.6mm, 1/40 Sec.

back into the business with him. Dad left his teaching post to become managing director of Orrs House Furnishers, in Greenock. He gave it so much 'push', that they opened a pram shop and another showroom. He negotiated an arrangement with a finance firm so that customers could buy furniture and carpets on Hire Purchase. Dad also streamlined the book-keeping system—he set up a card database of locally known bad debtors, from information gleaned from 'Stubbs Gazette' (which printed the names of people who'd incurred court decrees against them for non-payment of debt) and he commissioned a weekly advert in the Greenock Telegraph (locally known as 'The Tele'). His strapline was: 'Orrs House Furnishers: Good Quality at a Reasonable Price'. This immediately boosted sales and established 'Orrs' as a local firm renowned for excellent service and value. As Dad observed, often the best customers were those who had little money but faithfully came into Terrace Road to pay their weekly cash instalment. He recalled an occasion when a well-spoken, well-heeled couple came in and placed a very substantial order. However, Dad had his suspicions that their grandiose manner was not all it seemed. So he looked them up on his 'Stubbs Gazette' card index. Lo-and-behold, they were on record as bad debts! He confronted them with the evidence and that was the end of that!

It was Dad who suggested I might consider a career as a 'Commercial Artist.' He'd seen the sort of work the local commercial artists did to create advertisements for Orrs. It sounded appealing at the time and gave me something to aim for, even though life took a rather different turn.

I don't know whether it was Dad's army discipline, his own upbringing, or just his temperament, but he would brook no rebellion. When necessary, he had no hesitation about using corporal punishment. Unlike today, when the pendulum has swung to the opposite extreme, most parents of that era accepted that a judicious smack or the occasional 'tanning of the hide' were perfectly acceptable methods for managing children's behaviour. Now and then we pushed the boundaries beyond the limits of the normal checks and balances and sterner measures were required. Perhaps it's wiser to draw a veil over some of the reasons why this sort of punishment was meted out, save to say that if Mum ever said "I'll tell your dad when he gets home", our panicky reaction was: "No! No! Mum, don't tell Dad, please don't!"

Mum had a short cane made of ebony wood, which she called 'the rod'. If we misbehaved and ignored her warnings, she came after us with swingeing strokes, whacking the rod this way and that, at our buttocks, legs, or anywhere she could make contact as we swerved and jerked out of the way. We usually treated this performance as a joke, an exciting interlude which lent spice to the afternoon's entertainment. But as soon as she said "I'll tell Dad", the joke ended, and we abruptly came to heel. For a while, Mum kept a little book in which she entered 'a black mark' against our names when we didn't do what we were told. Too many black marks and Dad wanted to know why. So we pleaded with her: "No, don't give me a black mark, I promise not to do it again!" A 'thrashing' from Dad was an experience to be avoided at all costs, not so much because of its severity (and believe me, he made every whack count), but mainly because we dreaded his anger. He was never out of control, but the severity of his disapproval was such that it created a temporary estrangement between us and shut down his usual approachability. Fortunately, Dad only resorted to such treatment when all other sanctions were exhausted or when the crime was of such gravity that physical pain was the most effective method of teaching us a lesson. We certainly gained an experimental understanding of what the Bible calls 'righteous indignation'.

Dad was Sunday School Superintendent at Cedar Hall for a few years. Sometimes they had what was called an 'open school'. Instead of splitting up into separate classes, one of the teachers told a story to everyone. I remember Dad taking an 'Open Sunday' telling a story which involved a pair of antlers which Uncle Joe had given him from a deer he'd shot somewhere. I remember nothing about the story (!) but I have a vivid mental image of Dad bobbing around the platform holding the antlers on his head, pretending to be a deer.

Dad was an active participant in the Greenock Friday Night Class, an enjoyable mix of stimulating Bible discussion, talks, community singing, chorale groups and socialisation. I have a fond memory of the friendly atmosphere of those gatherings. Later, Dad took us to the Paisley 'YPMs' (young people's meetings). Although convened for the benefit of young people in the churches, brethren and sisters of all ages attended. In those days, there were no artificial barriers between young and old, which meant we were much more familiar with the older generation as three-dimensional individuals. As a result, I think we had a greater respect for them and a rapport with them which, it seems to me, is often missing nowadays.

Besides gathering fresh thoughts during the week to bring to God in appreciation of Christ at The Remembrance[2], Dad spent many hours preparing for various speaking engagements. He was always original and interesting to listen to. His thanksgivings on a Lord's Day morning were always fresh and often touched my heart.

When I was about thirteen, Dad decided to leave Greenock and move the family to Ayrshire where he'd applied for a post at Irvine Royal Academy. The Church held a farewell meeting for him. It wasn't until the night of the farewell that the reality suddenly hit him. He was moving away from people he knew so well, from the town where he was born and brought up, where he'd lived and worked and served God for so long. He became emotional and struggled to hold back the tears when he got up to say a few words of thanks.

I've never been entirely clear about the reason he made this move, which uprooted us from all that was familiar, and significantly affected each one of us.

∾

14 MUM

Mum with James, Jo, William and John

Mum always had a sunny, optimistic outlook. Even in her nineties, with various aches and pains and a seriously painful wound on her foot requiring twice-weekly dressing by the podiatrist, she maintained that happy personality. She loved each of us as only a mother can. When James, William and I were very young, she cared for her Aunt Mary and then her father at 19 Bentinck Street before they died. Later, when we were in our

teens, she brought her Aunt Nette from Edinburgh to live
with us and looked after her until she died.

~

Aunt Nette on her 21st birthday, 8th February
1917

AUNT NETTE TRAINED as a nurse and worked in
Lambeth in London when she was a young woman.
Later, she was a Matron in the Sick Children's Hospital,
Edinburgh, before taking up the post of Matron at the
Royal Blind School in Edinburgh, where she met and
married the blind headmaster, Hamish Lochhead. They
lived in a bungalow called 'Bruach na Luach' (Gaelic for
'bank, or border of worth, or value).

Every now and then, we drove through to Edinburgh to visit them at 11 Observatory Road, halfway down the steep road which leads up to the Royal Observatory on Blackford Hill. Aunt Nette always laid on a lovely spread for us when we visited.

She kept a few hens in a hen-run in the back garden and Uncle Hamish had a large vegetable plot right next to the house, so they always had plenty of fresh produce. Uncle Hamish had rope lines rigged up around his plot to guide him when he was cultivating the soil and looking after his plants.

When I stayed with her one summer, after breaking my cheekbone, she took me out to the plot and dug up fresh new potatoes for dinner each day. She served them with butter and they were mouth-wateringly delicious.

Uncle Hamish and Aunt Nette at the back of their house in Observatory Road, Edinburgh

~

THERE WERE one or two occasions when Mum's sunny personality was momentarily eclipsed. For example, she always had an irrational, almost superstitious fear of electricity. She became extremely worried when any of us tried to fix the wiring of a kettle or other electrical appliance. On one occasion, an electrician was doing some work in the kitchen and, having had a recent fright (the washing machine had been making a strange noise), she asked him if electricity could jump from one place to another. "Oh no, it canny jump. No, it canny jump," he said emphatically. "Hmmm, okay …" said Mum, weighing up this information. From her expression it was clear she didn't believe him.

Mum often took us for a walk to the Battery Park, along the Esplanade or halfway up the Lyle Hill to the Lyle Park where we enjoyed running about. Being a country girl at heart, she loved nothing better than to pick brambles at the end of the summer. There was a large bit of rough ground on the slope below the Lyle Park, where there were lots of large bramble bushes. She used Grandad's knobbly walking stick to pull the hard-to-reach branches closer to us and we picked the luscious black berries and filled our plastic containers with them. We always ended up with lots of scratches, but it was worth it for the lovely bramble jelly Mum made, using a recipe handed down from her Aunt Mary.

Mum loved to sing. Her PHSS[1] hymnbook is well thumbed and marked with umpteen favourites! She often brought to our notice the words of a hymn that had come to mind. She had a lovely soprano voice and, for several years, was part of the Scottish Singing Group, which made several excellent recordings under the expert musical direction (at different times), of Mark Bentham, Jim Cranson, and Martin Archibald. These are now available on Youtube courtesy of Martin Jones: https://www.youtube.com/watch?v=uJ4dPsxgx-U and here: https://www.youtube.com/watch?v=jS77XJdLTHU

For me, those precious recordings pull at the heartstrings. I'm sure I can hear her clear soprano voice singing those beautiful hymns.

'In the midst of the congregation will I sing thy praise.' (Hebrews 2:12)

One year when we were very young, Herbert Cameron, one of the Camp leaders, composed a song for the Scottish Campers. In my mind, I can still see and hear Mum and Dad heartily singing it in the kitchen:

> 'Oh comrade can you say, on this very day,
> That you're ready for the coming of the Lord?
> He is coming to the air,
> Saints will meet Him there,
> Are you ready for the coming of the Lord?
>
> Chorus:
> He is coming, yes He's coming,
> He will keep His parting word;
> What a promise He has given,
> He will take His own, to heaven,
> Are you ready for the coming of the Lord?'

Despite her friendly disposition, Mum was quite capable of standing up for herself and for her children. One day,

William came out to the back green, confident as ever, with his jeans tucked into his socks the way Bill Taulbut did when he went cycling. William was working on a makeshift repair to his bike when he noticed David Bruce watching him. "What are you looking at?" he said, and pushed his head against one of the four cast iron clothes poles that marked out the communal drying green. David's wail immediately brought his mother to the kitchen window, which was directly above ours. She shoved her ample torso out of the window and said "What's the matter, darling?" Before she was half-way down the stairs, William had made his escape into the shelter of our kitchen. When Mrs Bruce rushed out to the back green and discovered that David's assailant had disappeared, she marched over to our open kitchen window where a contented-looking William was standing beside Mum.

Mrs Bruce screamed "Smack him!"

"I've already smacked him," said Mum.

"Well, smack him again!" And she stormed off.

When I was about nine or ten, I was playing with some other children in Octavia Terrace. Jacqueline Ramage, daughter of Dr Ramage, made a nasty remark about Mum. I slapped her face hard. Off she went, crying and holding her face. I knew there would be trouble, so I went home and told Dad exactly what had happened. It wasn't long before the bell rang. It was Dr Ramage, complaining that I had assaulted his daughter. I overheard Dad saying: "he was only sticking up for his mother". I heard no more about it. I don't think Mum got involved on that occasion, but there were other times when an irate neighbour came to complain to Dad about something one of us had done.

On those occasions, Mum was the most disarming of women. She invited them in with a smile, made them a cup of tea and was extremely attentive while Dad sorted the matter out. They usually left on good terms!

With four energetic boys, followed unexpectedly a couple of years later by Elisabeth, Mum was under constant stress. When Grandad died, she lost control for a short but very intense period. I was only about five at the time but I clearly remember her, very agitated, in our hallway, shouting at Dad in a demented tone, "I believe he'll be sitting at the right hand of God!" Dad was so gentle in his response. He just put his arm around her and said, "Jean, Jean," and she calmed down. Mum did her best to keep up with all the housework and meals, but was often overwhelmed by it all. Eventually Dad drew up a rota and gave each of us a weekly job to do—cleaning the bath and toilet with Vim, sweeping and mopping the kitchen floor with flash and hot water, dusting, hoovering or whatever.

Mum loved the scriptures and the things of the Lord. She and Dad highly valued the privilege of being in the House of God. She used to tell us how her father read his Bible by candlelight before going out to work. His name was Peter Christison. He was born at Bowhill near Selkirk in the Scottish Borders. His father, James Christison, worked in the woollen mill at Walkerburn but died at the early age of thirty-four. His mother[2] raised him and his brothers and sisters on her own. Mum's father—Grandad to us—trained as a gardener, working for a time at the Logan Botanic Gardens in Dumfrieshire, before he was married. He used to cycle from there to the Church of God in Drummore (no longer in existence), to keep The Remembrance each week. During the First World War, both he and his brother John took their stand as conscientious objectors on religious grounds. Their brother William, who I know very little about, joined up. As previously mentioned, when the tribunal judge asked Grandad, "What would you do if the Germans invaded and began shooting your family?"—he replied, "It would be a quick dispatch to glory." He was willing to die rather than take up arms and was granted exemption from military service. The judge allocated him work of national importance in Forestry and after the war he secured a job as Head Gardener to Captain Murray Lockhart on Milton Lockhart Estate in the Clyde valley. Mum and her brothers, Jim, John and Peter, were born in the Gardener's cottage on the estate.

Mum's first job was as a housemaid in "The Big House", the mansion where the Lockhart family lived. She was saved through a Bible text on the wall that she read while making the beds. It read:

'My sheep hear My voice, and I know them, and they follow Me.' (John 10:27)

 Her mother Elizabeth died in tragic circumstances on 12th May 1939, when Mum was just eleven and a half. Her Dad was left with four of a family to look after, besides his gardening duties. Grandad did his best to look after them all, making basic meals such as porridge for breakfast and lentil soup for dinner. Eventually, however, it all became too much for him. The only solution was to cut short Mum's schooling when she was fourteen, so that she could make the meals and keep the house for her dad and three brothers.

Mum, with her dad and brothers outside their house in Unitas Crescent, Wishaw. My father took the photo.

Only a few years ago, Mum divulged the cause of her mother's death. Her mother had cancer—what kind, Mum didn't say—but apparently it was so painful that on at least one occasion she saw her mother run out into the garden, dancing around to ease the pain. On the day she went missing, they found her shoes on the bank of the river Clyde, which flowed through the estate. She couldn't swim. Her body was later found near the bridge at the entrance to the estate. At the graveside, her father quoted the words of Job:

"The LORD gave, and the LORD hath taken away; blessed be the name of the LORD." (Job 1:21)

∽

A YEAR or two after Dad died, I took Mum for a run in the car to Milton Lockhart. The big house had long gone. Incredibly, in the 1980s, A Japanese film star bought the dilapidated mansion and transported it stone by stone, across the Trans-Siberian Railway to Japan, where it was rebuilt. Milton Lockhart's original 'big house' now stands at the centre of a Japanese theme park. We drove over the bridge and parked the car outside the lodge gates. I opened the big iron gates, which were not locked, and we strolled through the estate. Mum pointed out the old walled garden, now overgrown, and recalled various landmarks. She pointed out the place where her dad kept bees and told me that she and her brothers were to run and tell him if they saw the bees swarming in the branches of a tree, so that he could come and collect them for a new hive.

Mum, beside the honeysuckle, near the ruins of the old cottage where she grew up, on Milton Lockhart Estate, Clyde Valley, Lanarkshire

I took her photo, standing outside the ruins of the Gardener's cottage where she was born. The estate was finally bought by Billy Allan, a Scottish Oil magnate (former

SNAPSHOTS FROM MEMORY 125

director of Partick Thistle Football Club), who later built a modern version of the big house, no expense spared. How true the words of King Solomon:

'There is no remembrance of the former generations; neither shall there be any remembrance of the latter generations that are to come, among those that shall come after.' (Ecclesiastes 1:11)

Mum's parents were numbered with the saints[3] in the Church of God in Crossford. (Sadly, it closed several years ago.) Mum told me how Harry Brindle, one of the overseers[4] in the Church, when his own daughters Ellen and Emily were going to be baptised, with the best of intentions, suggested it would be nice if she was baptised at the same time. Mum went along with the suggestion, but some years later, requested to be re-baptised because the first time she had done it out of a mis-placed willingness to please, rather than from personal conviction. She wanted to truly commit herself to the disciple pathway. Her request was granted. Mum had a very close friendship with Ellen and Emily all her life. When she got married, Ellen was her bridesmaid. She held their father Harry, in high esteem, as a shepherd hearted man who loved the Lord Jesus.

When Grandad retired from Milton Lockhart, the family moved to a council house in Lanarkshire town of Carluke. Mum got a job as a checker and postal packer in Smith's Clockwork factory in nearby Wishaw. She worked there until she and Dad were married in The Douglas Hotel, 193 Bath Street, Glasgow, on the 8th February 1956.

15 FRIENDS, NEIGHBOURS, CHILDHOOD PRANKS

Across the road, opposite our house on Bentinck Street, stood a large house with a gigantic 'Monkey-Puzzle' tree in the garden. The house had been converted into two flats. Two old sisters lived in the upstairs part of the house. The older of the two had a swept back mane of white hair and was rather eccentric. She had a permanently nervous look, as if the sun was in her eyes. On the odd occasion when she came outside, she skulked around like a fugitive fleeing an unseen pursuer. Once or twice a year, she plucked up the courage to come over and ring our bell. In a whiney voice which tailed off at the end of each sentence, she said: "Could one of the boys come over and sweep the floor?" I don't know why this job always fell to me—maybe because I was the eldest— but each time, I obediently crossed the road, opened the gate, skipped up the wide stone steps to the front door and rang the bell.

Miss whiney voice opened the door and showed me into her bedroom, which had a linoleum floor covering of indeterminate colour. "Would you please sweep under the bed?" she said as she handed me the brush. There were a couple of rectangular woven rugs which had to be rolled up first, then I swept all around the room, including underneath the dressing table, which had an assortment of ladies' perfume bottles, etc., on it. Then I skimmed the brush around the lino under the bed in a wide arc, bringing a plentiful, albeit distasteful, harvest of dust and grey hairs from underneath the bed. When the floor was swept and the sweepings disposed of, the old lady brought me a mop and a galvanised tin bucket filled with hot soapy water, and said, "Could you mop the floor as well please?" When I finished, she produced two shillings or half a crown from her purse and said "Thanks very much." I thanked her and went home, pleased to have earned so much so easily. Half a crown in old money— 'two and six' as we called it, was a respectable sum.

Two other families lived in our block of flats. We had the ground floor, the Bruces were in the flat above us, and the Hammonds owned the top flat.

Johnny Bruce was the eldest son in the Bruce family. He had blinded himself in one eye because of an accident at school. He was playing with an elastic band and a pencil when it backfired and hit him in the eye. Next to Johnny was Sandy, and David was the youngest. Johnny and Sandy had black hair, but David had sandy hair! Mr Bruce had an air of importance about him—he worked in the Renfrewshire Education offices. He smoked a pipe and drove a green Morris Minor shooting brake (the one with the ash wood frame). Mrs Bruce was a gym teacher. She usually wore a light blue P.E. Teacher's jacket. It had a pattern of blue stripes on it.

We spent a fair bit of time in the back green when we were young. Sometimes Mum opened the kitchen window and handed us each a paper 'poke'[1] with some sugar in the bottom and a stick of rhubarb. We dipped the rhubarb into the sugar and sucked it. A tasty snack to keep us going till lunchtime.

 One hot summer's day, Mrs Bruce was lying on a beach towel, sunning herself on the little mound in the back green. Johnny had been playing with a magnifying glass, setting bits of paper on fire. On the spur of the moment, a reckless idea came into his head. He put his finger to his mouth, signalling us to be quiet. He crept up beside his mum, where she was lying on her front with her eyes closed, presenting her bare, sun creamed back and legs to the sun. We watched silently as he crouched down and trained the magnifying glass on her ample calf muscle. We watched with bated breath as he carefully adjusted the sunspot to an intense, tiny white circle. Suddenly, her lower leg jerked back and she let out a howl of pain, which swiftly turned to rage as she realised what had happened. I don't remember what happened to Johnny, but I'm sure it wasn't pleasant.

The original residents of the top flat at 19 Bentinck Street were 'The McCowans', a family of boys who were older than us. They used to push James and me round the back green in our red Triang pedal cars. However, they moved away, and in their place came an English family who soon became known as 'The Hammonds'. Douglas and Martin Hammond were about the same age as James and me. They'd moved to Scotland from the Isle of Sheppey in England. They had an older sister named Ruth. She wore glasses and had red cheeks. Mr and Mrs Hammond also had several teenage foster children who lived with the family until they 'flew the nest'. Their names were Clive, Carol, Norah and Bill Taulbut. Clive wore pointed black 'winkle-picker' shoes, which, to me, looked really cool. Carol used to 'snog' her boyfriend in the entrance to the close before going upstairs after an evening out! One day Norah saw me walking up Bentinck Street with my shorts on and in her half English, half Scottish accent, exclaimed: "Oh, you've got knobbly knees Jo!" Both she and her brother Bill were a bit simple—'not quite the full shilling' as people used to say. Bill was a big strapping lad. When he left school, he got a job as a gardener.

Ruth Hammond married a German and went to live in Germany. One summer, her dad and mum took Douglas and Martin with them to visit her. They came back wearing leather 'Liebenhosen', the traditional garb of German boys. One year, a family of three African girls came to stay with the Hammonds for a few months. Their names were Ronké, Simi, and Beulah. Ronké was the eldest, a self-assured, confident girl. Simi was more reserved. Beulah, the baby of the family, burst into tears at a moment's notice! The Hammonds were Methodists and went to the Methodist Church, just across the road from Cedar Hall where we went, in Ardgowan Street. Their dad, Albert Hammond, was a Methodist preacher and also stood as a Labour Councillor in Greenock. Albert had glasses and a thick brown beard. He was a smiling, cheery man and was always friendly toward us. He drove a red and white Commer minibus. Mrs Hammond was a small, sharp featured but soft natured woman with a healthy complexion. The day they moved in, she came downstairs and introduced herself to Mum. "Anytime you run short of milk or sugar or anything, just come up and ask" she said. I used to enjoy taking their shaggy, multi-coloured mongrel for walks. Its name was 'Sheppey'.

Douglas and Martin were around the same age as James and me. We often played together in the back green, on Octavia Terrace or further afield. Apart from our friend-ship, one of the major attractions of the Hammond's household was their black-and-white TV. I got into the routine every Saturday evening of going up the stairs and ringing their bell. When Mrs Hammond came to the door, I would say "Is Martin coming out to play?" She invari-ably smiled, and said, "No, but you can come in and watch TV with him if you want." I always timed my arrival to coincide with the highlight of Saturday evening TV—'Doctor Who'. The entire family sat in the living room watching the latest enthralling episode where the Doctor and his assistant flew through time and space in the Tardis, fighting alien creatures such as the Daleks. In-evitably, just as the Doc and the good guys were in a ter-rible predicament, the weird 'Dr Who' theme tune came on and we'd have to wait until the following Saturday to see what happened.

Douglas was proud of his Dad's Gypsy origins and used to tell us of his previous life on the Isle of Sheppey in the South of England. Albert enjoyed watching professional wrestling on TV and I sometimes watched it with them. That's where I got the idea of wrestling with James. I used to get his head in an arm-lock and pretend to be Mick McManus shouting, "Hinya! Hinya!" as I jerked his head around. James just laughed. I suppose I could have hurt him if I'd been bigger and stronger, but the thought never entered my head. I was indulging my fantasy of being a world class wrestler.

Mr Hammond had an interesting collection of antique pipes, which included a few clay pipes. Douglas used to show us these and talk knowledgeably about them. Douglas liked to be the leader. If things weren't going the way he wanted, he exerted his authority. His catchphrase was "United we stand, divided we fall!" Martin was much more of a scallywag. When free of Douglas's restraint, he engaged in actions far more daring than Douglas would have tolerated. When you went somewhere with Martin, you never knew what he'd get up to next. As a result, he sometimes got himself and others into trouble. For example, there was an incident in Sammy George's typewriting school on Eldon Street, which involved a fire in the building. (Sammy George was a wee man who wore a grey raincoat and drove an old green Austin A30. Its exhaust was permanently exhausted because it made a dreadful racket every time he drove it. We used to call it 'the 'bih-bih' car' because of the sound it made.) Rumour had it that one of my brothers was involved with Martin in the fire-setting incident at Sammy George's place, although nothing was ever proven so far as I remember. Martin's default mode was to take the risk and enjoy the excitement of the moment, unlike Douglas. It certainly made life interesting.

One time we set off to climb the Lyle Hill from the rough, steep side of the hill which culminated in a small cliff at the top, not far from the big stone Cross of Loraine—the Free French memorial which overlooks Gourock and Cardwell Bay. When we reached the 'small' cliff, it turned out, as cliffs often do, to be bigger than we thought. I think it was James who first suggested we should turn back. But Douglas said "No! United we stand, divided we fall!" He insisted we stay together and find a way round the cliff rather than splitting up. On that occasion, it was probably the right decision. At other times, Douglas's presence was a definite hindrance.

For example, although Martin was never in the Cubs or Scouts, he took full advantage of 'Bob a Job' week—their annual charity fundraising drive—to make some extra pocket money. I remember going round with him one year. We knocked on a woman's door in Newark Street. She opened the door and in a bright, confident voice, Martin said, "Bob a Job?" She said, "Oh, great! Would you like to sweep up the leaves in my garage?" She opened the garage door, gave us a brush and shovel and left us to it. Once we'd gathered up the leaves, we rang the bell, collected our two shillings and went off, well pleased with ourselves. We tried several other houses without success. Eventually we ended up at a red sandstone tenement block at the bottom of Fox Street. We ran up the stairs and worked our way down from the top flat, ringing every doorbell. Unfortunately, no-one seemed to be in. On the landing outside the middle flat was a box of groceries. On the top were three square, grey paper mâché egg trays, filled with several dozen eggs, held together with elastic bands. Martin emptied most of the top tray, stuffing his pockets full of eggs. For good measure, he shoved two eggs through the letter-box. We didn't hang about. I felt sorry for the residents though, as I imagined their horrified reaction when they arrived home and discovered the damage. We walked along the Esplanade and tried our luck again. This time it was an old stone-built bungalow, on a level higher than the street. It had steep stone steps leading up from the pavement below, to the door. We pressed the doorbell and waited. No answer. Rang the bell again. Still no sign of life. So Martin took the eggs out of his pocket, gave a couple to me, and we pelted the door with the eggs and scarpered. I pitied the poor housewife, who had to clear up the mess.

On April Fool's Day in 1967, (a Saturday), William, Martin and James played a trick on an old woman who lived in Oakleigh Terrace. Her garden backed onto Madeira Lane, where the scene of operations began. According to William, I had used my paintbrush to write an uncomplimentary note addressed to the old lady, along the lines of, "We don't like you". What she'd ever done to warrant such nastiness, I don't know. The unpleasant fact remains—I had turned my artistic talent to a mean-spirited end. That morning, with mischief in mind, the three of them made their way to the end of Madeira Lane. William's recollection is that Martin placed my painted note on the doorstep of the woman's back door, knocked on the door and ran for it, while James and William hid from view outside the gate. However, as James remembers it, Martin started hammering the note on to the high sandstone wall, which had been skimmed over with a smooth concrete skin. They chatted and hammered, and now and then, a chunk of concrete fell off. Just as Martin got the paper to stick to the wall, the old lady came out in her dressing gown and said, "what are you doing?" When she realised what was happening, she shouted, "Get away from my wall!" and ran after them. She chased them halfway along the lane before giving up and returning to her house. Although it had started to rain, they slowed down, laughing at the escapade. As they crossed over Bentinck Street at the end of the lane, an old white Vauxhall Viva with a red stripe along the side jerked to a stop, wipers on. The door flew open, and the lady jumped out—still wearing her dressing gown. Martin said, "Quick, go through the churchyard." they jumped over the low sandstone wall into St Paul's churchyard. Undeterred, the old woman followed them, clearing the wall like a hurdler. They took off across the grass, through the gap in the fence at the other side and on into Mews Lane, which runs between the back gardens of the houses on either side of Newark Street and Octavia Terrace. Ten minutes later, they reached the end of Mews Lane and crossed the road into the Fort Matilda playing fields, where they hid inside the wooden ticket booth just inside the gate, in case the old lady kept up the pursuit. When sufficient time had elapsed, they felt safe enough to emerge and go home for lunch.

Mr More was one of our next-door neighbours. He and his family lived in the top flat of number 18 Bentinck Street. Mr More was from Wick in Caithness, and spoke with that distinctive north of Scotland accent which places a greater inflexion on certain words than the softer-spoken accents of the Sutherland folk. He had the job of going round the occupants of each flat every year to ask for payment of the 'Feu Duties', a curious carry-over in Scots Law from Feudal times, which requires payment of an annual fee to the landowner, (usually The Crown or its representative). Mr and Mrs More had a son named Stuart, who used to go up and down the hill on his scooter. Perhaps it was the Wick accent or what we perceived to be an over-confident personality, but we didn't like Mr More. Between ourselves, we called him "Mory". One day, Henry Eadie, a friend from school, came to play with me. Henry was a bit like Martin Hammond, a bit of a daredevil—always pushing the boundaries. For some reason, I had told him our nickname for

Mr More was 'Mory'. He thought this was hilarious and immediately cupped both hands to his mouth, looked up at the More's top flat window, and shouted, "MORY! MORY!" 'Shut up!' I said, wavering between laughing at his audacity and being embarrassed by his impertinence. We didn't need to antagonise the Mores any *more* than we already had. The memory of William's drum solo was very much on my mind.

A few months before, William had taken it into his head to have a drumming session in the back garden. He'd been watching a T.V. Western at his friend's house, in which the Red Indians did a war dance round the camp fire, chanting native American words in time to the drums. To William this sounded like, "Alamashey! Alamashey!" So, on the same mound where Mrs Bruce got more sun than she bargained for, he arranged an assortment of empty biscuit tins. He sat cross-legged on the ground and started hammering out a loud, fast paced, rhythmic wall of sound. In time with the beat, he shouted, "ALAMASHEY! ALAMASHEY! ALAMASHEY!" To us, it sounded great. Not so much to Mrs More. High above the cacophony of noise, from the top flat of number 18, we became aware of Mrs More rapping on the kitchen window, frantically waving in a way that could only mean 'cease and desist'. William knew fine she was there, but pretended he didn't. With a characteristic smirk, he increased the tempo, shouting even louder, "ALAMASHEY! ALAMSHEY! ALAMASHEY!" until Mrs More forced up the sash window, stuck her head out, and screeched, "STOP THAT NOISE!" Unfortunately, her intervention broke the spell of William's hypnotic beat—but it was fantastic while it lasted.

Another friend was Graeme Hoey. His parents and younger sisters Gillian and Jennifer lived in one of the new houses on South Street. Like us, they went to Cedar Hall, so it was natural we'd team up from time to time. I used to go up to Graham's immediately after breakfast on a Saturday morning. Invariably, his mother was still in her dressing gown but she always welcomed me with a cheery 'The early bird catches the worm!' I liked her. She had a positive outlook. Robert Hoey, Graham's dad, used to run a weeknight craft class for children. I remember spending ages, painstakingly gluing bits of Balsa on to semi-transparent paper to make a model aeroplane. I don't remember finishing it. The Hoey's emigrated to Canada, and we lost touch.

Dad and Mum encouraged us to save some pocket money each week. They opened a Post Office Savings account for each of us. Whenever we had some money to save, or wanted to take some money out, we went along to the Post Office in Brougham Street with our little savings book which had a blue plastic cover with a transparent plastic strip down one edge. The teller either took your money or issued the amount you wished to withdraw, entered the new balance by hand, then stamped the page with a round, inky black stamp. Before you could withdraw any money, you had to fill in a withdrawal slip. I remember going into the Post Office in Banff on holiday. It felt good to have a reserve of cash, although I wasn't the most frugal of savers. William was by far the best at saving money—and still is.

From the time we were about eight onwards, we were free to roam more or less where we wanted in Greenock, so long as we were home in time for lunch or tea. Looking back, I realise how fortunate we were. I regularly walked to the joke shop at the corner of South Street and Nelson Street, just opposite the Cemetery gates. Among the fascinating items for sale, such as fart cushions, pretend cigarettes and fake dog poo, you could also buy stink bombs—little glass bulbs filled with a noxious greenish yellow liquid. There was a baker's shop next to the joke shop. One Saturday morning after my visit to the joke shop, I joined the queue in the bakers, dropped a stink bomb and walked back outside to where my pals were waiting. We suppressed our sniggers as the ladies in the queue loudly began expressing their disgust at the smell. It was a moment we recalled with relish for a long time afterwards.

If you walked along Nelson Street, you came to the road that led to the West Station Cafe. They sold the best Italian ice cream in Greenock. Our church always bought a large canister of it to dish out at Sunday School trips and the Annual Camp at Auchenfoyle also gave them a good order during each of the four weeks—two weeks for boys followed by two weeks for girls, every summer.

∾

16 'ORRS', TERRACE ROAD, UNCLE WILLIE

When Dad was managing director of Orrs House Furnishers, there was a period when Dad was without a car. Uncle Willie brought Dad home after work in his plush grey 3.5 litre Rover P6. He parked at the top of the road and they sat there for a good twenty minutes or half an hour, talking over the day's business. I often went to meet him and jumped into the back seat of the Rover, where I enjoyed their conversation, savoured the smell of the red leather seats, and admired the beautiful veneered wooden dashboard. Years later, Dad told us, Uncle Willie never drove the engine higher than in third gear. He thought that was funny. It summed up Uncle Willie's cautious, canny nature.

In his book, Dad tells how his father and Uncle Wille had had a fight with each other in the street outside his father's shop in Terrace Road. Their dispute was about which of them owned the premises. Whatever the truth of the matter, Uncle Willie claimed victory and staked his claim. The Terrace Road showroom became the main part of his business. He had added several extensions over the years, upwards and outwards as the business expanded. This resulted in a rabbit warren of corridors, passageways, and stairs leading to unexpected corners. As you entered the building, you walked up a sloping, red carpeted floor. The distinctive smell of new carpets and quality furniture pervaded the place. Dad's office was off to the left as you walked up the passageway. To the right, facing down towards the entrance, was the window of the admin office, behind which worked a lady called Cathy, Dad's office manager. Cathy was a plump, cheery-faced lady with a jet-black mushroom of tightly permed curls. She was a sharp cookie who missed nothing. She was a highly valued and trustworthy worker.

Dad used to talk in reverential tones about the skill of Davie Rowan the joiner, a master craftsman employed by Uncle Willie, to work on pieces of furniture that customers brought in for repair. Dad often quoted a humorous saying of Davie's when talking about some apprentices: "He wouldnae know one enday' a hammer fae another if he saw wan!"

Bob was their carpet fitter. He was a capable, quick-witted, confident man. He came to our house a couple of times to fit a carpet. Unfortunately, Bob developed cartilage trouble in his knees, caused by the repetitive use of the 'kicker' tool, which was used to stretch the carpet. Nowadays, health and safety rules insist on the use of a mechanical stretcher. Back then, the 'kicker' was the carpet fitter's key tool. Cartilage problems were an occupational hazard.

When he reached his seventies, Uncle Willie sold the business to a Glasgow firm, which Dad told me was owned by a Jewish family in Glasgow. Sadly, this spelled the end of Dad's career as managing director of Orrs House Furnishers. The executives who arrived from Glasgow, ruthlessly set in motion a streamlining programme. They cut away everything that wasn't making a significant profit. When they terminated the employment of one office girl after another, Dad said, "Who's going to do their job, then?" — "You are", was the reply. It wasn't long before the pressure became too much and his health suffered. He developed disc trouble, for which the doctor prescribed a neck collar. Dad realised he was being pushed out and, gracious man that he was, rather than challenge their vicious tactics, decided to resign and go back to teaching Maths. In a brief space of time, (so it seemed), Dykes of Glasgow reduced Orrs from a respected family firm where people got superb service, to a cynical money-making machine where the only criteria for success was the profit margin. Inevitably, customer service suffered. Only a few years later, when they had stripped the business of its assets, the takeover outfit pulled out and sold off the various parts of the business. They sold the High Street gift shop and the pram shop as going concerns, and Terrace Road as a 'development opportunity' to a local builder. It was a sad end to a great local firm, which would have gone from strength to strength, if only Uncle Willie hadn't wanted to 'cash out' when he retired.

As boys, Dad used to take us to visit Uncle Willie in the tenement flat he lived in for many years. But after he sold his business, by arrangement with his nephew Robin, he moved to Gateside farm where he'd been born and brought up. Unfortunately, a woman who was renting some rooms at Gateside persuaded him to move back to

Greenock with her and her husband, where they'd purchased a substantial house on Finnart Street. Dad
strongly suspected Uncle Willie's money had paid for the
house. It created a tension between Dad and Uncle
Willie, which was a great pity, considering how close
they'd been.

~

17 CEDAR HALL

Our life revolved around Church. From childhood, we attended 'Cedar Hall' with Dad and Mum each Sunday. The address of the hall and the important legend that followed, is etched on my memory—5 Ardgowan Street—'the meeting place of the Church of God in Greenock'[1].

My earliest memories of going to church though, were not of Cedar Hall but of Caledonia Hall—'a large upper room furnished' (!)—in a building nearer the town centre which was knocked down many years ago to make way for the new town centre development. We sat on wooden 'forms'—plain wooden seats with a ledge on the back for books. After the Remembrance, before Sunday School, most folks stayed for lunch in the hall. The smell of tea being boiled in tea urns over the gas rings in the kitchen, then served in large brown enamel kettles, comes to mind. They poured the tea into white china catering cups —none of your disposable polystyrene or paper cups in those days.

The wooden forms and the huge round mahogany wall clock (with twelve black letters which read W-A-T-C-H-A-N-D-P-R-A-Y arranged around the Roman numerals on the clock-face), were moved to Cedar Hall, which was designed by David Baird, a talented architect in the Church of God in Paisley.

The tradition of staying for lunch in the hall continued. Hugh McNeil, who was blind, always called the happy murmur of voices to order by standing up, tapping loudly with a teaspoon on a cup and announcing: "Tea IS ready!" as he looked around the hall with smiling face. He or someone else gave thanks for the food, then Mum opened our packed lunches and handed out sandwiches and whatever else we'd brought.

Hugh's wife, Hannah, was a tall, motherly lady who wore her hair in a bun like many other women in our churches. The McNeils lived in Skye Crescent, Gourock. Danny was the eldest, followed by Eòghan and Ruth. They were all a few years older than us. We always enjoyed visiting them at their house. Their old Granny, who was suffering from what was then called 'senile decay' (or dementia) sat in a rocking chair. The McNeils had a cuckoo clock on the wall, which always fascinated us. We waited with bated breath for the cuckoo's emergence on the hour.

Eòghan's nickname was 'Yogi'. He was a quiet, friendly chap who was great at gymnastics. He and 'Young John Black' used to perform handstands for us outside the hall after the Sunday morning meeting was over. ('Young' John was so called, to differentiate him from his father John and his cousin John, (Jimmy Black's son), who later became known as John Black the Evangelist, because he went out full time in the Lord's work in Africa. Danny Mc-

Neil was good at football. He made some beautiful woodwork items at school, including a sideboard cabinet, which had pride of place in the McNeil's front room. Ruth was a couple of years older than me, an articulate, intelligent girl whose sense of humour and company we enjoyed.

Jack Erskine was one of the overseers of the Church. He wore horn-rimmed glasses on a weathered face, always wore a dark blue suit with a waistcoat and had a gentle sense of humour. He worked in one of the shipyards during the week. When it was his turn to read the announcements after the Remembrance, he announced the names of older ladies in the church who were unwell, like so: "we remember in prayer our sister Mistress Millar our sister Mistress Leitch, Mistress McNeill…" and so on.

One of the largest families in the church was the Black family, who were and still are, one of the driving forces behind much of the church's activities. They were relatives of my father and worked a dairy farm called Auchenfoyle (the old spelling of which was Auchenfoil), on the Kilmacolm Road, between Greenock and Kilmacolm. John Black Senior was Dad's cousin. His mother Mary and Dad's mother Janet were sisters. John Black's brothers were Jimmy, Willie and Hugh. Their eldest brother, Donald, was shot dead on the Kilmacolm Road a short distance from Auchenfoyle, while returning from a late evening visit to his sweetheart at nearby Mathernock Farm. He was only twenty-two years old. Dad's cousin John discovered his body next morning. The prime suspect was an eighteen-year-old farm labourer who worked at Mathernock. The family suspected he was jealous of Donald's friendship with the girl. He was acquitted of the charge of murder because of lack of sufficient evidence.

For many years Dad kept the old newspaper cuttings with photographs of the funeral cortege and the account of the murder and subsequent trial at Glasgow High Court in September 1931. However, when I looked for those cuttings among his files after he died, they were gone.

Jimmy Black owned East Green farm, which was always called 'The Green', situated nearer the village of Kilmacolm than Auchenfoyle. Willie went to the Church of God in Port Glasgow, so we only saw him occasionally when he came to visit in his light blue Volkswagen Beetle. Hugh lived next door to us for some years, in the middle flat of number 18 Bentinck Street. He was a history teacher and eventually became headmaster of Greenock High School. He had three daughters, Alison, Mary, and Grace. His wife Isobel was a kind-hearted lady who made us welcome and brought toys out of a cupboard for us to play with when we were very small. Hugh was the driving force behind Struthers Memorial Church, an independent Pentecostal Church in Greenock. They believed that 'speaking in tongues' was a desirable manifestation of the presence of the Spirit of God in the life of a born-again Christian. The Churches of God do not hold this doctrine. Our understanding of scripture is that the gift of 'tongues' was the miraculous ability to speak in a variety of other languages and be understood by everyone present. It was a sign of God's authority during the early phase of New Testament Churches of God and as the new movement became established, this sign of divine endorsement became redundant. In contrast, 'speaking in tongues' as practised in Struthers Memorial church and other 'charismatic' groups does not take the form of intelligible speech and is therefore quite different from the 'tongues' recorded in the New Testament, which were known languages. Prior to his final retirement, Dad went to work as a Maths teacher under the leadership of his cousin Hugh at Greenock High. He remarked on the friendly atmosphere among the staff there. It was a good school to work in.

John Black Senior was a big man in every way. Physically powerful through years of hard graft on the farm, he was one of the sincerest, straightforward, warmest-hearted men I ever knew. He thought of himself as a hard man, in the sense that he had little time for those who were prone to self-indulgence. But as a farmer, he had learned how to look after sheep and other livestock, and this awareness of the needs of his animals carried over into the flock that he looked after in the Church, in which he was an overseer. He had an open, cheerful personality coupled with a seriousness of purpose which you warmed to immediately. He usually thanked the speaker who had preached the gospel at Cedar Hall on a Sunday night and, I can hear him yet, closing his final appeal to unsaved friends by quoting the words of 2 Cor. 6:2: *"now is the acceptable time; behold, now is the day of salvation"*.

Jimmy Black was known to us as 'Cousin Jimmy.' He was born in 1915, and was three years older than Dad. An accident with a circular saw had left him with a stump of a finger in the middle of one hand. As boys, it fascinated us. On a Sunday, after the Remembrance, we used to go over to talk to him and touch the stump. He was amused by our interest. Physically, Jimmy was exceptionally strong. I remember one Sunday afternoon at Camp one year, because the weather was so good, they decided to carry some of the heavy wooden forms from the dining room to the field on the other side of the burn, where the camp leaders were going to sit in the sun and listen to an exposition of scripture by Jack Ferguson. The old wooden forms were ten or twelve feet long, solidly built, screwed onto cast iron legs. They needed two fit young men, one at either end, to stagger across the bridge with them. Jimmy picked one up, threw it over his shoulder and walked across to the field as if it was a scrap of timber. He must have been nearly seventy at the time. Cousin Jimmy wasn't a platform speaker. He was a practical man, not one to seek the limelight. But he had a roguish sense of humour and delighted in playing tricks on his friends. Roy Lees, who married Jimmy's niece, Mary Ross, visited us one time and enjoyed telling Dad and Mum, how, when he was courting Mary (she lived at Carsenowe, on the Kilmacolm road), he had stopped his car near East Green, to answer a call of nature. When he arrived back at the car, it was surrounded by enormous boulders! How he got out of that predicament, I can't re-member, but it gave us a laugh—Cousin Jimmy even more so. One hot summer's day when we were boys, Cousin Jimmy arranged with Dad and Mum to take us to the beach at Seamill. He had a lovely big Vauxhall Cresta, with bench seats front and back which we all piled into. At Seamill, he drove down the side of a field of potatoes to the beach. He opened the boot and took out a cast-iron pot and a garden fork. While we collected wood and made a fire, he dug up some Ayrshire potatoes from the field. We washed the potatoes in sea water, filled the pot with water and boiled them on the fire. Those freshly dug tatties, boiled in sea water, were the best I ever tasted.

When I was about fifteen or sixteen, two or three years after we'd moved away from Greenock, like many of the boys at school, I let my hair grow over my ears. I knew Dad didn't approve, even though he said nothing.

We had just moved into the house at John Knox Street in Galston, and the phone line hadn't been connected. One evening, Dad decided to phone Cousin Jimmy from the red public call box that stood at the junction of Wallace Street and Cessnock Road, just outside the old boarded up Cinema. He asked if I wanted 'to stretch my legs' and come with him.

The long-haired phase

I waited outside the phone kiosk while Dad spoke to Cousin Jimmy. After a bit he opened the door and said "Cousin Jimmy wants a word with you." We exchanged the usual pleasantries. He then said something about not becoming like 'those girlish pop stars' and in his gruff vernacular, ended with the admonition: "Be a man and stey a man!" Those words struck me forcibly, and it wasn't long before I went to the local barber and got my flowing locks chopped off.

Cousin Jimmy in his natural habitat

Some years later, I had the privilege of typesetting and publishing cousin Jimmy's autobiography, entitled *'Black O' The Green, Memories O' the Auld Days'* in which he relates many details and entertaining events that happened during his long life. In later years, after his wife May died, he used to sit in the porch of 'Shalloch Mor', the cottage he moved into when he handed over 'The Green' to his son Alan. I used to give him a toot and a wave when taking our children to Camp. He died at the ripe old age of 98, 'old and full of days'.

Stanley Barr was one of cousin Jimmy's friends. He had been born and brought up in the same part of Greenock as Dad. He told Dad that he used to envy the 'bogey' That Uncle Joe and Dad had made. Stanley worked at the Greenock IBM factory in Spango Valley. He had a droll sense of humour and an unhurried way of telling funny stories that built the fun towards the punchline. (It really is about the way you tell them). He told us about the American sailor who developed a varicose vein on the side of his face from chewing gum. Another time, he told us about a man who went to see his doctor. "What seems to be the trouble?" asked the doc. "Well, I used to be able to put my arm up to here"—(Stanley raised his arm high above his head) "but now, I can only put it up to here"—Stanley lowered his arm to shoulder height! We always enjoyed it when Stanley and his wife visited, because he kept us entertained.

Jack Barbour was another of Dad's friends. He and his wife Jenny had four girls: Sheena, Karen, Vivienne and Lynne. They three older girls were about the same ages as us boys. Lynne was around the same age as Elisabeth. Jack was a joiner to trade. He opened a small shop in Brougham Street, just along from the Post Office, where he displayed kitchen units which he sold and fitted for his customers. His business took off, so much so that he bought a substantial upper flat on Finnart Street which had beautiful views over the River Clyde and the hills beyond. Sadly, Jenny died while the girls were still in their teens. She was a kind, warm-hearted woman and always gave us a great welcome when we went to visit.

Sheena, Karen and Vivienne were always game for a 'carry on' and got us to play some hilarious games, including one called "Consequences'. We sat in a circle and passed around a piece of paper and a pencil. The first person wrote the names of two people, then passed it to the next one who wrote where they met, passed it on to the next who wrote what they said—next, what they did—and lastly, what happened—'the consequence'. Finally, the paper was unfolded and someone read the whole story out loud, to hoots of laughter at the entertaining fiction thus concocted, of people we knew, saying things that were completely out of character and having many ridiculous events happen to them. All good fun!

Every Lord's Day[2] morning we went to 'The Remembrance'. The seats were arranged in four sections, facing the space in the centre of the hall where the table was. Not being 'in the meeting' (baptised and added to the Church), our place as children was to sit on the long wooden forms at the side of the hall, just under one of the huge square windows. When we were older, we sat at the back, just inside the inner doors of the hall. In the middle of the room, was a table covered with a crisp white tablecloth. On the table, a loaf of bread on a plate, four white plates, a cut glass decanter of wine, and four matching wine-glasses. As was the custom throughout the Fellowship, the Remembrance always began with a brother rising to give thanks for the loaf. After the collective 'Amen', he broke the loaf into four pieces, placed one on each plate and handed them to two brethren designated to assist with distribution. They took them to the end of each of the four seating areas and gave them to the first person at the end of the back rows on either side. When the two assistants returned to their seats, the plates were passed along the rows, each person in the church breaking off a piece of bread and eating it. The plates with the remains of the four broken quarters of bread were returned to the table and the same brother who had given thanks for the loaf then went to the table again, took the jug of wine in his hands and gave thanks for 'the cup', just as the Lord Jesus had done on the night on which He was betrayed, when He said to His disciples: "This do in remembrance of me." After the Amen, the brother carefully decanted the wine into each of the four glasses. The same procedure was followed until everyone in the church had taken a sip of wine and the glasses were returned to the table.

After this we had a time of worship in praise and prayer, led by the brothers in the church. This usually began with a brother standing up and reading a verse or two of a hymn, then the entire congregation stood and sang in unison. The rich, four-part, unaccompanied harmony in Greenock was a treat to listen to. John Ross was the precentor. There was a pause while he hummed a couple of notes to himself to get the right note to start on, then everyone joined in as he began singing the first line. A hundred voices, including two families of muscular, deep-chested farmers, singing praise to God from the heart, was part of the warp and woof of our lives growing up. The Scottish poet Robert Burns wrote with sympathy of the great old hymns that were sung in his day, many of which we also sang. Those fine tunes became inseparably entwined with the words:

> Perhaps Dundee's wild-warbling measures rise;
> Or plaintive Martyrs, worthy of the name;
> Or noble Elgin beets the heaven-ward flame;
> The sweetest far of Scotia's holy lays:
> Compar'd with these, Italian trills are tame;
> The tickl'd ears no heart-felt raptures raise;
> Nae unison hae they with our Creator's praise.

FROM 'A COTTARS SATURDAY NIGHT', BY
ROBERT BURNS

After the Remembrance, everyone shook hands and asked after each other's welfare. The hall filled with a hubbub of friendly voices. We often went outside to the car park to look at the cars. Sometimes the young men talked with each other in the vestibule entrance area. 'Young John Black', who was very strong, sometimes got us to lock our elbows with our hands rigid at our sides while he grasped our fists in his hands and lifted us high above his head. If the weather was dry, the young men went out to the car park, kicked some tyres and talked about cars. The classic 'E' type Jag was THE ultimate sports car. Its top speed was 150 miles an hour and went from zero to sixty in just 6.4 seconds. No-one we knew owned one. Kenny McDonald had a racy-looking Mini Cooper. Jock Kerr had a wee grey minivan with wipers that didn't work. He had tied a piece of string between the wipers, with the two ends threaded through the driver's window and the passenger window. When it rained, he and his passenger had to open their windows a fraction and simultaneously pull the strings from side to side to wipe the windows as he drove along. We never thought to ask him what he did when he had no passenger. The mind boggles.

When the table had been put away and the collection money counted, those who were staying on for the ministry meeting and the Sunday School returned to the hall and had lunch together. Then the young men turned all the seats round to face the platform, ready for the ministry meeting and the Sunday School which followed.

∾

18   LET US TAKE THE LOAF

I wrote the following lines in May 2020, during the first 'lockdown' (horrible word), when our government banned church services and imposed excessive Health and Safety restrictions because of a so-called 'pandemic'. It struck me forcibly that a return to the simple dignity of the Remembrance, as we had known and practised it all our lives, was increasingly unlikely.

LET US TAKE THE LOAF

The Spirit moves him, and he says
"Let us take the loaf and give God thanks."
Goes to the table, takes the loaf in both his hands
Just as our Lord did at the first
'This do' said He, 'in memory of me.'

With reverent heart and holy awe
We bow, God's called out gathered ones
And listen as he gives to God the fruit of lips
Precious thoughts 'as incense beaten small,'

Thoughts of Christ that touch and thrill the soul
And tell again the story of His life, and love, and
  death.

The congregation says "Amen", and watch
Him break the loaf, symbol of the One
Of whom the scripture says:
'A bone of Him they shall not break,'
The Lamb of God, the Holy One,
Who died alone, our souls to save.

Each breaks and eats and passes round
The plate of broken bread. And as we eat,
Remember; think of Him who bore
Such awful grief; atoning sacrifice of love!
He took the sinner's place, laid down
That perfect life upon the cross—for me!

"We'll also take the cup," He says and rising
To the table once again, he goes
This time to take into his hands the cup,
A jug of wine, emblem of Christ's blood.

In Spirit, as before, we enter heaven above
And every heart and mind, afresh is gripped;
Captivated by the thought that God's own Son
Came down so low, endured for us such
  untold woe.

But even as we think such solemn thoughts,
This glorious truth breaks through the gloom:
This first day of the week is resurrection morn!
It is the day the Lord has made! Praise God!

This is the day our Saviour burst the bonds of
    death,
And rose triumphant from the grave,
Eternal in His strength to save!

"Amen!" the glad refrain goes up to God,
We watch again, as wine is poured from jug
    to cup—
Symbol of His life poured forth, redeemed by pre-
    cious blood.
We pass around the cup, and as each drinks,
We meditate on Covenant blessings New, forever
    ours in Him.

'No longer heirs of wrath, the smile of peace we
    see,'
Glad songs of love now rise from grateful souls
    set free.
Thanksgiving follows on, in prayer as well as song,
And then, in closing, sometimes sing,
Horatius Bonar's lovely hymn:
"Too soon we rise, the symbols disappear,
The feast, though not the love, is past and gone;
The bread and wine remove, but He is here,
Nearer than ever, still our Shield and Sun."

∾

19 SUNDAY SCHOOL AND CHURCH MEETINGS

Sometimes we stayed for the ministry but often, we went for the ride, with young John Black in the Bedford Van, to collect the Sunday School children from Renton Road and Leven Road and various other streets in the East End of Greenock. Renton Road and Leven Road were two very run-down streets lined with council flats on either side. There was graffiti on the walls, broken bottles, cans and bricks lying in the gardens and on the road. Several houses were boarded up. The children we picked up were a motley crew who spoke with a tough East End accent. I still remember the rank, unwashed smell that pervaded the vehicle as the children crammed onto the bench seats beside us.

Their names somehow seemed to fit like a glove. There was Joe Easdale and his tall, lanky brother, George. Joe's breath stank, but he had a sharp sense of humour and was always cracking jokes. Then there was Charles McLuskie, Jim Lafferty and John McQuillan, who, for some long-forgotten reason, punched me in the face one Sunday, outside the hall. There were also as many girls as there were boys at Sunday School—but they weren't on my radar till much later.

Lex Forbes was the Sunday School Superintendent for quite a few years. He was the manager of a furniture shop in Port Glasgow, or 'The Port' as we called it. Lex composed a daft little chorus which we all enjoyed singing[1]. It went like this:

Have you got the sunshine smile?
Have you got the sunshine smile?
Wherever you may be,
Or whatever you may see,
Have you got the sunshine smile?

The last verse (I forget the middle one) went like this:

Have you got the sunshine Ha Ha Ha ha Hee?
Have you got the sunshine Ha Ha Ha ha Hee?
Wherever you may be
Or whatever you may see,
Have you got the sunshine Ha Ha Ha ha Hee?

Jim Lafferty's big sister Liz thought it was hilarious and could hardly sing it for laughing.

John Black (later known as 'John Black the Evangelist')—was my first Sunday School teacher. Sunday School always began with communal singing of hymns and choruses from the big flip-chart hymn sheet, which was mounted on a large wooden easel. (View the digital version of that venerable hymn sheet on https://oldchoruses.wordpress.com). After the opening prayer, and sometimes a quiz, we split into various parts of the hall and ante rooms for classes. Because the Sunday School was so large in those days, John had to take his class in the back of the Bedford Van. One day, he told us the story of Moses. To ensure everyone had been listening, he asked the usual questions afterwards. "Charles, what was it that Moses' mother made for him when she hid him in the bulrushes?" Charlie McLuskey looked blank for a moment. Suddenly he came out with "A wee hing-me" and waved his hands back and forth expressively, outlining the shape of the 'hing-me'. John laughingly replied, "A wee hing-me? Awrrite, gies a rope and we'll hing 'im!" Charles got the joke immediately and laughed as hard as the rest of us.

Jim Lafferty had a big, broad, smiling face. His party-piece was speaking in an explosive, deep, hoarse voice. We often asked him to say something just to hear the funny, rasping phrases coming out of his mouth. Unknown to him and to us, he was doing permanent damage to his vocal cords.

There were two highlights in the Sunday School year; 'The Sunday School Treat' in December and the 'Sunday School Trip' in the summer.

December was the month of the annual 'Treat'. In the run up to the big night, the Superintendent made a list of the various items the teachers of each class were proposing to present. These included recitations of poetry, selected scripture portions, singing items, acting out a Bible story, or quizzes. There was usually a big turnout of Sunday School parents and saints from the church, besides the children and teachers. One year, when James and I were about four or five, Dad got us to learn and practice reciting verses 7-10 from Psalm 24. We learned it this way:

Jo: Lift up your heads, O ye gates; and be ye lift up, ye everlasting doors: and the King of glory shall come in.

James: Who is the King of glory?

Jo: The LORD strong and mighty, the LORD mighty in battle.

James: Lift up your heads, O ye gates; yea, lift them up, ye everlasting doors: and the King of glory shall come in.

Jo: Who is this King of glory?

Jo and James: The LORD of hosts, he is the King of glory. Selah.

After all the class items and recitations were finished, a specially invited speaker from further afield gave a gospel message. They often illustrated their message to hold our attention. Speakers like Charles Early from Bargeddie in Coatbridge had a particular gift for speaking in an entertaining way, which captivated the audience from the start. Charles was a small, slim young man with glasses and a neatly clipped moustache. Smartly dressed, he had a twinkle in his voice, which made you warm to him immediately. He could hold an audience of two hundred in the palm of his hand as he got one laugh after another with his witty remarks, finally using his humorous stories to illustrate and drive home a more serious aspect of the gospel message. Billy Smyth from Glasgow was another. He had been a 'Teddy Boy' in Belfast before he got saved and had that typically dry and incisive Irish humour, which everyone enjoyed. Billy worked as a graphic artist for the Honeywell plant near Motherwell and used his artistic skills to illustrate his message. With his colourful visual aid, he told a story about 'Marmaduke the monkey' which is still vivid in my mind — except I have no recollection of how he applied the story of Marmaduke to the gospel message! Billy also illustrated many stories in 'Eagles Wings' over the years, the monthly children's magazine produced by the Churches of God. At the end of the Sunday School treat, David Black, Young John and Willie Kerr or Danny McNeil had the job of handing an apple and an orange to every child as they left the hall. There was a box of apples on one side of the double doors and a box of oranges on the other. It was a lovely end to a memorable and happy occasion.

The Sunday School year ended in June, coinciding with the start of the school holidays. Around the last Saturday in June or the first Saturday in July, we had our annual 'Sunday School Trip.' This was a ticketed affair—every eligible child got a free ticket, which entitled you to a box of sandwiches, a cake, a packet of crisps, a bottle of lemonade and an ice cream. Only children who attended regularly had a free ticket. Everyone else had to pay. The venue for Sunday School trips was invariably a park in some outlying place, such as Lochwinnoch or Rouken Glen park in Glasgow. One year we took the little 'Granny Kempock' ferryboat from Princess Pier and sailed across the Clyde to Helensburgh where we walked up the streets to the local park. Many denominations organised Sunday school outings around the end of June, so these

parks usually had to be pre-booked with the town council, who allocated a designated area for each group. We
also arranged with a local church hall or community
centre to get the use of electric facilities for heating the
tea urns. These halls doubled as a fall-back wet-weather
venue, just in case it rained on the day. The morning of
the 'The Trip' was one of mounting excitement. We usually had to be at Cedar Hall at 12.00 noon. We left the
house around 11.30am and walk to the hall to join the
crowd of children and adults milling around in the car
park waiting for the double-decker buses to arrive. There
was sometimes a mad rush to get on and the older folks
had to exercise a bit of crowd control. The important
thing was to get a seat next to a window so that you
could unroll the coloured paper 'streamers' that you'd
brought, and feed them through one of the sliding windows on the bus. A tremendous cheer went up as the
bus driver finally started the engine and drove off,
streamers flying from every window.

When we arrived at the park, we helped to carry the various boxes of prizes, games equipment and foodstuffs to
the designated area.

We had various races, including the sack race, flat race
and three-legged race. There was always a ladies race
and a men's race, which was fun to watch and was entered into with enthusiasm by the parents. One of our tra-
ditions was 'The Sweety Man'. Before the trip, some
ladies in the Church sewed lots of wrapped, boiled
sweets onto an old shirt. At a suitable lull in proceedings,
a sudden shout went up: 'The Sweety Man!' and a young
chap dashed out from behind a tree or somewhere,
wearing the shirt and carrying a big bag of sweets, from
which he scattered handfuls across the grass to slow the

mad rush of children chasing him over the field. A crazy moment of great fun.

Robert Hoey started a mid-week craft class for the children of parents in the church. He started us building model aeroplanes, made from balsa wood and tissue paper. I couldn't remember the details, but I remembered there was a bit of bother at that class, involving Hamish Murdoch, one of the brethren who helped out with the model making. I am indebted to James's amazingly detailed memory for the following account of what happened.

"I could put it this way. You and I attended this class and so did Peter Groveh, Felix's son from Auchenfoyle." [Felix was a German prisoner of war (POW) who stayed on at Auchenfoyle after the 2nd World War. He and his family lived in the cottage just along the road from the farm. But I digress—back to James' account of the craft class.] "Peter broke your model whether unintentionally or intentionally doesn't matter. Next thing was, you went over and broke Peter's model—intentionally. This was enough to get you put out of the class by Hamish Murdoch and Robert Hoey. You crept back into Cedar Hall and hid in the cloakroom while Robert Hoey called me out from the class and told me that you Jo were now banned from the class. The details of what happened next are hazy, but I do remember Robert Hoey basically telling me, that if I sided with you, I too would be banned from the class. My mind was clear. I chose to accept that I would forfeit my place in the class because I wanted to keep you company. Then you tried to sneak back into Cedar Hall and that's when Hamish Murdoch came roaring at you and grabbed you in a bear hug and then made sure we left the premises. So we walked home to Bentinck Street. A few weeks later, Robert Hoey came to speak with Dad over a cup of tea and biscuits in the sitting room, and we were called in to apologise and received Robert's forgiveness. So we were welcomed back to the balsa wood class!"

As we grew older, we started attending the Friday Night Class and the Saturday afternoon YPMs, both of which were held once a month.

Apart from the weekly Remembrance, informally known as 'the morning meeting', the three other important regular meetings of the church were the ministry meeting, the prayer meeting and the gospel meeting. They usually held ministry meetings on a Sunday afternoon and depending on how interesting—or otherwise—the speaker was, occasionally the heads of some hard-working members of the congregation dropped onto their chest as they caught up on the sleep they'd lost during the week.

When Hugh McNeil took 'the ministry' (as the ministry meeting was commonly termed), he read with his fingers from an encyclopaedic sized Braille Bible. He kept a set of oversized Braille volumes of each book of the Bible in a cupboard at the back of the hall, and from these, selected whichever book he was going to speak from, to take to the platform with him. He read fluently, staring straight ahead, his fingers flying back and forth on the thick brown card pages as he read his way along and down each line of raised Braille dots. This unique skill fascinated me.

From time to time, visiting guest speakers were invited to take 'the ministry.' I remember one old brother from Canada, who, as he finished up, spontaneously burst into the words of a well-known hymn and everyone joined in with him. It was a lovely, unforgettable moment (although I forget the hymn he sang!)

Gospel meetings took place on Sunday evenings between 7.00pm and 8.pm. No such thing as a half hour gospel message in those days! But back then, we had several gifted preachers—especially the full-time evangelists—who, unlike most of their counterparts today, possessed the ability to hold us spellbound with the power and persuasiveness of their preaching. The time flew by —we could easily have listened to them for another hour. What made them such compelling speakers? They were men of prayer, steeped in the Word of God. While they were relaxed and willing to share a laugh in an informal setting, when it came to their preaching they were deadly serious. There was no flippancy about them on the platform. Their lives were consistent with their calling. They were dedicated, without reserve or compromise, to the service of God. Such self-sacrifice came at significant cost to them and their families, and will be amply rewarded in a day to come.

Before the Gospel meeting, we had a prayer meeting from 6.00pm till 6.15pm and then went out to one of the street corners downtown for an open-air meeting at which interested listeners were invited to come back to the hall with us for the gospel meeting. But I don't ever remember anyone responding to the invitation.

Various local and invited speakers were rostered for these meetings. One speaker had a habit of adding an extra syllable at the end of words ending in the letter 'n'. For example, when reading the verses of the hymn he'd chosen, in which the last line of each verse and the chorus was 'Call them in', Without fail, every time he ended each verse with "Call them in-eh." To my young ears it was so unusual that afterwards, every time I saw this brother, in my mind I heard him say: "Call them in-eh, Call them in-eh".

My favourite gospel song was number 44, 'Come weary one and find sweet rest, Jesus is passing by.' I liked the way the words 'passing by' were repeated as a refrain in the chorus. It had a great rhythm to it. There were several well-loved hymns in that hymnbook which didn't survive the revision of our Gospel Hymnbook, which was completed by the Fellowship Hymnbook Committee in 1978. I suppose we had to move with the times and as well as adding some great new hymns, it was time to shed some rather dreary ones, which it has to be admitted, were out of date. In the process, however, we lost some that were were full of precious gospel truths. To quote just two examples:

The very first song in the book tells the story of Zacchaeus—'A certain man of whom we read'—was one of Dad's favourites. The chorus says:

> 'Oh yes, my friend, there's something more,
> Something more than gold:
> To know your sins are all forgiven
> Is something more than gold.'

Another one, number 237, written by Horatius Bonar, one of the hymn-writing giants of the 19th Century, emphasises the substantial, Bible based love of God (contrast this with the wishy-washy ideas about God's 'love' that abound today):

> The love of God is righteous love,

Inscribed upon Golgotha's tree,
Love that exacts the sinner's debt:
Yet, in exacting, sets him free.

Chorus
O wondrous love! For sinners given,
To save from hell, and bring to heaven;
O tell the virtues all abroad
Of Love divine—The Love of God.

Love that condemns the sinners sin,
Yet in condemning, pardon seals;
That saves from righteous wrath, and yet,
In saving, righteousness reveals.

No not the love without the blood,
That were to me no love at all;
It could not reach my sinful soul,
Nor hush the fears that me appal.

I need the love, I need the blood,
I need the grace, the cross, the grave;
I need the resurrection power,
A soul like mine to purge and save.

'No, not the love without the blood…' Yes, it took the blood of the Spotless Lamb of God to save a hell-deserving sinner like me. When I was around eleven or twelve, Jack Barbour preached a gospel message on the coming again of the Lord Jesus to the air. I was troubled in my heart. I knew James and William were both saved —but I wasn't sure, and I had put off making a personal decision. What if the Lord came back tonight and took them and Dad and Mum to heaven? I would be left behind. How thankful I am that the Spirit of God spoke to me through the word of God and through preachers like Jack Barbour. God gave me several opportunities until, finally, the moment came when I took that momentous step of faith.

20 AUCHENFOYLE CAMP

Auchenfoyle Camp was a special place. Situated between Greenock and Kilmacolm beside a meandering stretch of the river Gryffe, the campsite is surrounded by fields in a peaceful corner of the Gryffe valley, sheltered by Cairncurran and Corlick, the two nearby hills. The river was known to every camper as 'The Burn', the Scottish name for a small stream not large enough to be classified as a river.

Auchenfoyle Camp, circa 1968

The site was owned by John Black Senior, who gave it to the Churches of God in the 1940s for use as a Bible Camp where young people attending our Sunday Schools could learn more about our Saviour's love and where young Christians would be nurtured and encouraged in their Christian lives.

We went to Camp from the age of ten onwards. From the Kilmacolm Road, just before the entrance to Auchenfoyle farm, we drove down a rough track at the edge of a field, over a cattle grid and into the Camp site. On arrival, we jumped out and ran over the wooden bridge, constructed from railway sleepers fixed to two steel girders. It was open on both sides—no handrails. To the left, over a small iron bridge, was the toilet block. To the right stood a long, single storey, whitewashed brick building with a corrugated iron roof. A verandah supported by iron posts ran the length of the frontage. This building housed the cookhouse, the wash-room and the plant room. The adjacent washing up kitchen and dining hall were accessed by a couple of steps and a small corridor at the end of the verandah. Formica-topped tables lined the front of the verandah, between the cookhouse and the dining hall. A dividing wall separated the dining hall from 'the brick tent', where the Camp leaders slept on camp beds and where the tuck shop items were stored—crisps, sweets and bottles of lemonade.

From the dining hall end of the verandah, a narrow concrete path curved through the grass towards the tents. The white canvas ridge-pole army tents were pitched in two rows facing each other along the side of 'The Burn' and a grassy path (which became muddy when it rained) went up the middle towards a larger meeting tent at the end of the tents. It was further back from the tents we slept in.

On arrival at Camp, the first thing you had to find out was which tent you were in and who else was in it. The noticeboard in the dining room listed tent numbers, the 'monitor' (or tent leader) and the names of boys allocated to that tent. There were usually five or six boys in each tent. The monitor was an older teenager or brother from one of the churches. He slept across the back end of the tent and we arranged our palliasses on the wooden boards of the tent, across the way or longways from the door. During the day, we piled the palliasses on top of each other at the sides and back of the tent, which gave more room to sit and relax. (In later years, plastic covered foam mattresses replaced the palliasses). The camp leaders had an 'inspection' during breakfast or lunchtime each day to award or deduct points in the 'Tent Tidiness' competition. They announced the points after breakfast each day and there was keen rivalry between tents to see who would get the prize for the tidiest tent at the Friday goodnight meeting. This was a big occasion, because parents and other visitors from the Churches descended on the campsite and filled the hall for the evening programme.

There was a different set of camp leaders for each of the two boys camp weeks. But for many years, those leaders were wedded to their own particular week. They therefore imparted their own style of leadership and brand of humour, and each week seemed to attract a group of monitors and campers who also lent a particular atmosphere and culture to the week. In those days, my brothers and I always stayed for both weeks of camp. The transition period between the end of week one and the start of week two was always quite an adjustment. To me, the first week always seemed more adventurous and attracted people who had that sort of outlook, while the second week had a tamer, more family feel to it. The Grays from Wishaw dominated the second week. Tom, David and Isaac Gray all went to the second week. David Gray and Ken Robertson from Glasgow were the week two Camp leaders. David was an auctioneer and had a quick, intense way of speaking, coupled with a ready sense of fun. He and his brothers were shepherd-hearted men who loved the scriptures. They made a deep impression by the winsome, passionate way they spoke about the Lord Jesus. Ken was a quiet, well-spoken man whom we knew as 'Uncle Ken'. I believe he was an executive salesman with the paint company Sandtex. I remember him speaking in Greenock about a visit he had made to a chapel to discuss his company's contract with the Roman Catholic priest. A little girl was present at the time and when she saw Ken standing behind the altar, exclaimed in horror: 'Oh, he'll go to Hell!' Such was the superstitious fear instilled into her.

The first thing you did after dumping your suitcase or haversack in your tent was to make sure you had a palliasse to sleep on. A palliasse was basically a large canvas bag filled with straw. Sometimes there wasn't enough straw in the palliasse and you woke up feeling the hard wooden boards under your shoulder or hip bone.

The dining hall had a row of tables along each side of the hall with long wooden forms to sit on. Mealtimes always began with the singing of "Oh God to Thee we raise our voice…". If you didn't know it at the start of the week, you knew it by the end. I can still hear Ken Robertson's voice saying "All stand." We'd jump to our feet and fifty or sixty voices lustily sang out[1]:

> Oh God, to Thee we raise our voice,
> In thanks for these good things.
> Thy kindness makes our hearts rejoice,
> Each hour fresh token brings,
> Yes, for Thy mercies every one,
> A gladsome song we lift,
> But chiefly for Thy blessed Son,
> Thy richest, greatest gift. Amen.

We'd sit down and the camp leader nominated one of the monitors to give thanks—"So and so will give thanks for the food." After he'd given thanks, the leader said: "Table one"—and table one's boys came out and lined up with their plates in front of the serving table, where two or three monitors dished out the dollops of food onto their plates. If there were leftovers after they served everyone, the servers came round the tables with trays of extras, asking if anyone wanted a second helping. They repeated the same procedure for pudding. One of our favourites was 'Shepherd's Pie'—which was just mashed potatoes and corned beef all mixed up together. You got a great dollop on your plate. It tasted so good!

After the meal, the command "All Stand" had us on our feet again to sing our thanks in these words:

> Let us with a gladsome mind,
> Praise the Lord for He is kind;
> for His mercies aye endure,
> Ever faithful, ever sure.

He hath with a piteous eye,
Looked upon our misery,
For His mercies aye endure,
Ever faithful, ever sure.

All thing living He doth feed,
His full hand supplies our need,
For His mercies aye endure,
Ever faithful, ever sure.

After lunch, there were usually some announcements. George Millar, a well-built, lugubrious man from Kirkintilloch with a twinkle in his eye and a great sense of humour, always went to the first week. He was in charge of announcements during the first week. He handed out the postcards or letters that arrived for the boys and made a big thing of reading out their names. It was something special to get a letter from home and even more fun when George read out the message on someone's postcard, especially if a girlfriend had sent it. That was often an excuse for a slow hand-thump on the tables. Someone spontaneously started slowly thumping both hands down on the table—the cue for the rest of us—we gleefully joined in and thumped in unison. 'Boom…. Boom …. Boom…. Boom'—the tempo increased until we ended in a frantic crescendo of mad hammering on the tables, plates and cutlery jumping up and down with the din. The leaders took it all in good part and George handed the boy his postcard with a smile.

Duties were allocated by tent number, and rotated each day. Potatoes, Dishes, Pots, Table Setting and Hall Cleaning were the main jobs.

Being on potatoes meant sitting in or near the verandah peeling a mountain of spuds for the following day's dinner. There was an old rusty hand-cranked potato peeler machine, which you filled up with potatoes, then sprayed water into it from a hose as someone cranked the handle for all they were worth. The potatoes rumbled around the interior of the drum, which had a rough lining made of abrasive material. This scrubbed off the skins but left the eyes intact. Our job, sitting in a semi-circle round an assortment of buckets and a giant steel potato pot, was to cut out the eyes and any bad bits using a hand peeler. The downside was that you'd still be sitting there at least half an hour after everyone else had finished their duties, digging yet another eye out of a potato and throwing it with a splash into a water-filled plastic basin. The upside, though, was that once the potatoes were done, you had no more duties that day.

Cleaning the pots included pouring all the unused tea and tea-bags from the teapots from the middle of the bridge into the burn. You also had to scrub clean every cooking utensil, pot, and tray that the cooks had used after each meal—including the huge porridge pot after breakfast.

When the weather turned wet, cold or windy, you were thankful to be on dishes, because you were sheltered from the elements, unlike the huddle of boys on the verandah, peeling potatoes or washing out pots.

One year, there was a sizeable contingent from Glasgow. I got to know some of them and enjoyed the back-and-forth nonsense and verbal ribbing that went on. James Munn was one of them (everyone called him 'Munn') and big 'Jumbo' from Merrylee was another. They introduced some of us to a rather dangerous game—induced fainting. You had to inhale and exhale as deeply as possible for a minute or two, then hold your breath while Munn gave you a bearhug. Within seconds you became dizzy, saw stars and momentarily passed out. 'Miller', another Glaswegian, was a red-cheeked chap with a mop of curly black hair. His speciality was stamping on the flies that landed on the little iron bridge over the rivulet that divided the toilet block from the end of the cookhouse area. There was a mini bluebottle bloodbath on the bridge by the time he was finished.

After duties, around 10.00am, a boy—usually the youngest boy in the camp—had the job of going around ringing an old school handbell to announce the start of morning classes. The boys congregated in the dining hall, now rearranged by the table serving team, with seats facing one end of the hall instead of on either side of the tables. Morning class proceeded by singing choruses, listening to a story from the Bible, followed by a quiz or workbook activity. While the boys were in the hall, the older men met in the large meeting tent at the end of the ordinary tents, where they spent an hour each day studying and discussing a particular topic, character or book from the Bible or listening to a ministry message from a gifted Bible teacher.

Young John Black (now called 'Farmer John') was good at gymnastics. He walked on his hands all the way down the path leading to the tents, along to the end of the tents and back. We didn't just stand in awe of his physical prowess, but admired his manly bearing and straightforward, no nonsense way of speaking. Along with his brothers Davy and Donnie, they made a formidable impact on everyone who came into contact with them. They were—and still are—out and out for the Lord, with a great desire to reach out with the gospel message to others. The impact they've made on many in Greenock and latterly, in their work among recovering drug addicts at 'The Haven'—a Christian rehabilitation centre which they helped to set up next door to Auchenfoyle, is incalculable. *"The day shall declare it."*

Sports and games took place after morning classes and in the afternoon. The 'Sportsmaster'—usually an athletic young man who was good at organising, worked out the draws for the football, table tennis and other sporting events which took place over the week. Football was by far the most important, and generated the fiercest rivalry between tents. As the week progressed, and one team after another got knocked out, the excitement grew over who would play against who in the quarterfinals, semifinal and final. The games were all played on the football pitch on the other side of the burn. There were proper iron goalposts at either end. At the start of the first week of Camp, John or David Black came over on a tractor and mowed the grass on the football pitch. The football final was the climax of the sporting week, usually played on Thursday afternoon or evening. Everyone lined the side of the pitch to watch the finalists battle it out. One year in week two, Tom Gray, the eldest brother of David and Isaac Gray was in goals in the final. He made several great saves against the onslaught of shots at goal from powerful players such as Danny McNeil and Ian Stewart. Suddenly, there was a shout of alarm. Tom had dived for the ball and hit his head with a sickening thud on the goalpost. He lay motionless on the ground. When he came round, he was taken to hospital suffering from concussion. An abrupt end to his illustrious football career.

Thankfully, he came back to camp again the next year, but I don't think he ever played in goal again. Another accident was more gruesome. David Barron from Glasgow was messing about in goals, playing a friendly game of 'three-and-you're out' with a couple of boys one day, when he jumped high with arms outstretched to save a ball. His wedding ring caught on one of the iron net pins welded to the back of the bar and severed his ring finger clean off. His finger fell into the long grass at the back of the goalposts. "Help me look for my finger," he said. They searched all over that grassy patch but, unfortunately, did not find it.

Other tournaments that took place were table tennis, chess and pillow fighting. The pillow fight tournaments took place outside the verandah and were savage affairs. Two people sat opposite each other on an iron pipe laid across two X shaped wooden trellises, about four or five feet off the ground. The protagonists balanced themselves facing each other on the pipe which had some old cloths tied round it to create two makeshift saddles. On a signal, they started laying into each other with their pillows. The first person to lose their balance and fall off was the loser. Ken Robertson senior, was game enough to enter the lists one year but his son Bryan wasn't so sure about the wisdom of that decision, and remonstrated with his dad not to be so foolish at his age. Fortunately, the only bruises Ken suffered were to his ego when his youthful opponent, whose name escapes me, knocked him off his perch.

∾

21 MORE CAMP MEMORIES

One year at Camp, we were sitting at lunch in the dining hall when a boy stood up on the wooden form to look out of the window. (The windows in the dining hall were above eye level when we were sitting down). To his amazement, he saw a big black gorilla running about in the field on the other side of the burn. Immediately everyone crammed around the windows to catch a glimpse before the leaders said, "right, back to your seats, boys." Strangely, the gorilla always appeared while everyone was in the dining hall at lunchtimes. Only a few of the monitors were in the know, but there were a few stories doing the rounds that the hairy creature had escaped from a circus van. Eventually, we discovered it was Rodney Johnston dressed up in a very lifelike gorilla suit!

Another surprise event happened to Neville Coomer, when he retired from leading the first week of boys camp after more than 20 years of service. Neville, unsuspecting, was called into the hall, where his fellow camp leaders conducted a light-hearted presentation ceremony. Suddenly, things got out of hand. Who started it I don't know, but out of nowhere, a complete 'free for all' began and poor Neville found himself on the receiving end of dollops of tomato sauce, handfuls of flour and custard being flung at him from all directions. For a few glorious minutes, it was mayhem. Eventually, order was restored. To his credit, Neville took it all in good part, but I think everyone knew it had gone too far.

As a boy, I rather resented Neville's position of authority at camp. That he was 'a posh Englishman' had everything to do with it, such is the parochial prejudice and pride that lurks in the Scottish national psyche. Little did I know, I would later be indebted to the Christian kindness that Neville and his wife Helen showed me during my art student years in Dundee. Sadly, Helen died a few years ago. Now, having spent the last twenty-two years in fellowship with Neville in the Church of God in Buckhaven, I know him as a true friend. At ninety-three, he's still going strong, working on his farm despite the aches and pains of old age, and as positive in his attitude to life as ever. He had an English public-school education and was always a 'go-getter' with a strong work ethic. He was and is a born salesman, and with his innate ability to persuade others to see things from his point-of-view, could easily have been a successful politician. When I was writing this chapter, we were still in 'lockdown' because of the Coronavirus scare. Nothing daunted, Neville worked with me on Google Hangouts and via email, to publish a book featuring photographs of the Bible Prophecy chart, which Neville and Helen had commissioned me to paint for them several years ago. We published it on Amazon last year, with relevant explanatory scriptures alongside the chart. It gives a useful visual representation of God's dealings with men through the ages, and points to aspects of God's eternal purposes as outlined in the Bible. You can buy a copy on Amazon by searching for the title, 'Bible Prophecy Panoramic Chart: God's Purposes through the Ages'.

∾

IF THE WEATHER was good at camp, we went swimming at least once in the week. Nowadays, a coach takes campers to the swimming baths in Greenock. Alternatively, they go across in the ferry to Millport near Largs and cycle round the Island of Greater Cumbrae. We had to be content with a walk over to Auchenfoyle Farm, where there was a wide stretch of the river just beyond the bridge. A pile of gigantic boulders between the edge of the field and the opposite bank formed a dam with a deep pool behind it. This was our swimming pool. Most boys got changed behind the bushes at the side of the field. I preferred to walk across the top of the dam, and up the far bank, to get changed just inside the big wooden shed that housed the farm sawmill. I can still recall the sweet, fresh smell of sawdust and the excitement of getting ready to plunge into the icy waters of the Gryffe. Actually, I never plunged. I usually walked in, gradually getting used to the cold before submerging my shoulders and swimming around with the others.

At suppertime we got cocoa instead of tea. The warm, sweet mixture of milk, water and cocoa powder had a comforting taste. While supper dishes were being done, another team quickly reorganised the seating in the hall for The Goodnight Meeting. The youngest camper then walked down to the end of the tents and back again, ringing the hand-bell, and we trooped into the hall and sat down on the wooden benches, facing the gable end. The singing leader took us through the two new Camp songs for that week. At the beginning of the week, no-one knew the tune. The singing leader started us off on the sol fah tonic scale, just learning the melody, repeating the first verse a few times, then the chorus until we got it. By the end of the week we'd learned it so well we enthusiastically 'raised the roof' with our singing.

One highlight of the first week in those halcyon days was the humorous poems written by Eric Archibald and Charles Early, which were recited to a packed hall on the Friday night. Each year, Eric and Charles used to sit on the other side of the Bridge, composing their poem — they were so well written and had everyone in fits of laughter as they commented in verse, about the events and characters which had made their mark on us that week.

I contacted Eric recently to find out if they had preserved any of their poetic gems for posterity. Sadly, it seems not. In his email reply, however, Eric reminded me of the following incident. (Eric, you must understand, is a Classical Greek scholar):

> "If it were not for Charles, I would not have been involved, in fact as I recall it, he mostly composed them. One day he asked me to turn something into Ancient Greek, and pretend it

was discovered. I obliged, and unknown to me a group including Charles partially charred the page at the cookhouse fire, and got me to re-translate it publicly, which I did. It was some fable about it being dug up in Egypt. They then had a look, and when they found it was still written in Greek, they didn't know what to think, being reluctant to regard me as a liar.

Unfortunately, a sort of superstition took hold that was enhanced by people at random howling in the darkness that night round the tents, a noise resembling a wolf. At that stage I was conscience stricken because I believed it was interfering with the spiritual message of Camp, which, being out of context of their normal home life in many cases, made it a serious matter to be playing about with their trust in what was said to them. I let them know at the end of the day that it had been meant only as a joke, but felt that they were thereby less inclined to credit any of what they were being told. I think you can understand what I was going through. Perhaps I underestimate the perceptiveness of youth, and their capacity to take it in their stride."

Thinking of the studious and brilliant Eric, reminds me of his equally erudite brother Martin, who in his working life was an English teacher. One memorable Camp week, it rained and rained and rained. After several days, it was becoming impossible to prevent our clothes and sleeping bags from getting wet. Even the covers on my Bible were soggy. The ringing of the bell summoned us to the dining hall, where we crammed in to watch yet another session of table tennis. The rain was hammering on the corrugated iron roof as if it would never stop. Suddenly and with great feeling, Martin started singing in his uniquely proper, Glasgow University voice:

A wet camp is a happy camp,
A wet camp is a happy camp,
A wet camp is a happy camp,
And so say all of us!

 Suffice to say, not all of us joined in with quite the same level of enthusiasm—but it raised a laugh and increased our admiration for Martin's indomitable spirit.

Aeneas Kinghorn and Jim Carlin were two young men who came to camp from Wishaw one year. Jim lived in Bellshill. He didn't live long because he got leukaemia and died in his early twenties. Aeneas was a regular camper. He was always friendly and, being older than the boys, was trusted by the camp leaders to accompany some of us on a midnight walk along the Kilmacolm Road one night. We walked up the hill past Faulds Farm (where some of my forbears on Dad's side came from) and round by the old quarry. As we came to the quarry, someone started telling a story about a man who hanged himself there many years ago and suggested it might be haunted. A thrill of fear gripped me as we walked on and I nervously looked back at the black hole of the quarry over my shoulder—just in case. In the darkness of the night, I was glad of the company.

 On the Thursday night of camp, we had a 'Testimony Meeting'. We stacked up the tables at the end and sides of the dining hall and arranged the forms around the walls so that everyone sat facing the middle. One or two older chaps kicked off proceedings by telling how they got saved, then the meeting was open for anyone to stand up and tell their story. It was always compelling to hear men and boys, some of whom were unused to public speaking, plucking up courage to declare 'what great things the Lord had done for them'.

As it says in Romans chapter 10 verse 9:

> 'if you shall confess with your mouth Jesus as Lord, and shall believe in your heart that God raised him from the dead, you shall be saved: for with the heart man believes unto right-eousness; and with the mouth confession is made unto salvation.'

On Friday afternoons we piled onto a private hire coach and went to Greenock, where we shopped for our Friday night 'Beanfeast'. Our tent monitor usually discussed with us what to buy and we clubbed together and put some money toward the cost. Some years the boys in my tent went over the top, buying far too much and had so much left over, we ended up slipping on discarded bits of cake which fell on the floor of the tent, which we were too tired to clear up till we got up on Saturday morning. The 'Beanfeast' always took place after the Friday night visitors to the 'goodnight meeting' had gone home.

Around 6.30pm, a crowd of visitors invaded the camp-site. A succession of cars bumped along the dirt track, carrying parents and friends from our churches in the West of Scotland, and parked in the field on the other side of the bridge. At 7 o'clock the bell rang and everyone crammed into the dining hall, which was re-arranged to seat as many folks as possible for the final goodnight meeting.

The first part of the programme was a variety programme —humorous tales or poems about things that happened during the week, 'party-pieces' from tent groups and awarding of the sports trophies. The 'monitors hymn' was always a treat to listen to—they had practised it all week, learning the four-part harmony for tenor, alto, bass and soprano. After that, a brother presented a gospel message, often illustrated, with an appeal at the end, for anyone who wished to talk further about their spiritual welfare, to speak with a Camp leader afterwards. By the end of the meeting, the heat of 200 bodies had built up, and it was a relief to stream out onto the verandah for some fresh air and a chat with the visitors—especially any girls who had come with their parents. We served the visitors with a cup of cocoa and something to eat before the bell rang to signal time up for the visitors.

A Friday night bonfire at Auchenfoyle Camp

As soon as they had gone, we headed over to the patch of ground beside the football field, where during the week, John, Donnie or Davy Black had been ferrying tractor-loads of scrap wood, building the Friday night bonfire. We'd watch Donald Gillies or one of the other older guys throwing petrol on the base of the pile. Then, to a warning cry of 'STAND BACK!' Someone lit a match and 'WHOOF!' the whole thing went up. After standing round warming our backsides at the fire, we'd drift over to our tents—or latterly to the dining hall—where our tent monitor started dishing out the Beanfeast goodies.

One year, Danny McNeil was my tent monitor. He loved Carnation® milk and tinned fruit, and made sure those items were on our Friday afternoon shopping list! Danny had set out plastic bowls and spoons on the wooden floorboards of the tent. He opened the tins of fruit with a tin opener borrowed from the kitchen and carefully spooned out equal portions of fruit into each bowl. One of us pierced two holes at either side of the tin of Carnation® milk and poured the thick, sweet contents on top of the fruit. The full, round taste of tinned peaches, syrup and a generous helping of the evaporated milk was delicious and very satisfying.

Over the years, the Camp Committee gradually improved the facilities. One year the Blacks laid a line of great boulders alongside the burn, near the boundary chain that curved low over the Gryffe, at the far end of the camp. The idea was to reclaim a piece of land that was marshy because of overspill from the burn. When first constructed, the new wall was quite visible, although you'd hardly notice it now because of the natural growth of vegetation around it. Anyway, Malcolm MacDonald decided to commemorate Jack Ferguson's legacy by carving an inscription on one of the large stones. Every day, he sat on a stool in the shallow water, and attacked it industriously with a hammer and chisel. He stuck at it until it was ready for the grand unveiling ceremony. It read: 'The Fergie Wall'. I think he also carved the date, but I couldn't find it when I went to look for it a year or two ago.

22 SAVED AND BAPTIZED

A few years ago, I unearthed a rare document from Dad's filing cabinet. Two sides of a sheet of lined paper from a school jotter, written in a round, schoolboy hand. It was my testimony, the story in my own words of how, as a boy of eleven, I came to put personal faith in Jesus Christ as my Saviour.

My transcript reads:

> On the 19th January 1969, I was saved. I had been hearing a man recounting a story which he said happened to him when about 15. His story says that he was sleeping in a dead person's room and when nobody was there the bed-covers were pulled down. He pulled them up again and it went on like that until he started to pray. After he had prayed the 'ghost', as he called it never bothered him again. I was frightened quite a bit when I heard it and not being able to sleep, I went through to the kitchen

where my mum told my father when he came in that I was needing a little talk with him. My father told me not to worry because anybody who trusts in Jesus can not be hurt. He gave me the text 'nothing will in any wise hurt you' and I went to bed again. I prayed and asked to be forgiven and that I might be saved and know it. I was saved then. I went through at once and told my mother and father and when my father and mother heard it they were very glad. My father told me that Jesus had been waiting for me to take that step for a long time. That is how I was saved.

On the 14th January 1969 I was saved. I had been hearing a man recounting a story which he said happened to him when about 15. His story says that he was sleeping in a dead person's room and when nobody was there the bed-covers were pulled down, he pulled them up again and it went on like that until he started to pray. After he had prayed the "ghost" as he called it never bothered him again. I was frightened quite a bit when I heard it and not being able to sleep I went through to the kitchen where my mum told my father when

A few years ago, I gave my testimony at a family service. I wrote out the story of my life before conversion, to put the handwritten account into context. I know I've covered some of these details elsewhere in this book, but I think it's useful to have it all in one chapter.

he came in that I was
needing a little talk with him
My father told me, not to
worry because anybody who
trusts in Jesus can not be
hurt. He gave me the text
"nothing will in any wise
hurt you" and I went to
bed again. I prayed and
asked to be forgiven and
that I might be saved and
know it. I was saved then.
I went through at once
and told my mother and
father and when my father
and mother heard it they were
very glad. My father told me
that Jesus had been waiting
for me to take that step
for a long time.
                    That, is how
I was saved.

~

MY TESTIMONY

I was born and brought up during the 1960s in the ship-building town of Greenock, on the West coast of Scotland.

Both parents were Christians, numbered with the Church of God in Greenock–which meets at Cedar Hall, 5 Ardgowan street. I'm the eldest of five children–three brothers and a sister. As children, we sat on Dad's knees while he told us a Bible story before going to bed. No-one brought those stories to life the way he did! For example, when telling the story of Samson and the lion, we waited with bated breath for the bit where the lion jumped out from the side of the road. Dad roared and rose up off the chair with us still on his knees! What excitement!

On Sunday mornings, we sat beside our parents on the wooden forms in Cedar Hall where the church met each week to remember the death and resurrection of the Lord Jesus. When we sing certain hymns even today, they take me back there in spirit. My parents often invited friends home for supper after the Gospel meeting—the "sing-songs", conversation, and hearty fellowship of those days is a precious memory.

Over the years, I heard many gospel preachers. I was familiar with the message of salvation through faith in Christ and with the account of God's dealings with men in the Bible. When I was ten, I went to summer Bible camp at Auchenfoyle Farm between Kilmacolm and Greenock, which was run by our churches. In those days we slept in old army tents–fine if the weather was dry, not so pleasant when it rained. After supper, we had a good-night talk before going to bed. Each night the gas mantles in the "brick tent"—our all-purpose meeting room, dining room and games room—had to be lit by hand, one by one. I remember the hiss of the gas lamps and the thump, thump, thump of the petrol generator, powering the light bulbs in the tents, as we sang the camp hymns and listened to the goodnight message. The speakers brought before us the love of God in sending His Son to die on the cross and the urgent need to get right with God by trusting Christ as our own personal Saviour. At the end of each goodnight meeting, the leaders invited us to stay behind and have a chat. I always avoided this and made my escape with the rest of the boys to my tent!

Although I had always believed the Bible, there was an internal conflict—was I saved? Had I trusted the Lord Jesus as *my* saviour? Where was *I* going to spend eternity? For two years, I put off the decision. After returning from Camp in 1968 (aged eleven), I heard several preachers speak of the return of the Lord Jesus to the air. Even though I'd heard it before, I couldn't get it out of my mind. I believe the Spirit of God was speaking to me. Two of my brothers were saved. If the Lord came today, I knew they would go to be with Him and I would be left. One night a few weeks before my twelfth birthday, I was troubled by an incident which happened to the father of Jim Lafferty, one of the Sunday School boys. Mr Lafferty had been at our house for supper and told us how, as a boy of fifteen, he'd been troubled by a 'ghost' when he slept in the room of someone who'd recently died. According to my written account, this bothered me so much that I got up out of bed and spoke to Mum about it. She asked Dad to have a word with me. Oddly, I don't remember that part of the story — but I clearly remember lying awake, turning everything over in my mind. Finally, I said to myself: "This is silly! I know how to get saved–I know John 3:16 — 'For God so loved the world, that he gave his only begotten son, that whosoever believes on him should not perish but have everlasting life' — Why don't I just do it now?" So, there and then, I turned over on my pillow and accepted Jesus as my Saviour. I can't remember my exact words, but I remember the great sense of peace that came over me at that moment. I knew a transaction had taken place between me and God. I got out of bed, went through to the kitchen and told Dad and Mum I'd got saved. They were very pleased to hear this.

I started reading my Bible regularly. A couple of years passed. In 1970, age thirteen, I took my fishing rod to Camp. One afternoon, George Millar, one of the Camp leaders who'd also brought his fly rod with him, asked me if I wanted to come with him and see if we could catch something. Little did I know, he was intent on catching a different kind of fish. As we walked along the banks of the Gryffe, he asked if I'd thought about getting baptised. I don't remember my reply, but he asked me to consider it seriously. Then, as only George Millar could, he said "I hope, when you come back to Camp next year Jo, you'll have been baptised." He left it at that and we spent the rest of the expedition fishing for trout. However, George gave me plenty to think about. I didn't know what I would say to him if I hadn't been baptised by the time next year's Camp came round, but I pushed the thought out of my mind. I went home, went back to school, and life returned to normal. Around the turn of the year, in my daily Bible reading, I came to the story of the Ethiopian eunuch in Acts 8. I read "Behold, here is water, what doth hinder me to be baptised?" The words seemed to leap off the page. I said to myself, "there's a baptismal tank at Cedar Hall. What's to stop me being baptised?" John 14:15 had also been on my mind: "If ye love me, ye will keep my commandments." I resolved to speak to one of the overseers of the Church, which I did on the following Sunday. He arranged with my father to come and visit me with another overseer. They asked me what had brought me to this decision, and I told them how I'd been reading the story of the eunuch in Acts 8, and wanted to obey the Lord's command by being baptised. Not long after this, I was baptised in the tank at Cedar Hall and the following week added to the Church of God in Greenock. I don't remember any follow-up from George Millar when I went to Camp in 1971, but he was only one link in the chain of my decision to become a disciple (a committed follower of Jesus Christ). Some years later, like the Jews in

Beroea, I studied the scriptures more carefully and examined the teachings of the Churches of God 'to see if these things were so'. I satisfied myself that the practice and teaching of the Churches of God were closely aligned with the teachings of Christ and His apostles in the New Testament. I count it the highest honour to serve the Lord in His House and hope that I can continue to do so until faith gives way to sight.

One thing have I asked of the LORD, that will I seek after; that I may dwell in the house of The LORD all the days of my life, to behold the beauty of The LORD and to enquire in his temple." (Ps 27:4)

〜

WHEN WE MOVED from Greenock to Kilwinning in Ayrshire, we transferred to the Church of God in Kilmarnock. Willie Gilmour, one of the older overseers there, was a big-hearted man who gave great encouragement to us as teenagers, taking our first steps to take part in the remembrance. He said to James, William and myself — 'I want you each to choose a hymn and give it out next week.' He knew how nerve-wracking it was for young men learning to speak publicly for the first time, and this was his way of helping us overcome that initial fear. Each of us had our hymn ready and at an opportune moment in between thanksgivings, each of us got to our feet and read out our chosen hymn. It was typical of Willie Gilmour's practical approach to life. He got us over that first hurdle of taking part audibly in the church. It wasn't long before we were bringing a few thoughts in thanksgiving. Later, we were introduced to speaking in public at the evening gospel meeting by 'sharing the meeting' with an older brother.

One significant innovation before digital audio streaming came along was the development of 'taped ministry.' Recordings of conference speakers and some gospel preachers were made available on cassette tape for a nominal cost. Dad bought several of these from Billy Bell, the brother in Kirkintilloch, who took on the job of recording the speakers and compiling the tapes. One of these was an old recording, transferred to cassette tape from a reel-to-reel tape recorder. Jack Miller had recorded it in the 1960s, of his father John Miller, an outstanding Bible student who was a full-time evangelist and teacher among the Churches of God. He was a powerful orator and even though the recordings had a lot of background noise, James and I found those tapes fascinating to listen to. John Miller was a master of his subject, and the way he presented the message was as important as the message itself. Over and over again, we listened to his address entitled 'From Egypt to Canaan', until we could imitate him and recite his declamations back to each other.

From Kilwinning we flitted to Galston in the Irvine Valley. We transferred to the Church of God there, where the local overseer, Jimmy Barr and his wife Elsie lived. They had a small shop on the corner of Henrietta Street and Polwarth Street, at the crossroads of the town, which was always known locally as 'The Cross'. Jimmy was a small, heavyset man with deep-set eyes and a determined jaw. He was a time-served Joiner, but like many tradesmen, was a 'Jack of all trades' and could turn his hand to several building construction skills. His sister, Mary MacArthur, was a widow. Like Jimmy, she had similar facial features. She lived in Newmilns, the next village farther up the valley. Our private nickname for Mary was 'Haystack' — borrowed from one of the TV wrestling champions of the day, who went by the name of 'Giant Haystacks'. Not to put too fine a point on it, Mary appeared to us to be a female version of 'Giant Haystacks'. She was as broad as she was long. However, Mary was one of the most hospitable people you could ever meet. She loved having us visit her in her council house in 'Gilfoot', the small estate on the edge of the village. She was a strong woman who was forthright in her opinions—but she always tempered this with a willingness to laugh at herself and see the funny side of things. Mary had been a talented singer in her youth and still had a powerful altosoprano voice. After serving us with tea and cake or biscuits, she used to sit down at her piano and play and sing hymns. Now and then, in the middle of singing, she'd have to clear her throat, but she just paused for a moment to shift the phlegm, and kept on singing. Happy memories.

'Church Lane Meeting Room' was the little hall in Church Lane, Galston, where the church met for their services. It had a musty smell about it. The rows of solid folding wooden seats were screwed into the floor with wrought iron feet, and lent a rather down at heel air to the place. A double row of brown, oval shaped, metal electric heating pipes, ran round the walls, including the wall at the top right-hand corner of the hall, where the baptismal tank had been installed, underneath the floor. When Dad arrived, with Jimmy's blessing, he began a renovation programme, taking out the old seats and replacing them with blue plastic stacking seats, which were easier to manage and reorganise for different functions. He also laid a hard-wearing carpet which was more welcoming than the tired old lino tiles that had been there since 'the year dot'. On a Lord's Day morning we arranged the seats in a square around the table. After the remembrance, we rearranged the seats for Sunday School and the Gospel meeting in the evening. The old wooden lectern had a hand-lettered quote on it. It was the motto of William Carey, who took the gospel to India during the 19th century. Embossed in gold letters it read: 'ATTEMPT GREAT THINGS FOR GOD; EXPECT GREAT THINGS FROM GOD'. Little did we know what highs and lows lay ahead in our service for God in Galston.

~

23 FARM DAYS

When we were about eleven or twelve, towards the end of the summer holidays in Greenock, James and I would have an early breakfast and cycle up to Auchenfoyle Farm. From there, Davy, John or Donnie took us in the lorry, or sometimes on a tractor pulling a trailer, to Newmains Farm, near Glasgow airport. John Black Senior owned Newmains until it became the subject of a compulsory purchase order by Renfrewshire Council, who wanted to build an industrial estate on the land. I remember him telling Dad, that the year after they made the compulsory purchase order, he had ploughed the land and sown seed as usual. He got two more years of crops from it before work on the industrial site began. They were large fields of rich soil and produced bumper crops of wheat and barley each year.

Our job when we arrived at Newmains, was to walk up and down the field, rolling in the bales of straw deposited by the baler, to form one continuous line of straw bales, so that the tractor-drawn elevator could lift them more efficiently. The baler, drawn behind the tractor, mopped up the swathes of straw left behind by the combine harvester. It had a complicated arrangement of metal arms which paddled back and forth in a rotary motion, picking up the loose straw, compacting it and tying it securely with nylon baler twine. Whenever the newly created bale was complete, it was shunted into a metal channel behind the previous one and, inch by inch, pushed along until they fell off the end of the baler chute onto the ground. Unfortunately, this didn't happen quickly enough and there were considerable gaps between each bale—hence the need for a couple of boys to walk up and down the rows ahead of the elevator to bring the bales into one long line. It was hot, tiring work, hoisting each bale off the ground and humphing it across the stubble and dumping it down in line with the others. The dry, sharp ends of straw scratched our wrists—and the tops of our bare thighs if we were daft enough to wear shorts —till our skin was criss-crossed with red marks. But we got a great suntan! When the sun came out, we'd take our shirts off and by the end of the week were almost as brown as Donnie. Well, not quite. Donnie's back was dark, dark brown, almost black, he was so burnt with the sun.

We usually had a short mid-morning break for a quick cup of tea, but by the time lunchtime came round, we were glad of the chance to sit down and open the packed lunch Mum had made.

One time, Davy Black took a shotgun with him and shot a few pigeons in the adjacent fields in the morning. At lunchtime, we all went back to Newmains farmhouse, where one of the ladies—I think it was Aunt Betty—had plucked and cooked the pigeons for lunch. All the Blacks sat round the kitchen table and enjoyed a hearty lunch of freshly cooked pigeon. I hung about the kitchen doorway for a bit, hoping that someone might say "Would you like to try a bit of pigeon Jo?"—to no avail. I suppose if they'd offered me a bit, they'd have had to extend the same favour to James as well, and since pigeons are fairly small, there was probably only enough for the men. James and I sat in the yard and enjoyed our packed lunches in the sunshine.

It wasn't long before we were on our feet again and on with the work. Donnie stood on the back of the trailer with two iron hooks in his fists and stacked the bales into position as they came off the elevator. He gradually rose higher and higher as he laid down layer after layer of bales until he was too high to reach down and take the bales off the top of the elevator. The elevator was then disconnected and young John used a pitchfork to lift each bale high above his head so that Donnie could complete the topmost layer. When work stopped at the end of the day, it was a great release to jump up onto the mudguard of the tractor beside John or Donnie, who drove the trailer stacked high with bales back to Auchenfoyle. Sometimes we lay on the very top of the stack of bales on the trailer, overlooking the tractor. Our route took us back through Houston, Bridge of Weir, up past The Green, Gateside, The Faulds Farm and on to Auchenfoyle. Just as well we weren't on top of the trailer the day that Donnie took the corner in Houston too sharply and the trailer tipped over and spilled bales of straw all over the road!

When we arrived back at the farm, Ettie, John Black senior's wife, said to John or Davie, "Did these boys work hard?" And they replied: "Aye, like Blacks!" We took that as a great compliment, only dimly aware of the humour implicit in that now unsayable double entendre. Ettie reached for a jar on the mantlepiece and took out a ten-shilling note or a pound note for each of us. We went home with money in our pockets, tired, but full of the satisfaction that comes from doing an honest day's work.

Sometimes we just went up to the farm for a visit. On one of those occasions, Kenny McDonald, son of Betty the milkmaid—who we called Aunt Betty—was working on his car engine. We were standing watching him when he said to me "Haud that a minute Jo." I obediently held the bit of battery terminal wire—and got a massive spark of electricity as he touched it with the tool he was using. I jumped back in surprise, to Kenny's great amusement. "Did you get a wee shock?" he asked with mock concern. "Hmm", I said to myself, "I'll need to watch him."

One day I was sitting in the Bothy at Auchenfoyle, chatting with several boys who'd come up from Greenock to work on the farm. 'The Bothy' was an upstairs room in a separate part of the building, accessed from the inner courtyard next to the farmhouse kitchen. Suddenly, the door opened and Donnie came in. "Right! Time to get some work done here." The idle chit-chat was cut short and and off they went to earn their day's wages!

～

24 HOLIDAYS IN SCOTLAND

Every summer, during his eight-week school holiday, Dad packed the car, and later, our Volkswagen Caravanette, and we went off for a week's holiday.

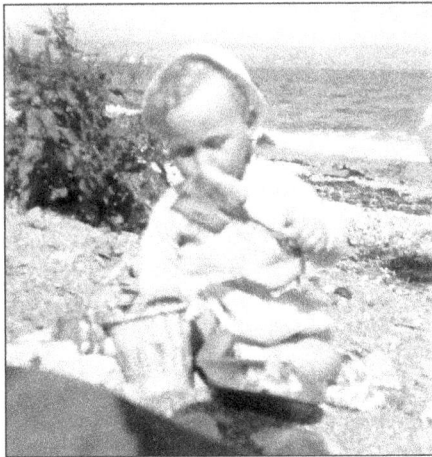

On Carradale beach with rubber bucket and spade. Dad put a baby jellyfish in the bucket. I didn't like it so I threw it out!

Apart from the hazy memory of playing with a plastic
bucket and spade on the beach at Carradale, one of the
earliest holidays I remember was when we went to stay
with Dad's cousin Jenny Kerr and her husband Willie at
Gryffe Neuk for a few days. They had a tomato growing
business on their smallholding—apparently Jenny's
mother (Granny Black), had given the house its name
when they built it in a 'neuk' (a corner) beside a bend in
the river Gryffe. Cousin Jenny, as we called her, was always pleased to see us and had a quick reply for any
witty remark. Her husband Willie was a hardworking man
who was intensely practical. They had three of a family:
William (who later changed his name to Bill), Mary and
Jock. Willie Kerr was a kind-hearted man and one of the
most upright, straight talking, honest men I have ever
known. My father counted him as a true friend. When we
went upstairs to bed on our holiday at Gryffe Neuk, we
passed William's (Bill's) bedroom, which was under the
eaves at the front of the house. His door was open, and
he was sitting up in bed reading his Bible. He gave us a
cheery "Goodnight" as we passed. He had an enquiring
mind and was a first-class engineer. In his early twenties,
he set off for India by hitch-hiking across Europe,
working on a kibbutz in Israel to earn money for the next
leg of his journey and eventually, after many adventures,
reached India. He visited us at Bentinck Street more than
once in between his globetrotting travels and showed us
slides of the people he'd met and the places he'd been.
One time, he had to spend the night in his sleeping bag
on a beach in Israel, but stayed awake all night to protect
his belongings from some Arabs who sat nearby, waiting
for him to fall asleep! We enjoyed hearing his tales. Bill
lost his life suddenly just over a year ago, aged seventy-
seven, in a Paramotor hang-gliding accident. Adven-

turous to the last, but an immense loss to all who knew him.

In the morning, when we came down to breakfast at Gryffe Neuk, we sat round the table in the kitchen with the family. Cousin Jenny had made porage for us and had set a cupful of milk beside each bowl. We usually poured our milk from a jug at home, so this was a novelty for us. Pouring the milk from cup to bowl without spilling it was a challenge! There was a small bridge over the Gryffe at the entrance to the house. Moored in the water was a flat-bottomed, home-made 'punt'. Dad took James and me out on the punt one day, which was great fun. We had to keep our heads down when we went under the bridge!

Mary took us into the tomato house one day and showed us how they nipped off the un- wanted tomato shoots to get bigger crops. I don't recall any interaction with Jock on that visit but we always enjoyed talking to Jock after the morning meeting at Cedar Hall — he was always ready to see the funny side and had an un- inhibited, full on laugh that only encouraged me to think

The Black Phantom, home-made 'punt' on the river at Gryffe Neuk

of another funny remark, just to make him laugh! Jock drove a grey Mini-van. When the market for Scottish grown tomatoes became less profitable, Willie Kerr sold Gryffe Neuk to Kenny McDonald and built a bungalow beside the farm cottage that Felix and his family had lived in, along the road from Auchenfoyle. Willie Kerr was responsible for erecting the sign in the roadside field next to his property, which read 'CHRIST DIED FOR OUR SINS'. Jock got a job in Johnstone, working for his brother Bill in his sign-writing and engraving business.

One year, when we were about to set off for a holiday 'up North' at Uncle Hugh and Aunt Nan's, we were all sitting in the Volkswagen Caravanette ready to go. The sliding door was still open and Dad was standing talking to Mr More. ('Mory' to us!) We heard Mory saying to Dad, "D'you think you'll make it?" We roared with laughter at the stupidity of this remark. Of course, Dad would make it! He would drive till midnight if he had to! Mr More heard us laughing and gave us a sidelong glance as he wished Dad a pleasant trip. Such was our scorn for the man from Wick.

Uncle Hugh had inherited the croft from his father. It had the Gaelic name 'Badfluich' which, (according to an old book[1]) is actually spelt 'Badfliuch' and means 'wet place'. (The Ordnance Survey map spells the name of the nearby wood as 'Badfluich', so the 'u' and the 'i' must have been transposed before Dad or we arrived on the scene!)

The cottage was a simply furnished, homely place. Aunt Nan cooked the meals on a cream-coloured Rayburn stove. She made the most delicious pancakes and scones. Uncle Hugh was away on the river all day, showing the toffs from London how to catch fish. He sometimes brought home a freshly caught salmon which Aunt Nan cooked for tea, accompanied by their delicious homegrown potatoes and vegetables. An old grey Massey Ferguson tractor sat outside Uncle Hugh's Nissan hut workshop, which housed his circular saw and various farm tools. We loved to sit on the tractor and pretend we were driving!

From Badfluich as our base, Dad took us on various outings. One day, he bought a ball of string and some fishhooks, cut down some tree branches and made fishing rods for us. We took these to a small loch where we went out on a boat to fish for perch. I think we used bits of bread for bait, but apart from a few bites, we caught nothing. There were always plenty of walks on the single-track roads there. Sometimes we walked to the Post Office at Altass, a small hamlet of a few houses about a mile from Badfluich. Dad also took us to visit Edie Ross, an old lady who was a relative of his father and lived on a small croft at the bottom of a field near Altass. She kept a few sheep and had one that was so tame it trotted over to her whenever she called it. Another relative was Jess, who lived in Tain but later retired to a family cottage near Altass. Norma and I visited her before our family was born and found her in the garden picking blackcurrants at ninety years of age.

Dad also showed us the pool in the river near Badfluich where, as a teenager, he caught a salmon by damming up the pool with stones and chasing the salmon into a corner. He had nostalgic memories of his father bringing him and his brother Joe in the 1930s to stay at Badfluich with their Uncle Heckie Mackintosh, Hugh's father. I think losing his father so young made those memories even more important. Dad's father died from stomach cancer aged fifty, when Dad was only twelve.

Dad, with the salmon and a small trout he
caught near Badfuich.

~

ONE YEAR we had a holiday in Banff, near Macduff on
the Moray coast. There was a Church of God in Macduff
which we attended on the Sunday. We knew some boys
there because they'd been to camp. Robbie Mitchell was
one of them. He became a fisherman like his father, Jim.
One of their crew—the cook Colin Chinchen had been
my monitor at Camp. They all spoke with that distinctive
North East accent known as 'the doric'. When one of
them first asked me "Fit like?"—meaning "how are you?"
I wasn't sure what to answer! A vital element of those
holidays was the opportunity to spend our 'spending
money'. We spent a considerable amount of time in various shops, examining fishing nets, toys of one sort or
another, penknives, comic books and whatever else interested us, before deciding what to buy.

We spent many happy hours on the beautiful sandy beaches at Whitehills and Cullen. I remember we met up with Guy Jarvie's brother Bob, on holiday from Glasgow, on one of those occasions. He sat in a deckchair with his trouser legs rolled up and enjoyed our company. He had a very individual sense of humour, which we also enjoyed.

Another day, we went to the outdoor swimming pool at Tarlair, just outside Macduff. I was playing on a boat with another boy. I don't remember this, but James says I tipped the boy into the water. He must have fought back because we both finished up in the pool!

One of the brethren in Banff assembly was Albert Robertson, a well-known dentist. He and his wife invited us round for dinner one evening during the week. Their son Jonathan was a student at Glasgow School of Art. There was a sculpture he had made of a fisherman in an alcove on the stairs of their house. One of Albert's hobbies was movie making. He had created a little projection room, complete with a couple of rows of folding cinema seats. After dinner, he took us into this room and showed us black and white films of early Camp days, including a sequence with Jim Watt as a young man, energetically swinging an axe to cut down a tree. Jim had been born and brought up in Macduff. He trained as a dental technician and moved South to Kilmarnock, which is where we got to know him, at the church there, with his wife Sarah and their daughters, Deriele and Michelle.

～

JAMES REMINDED me of the holiday we spent in the border hamlet of Darnick, near Melrose, at Aunt Ina's old cottage. Aunt Ina had died and Aunt Nette looked after her cottage until she sold it. As James recalled, we hardly slept the night we arrived, because of all the old clocks that chimed every hour! The next day, Aunt Nette arrived and stopped all the clocks. James said she had a chuckle when she realised we'd been kept awake with their chiming! My abiding memory of Darnick, apart from visiting Melrose Abbey, where the heart of Robert the Bruce is buried—which fired my imagination—was of being attacked and relentlessly bitten by flying ants one boiling hot day as we walked along one of the country lanes. There was no escaping the fierceness of their bites.

When Dad was studying for a postgraduate qualification at Moray House, Edinburgh, he had to attend a summer course for a few days. I was about ten or eleven. He combined his course with a family holiday at a caravan site in Penicuik, near Edinburgh. One sunny day, we went into Princes Street Gardens. At that time there was a putting green there. Mum sat on a wooden bench and watched while James and I played a round of putting. Without warning, James tried a golf shot on the ball. He didn't realise I was standing behind him and swung the club back to take the shot. The metal club smashed into the side of my face. I blacked out momentarily and when I came to, found myself in a half-kneeling position on the green, clutching my face in agony. Fortunately, a male nurse was sitting nearby. He came and checked me over. "It's probably only a bruise," he said. I knew it was more than a bruise. Mum hailed a taxi on Princes Street, put James and me into it, and told the driver to take us to the Royal Infirmary.

Someone took me into the emergency room, leaving James on his own, wondering what was happening. I was sitting waiting for a doctor to return with the result of an X-ray, when a nurse brought a visibly upset James in to see me. I think he was just so relieved to find me still alive! The X-Ray revealed a broken left cheekbone, which required an operation to lift it back into place and a brief stay in hospital afterwards. A nurse shaved the hair off the left side of my head and I was given a general anaesthetic. An incision was made above my left temple to allow the surgeon to insert an instrument to lift the bone back into position.

I woke up in the ward, where a beautiful nurse with a lovely Stornoway accent was keeping an eye on me. I spent the next three or four days there, alongside some other patients, one of whom had broken his jaw. His teeth were wired together while the bone healed. He had to suck liquidised food through a straw. Dad arranged for me to spend the rest of the holiday at Aunt Nette's. for me, it turned out to be a most enjoyable holiday. Aunt Nette was glad of the company, since Uncle Hamish had died several years before. She allowed me to watch her black and white T.V. in the evenings. She sat and watched an interview with the actor Peter Ustinov one evening and said she had really enjoyed it. During the day, I took Jonathan, Aunt Nette's Scottie dog, for long walks up past the Observatory and down through the woods on the other side of Blackford Hill. One day I watched a squirrel gathering nuts on a tree stump there. It was a special moment.

~

25 MORE HOLIDAY MEMORIES

Another memorable holiday took place in the summer of 1969 on the Isle of Man. To get there, we had to take the ferry from Ardrossan to Douglas, a journey of several hours. As usual, we spent the first hour exploring the ship, running up and down from below deck to the upper decks, where Dad and Mum were sitting behind the great painted funnels, enjoying the sun and the sea breeze. It so happened that Elsie Gilmour, an English lady who'd married a Scotsman from the Church of God in Kilmarnock, was already sitting on deck when we boarded. She was visiting relatives on the Isle of Man. Dad and Mum were so pleased to see her and enjoyed her company for the duration of the crossing. When we arrived at Douglas, we headed back down to the car deck, piled into the VW Caravanette and drove to the Glen Dhoo Drive-in Campsite on the outskirts of Douglas, where we helped Dad put up our ridge pole tent. The tent was sleeping quarters for us boys for the rest of the week. Elisabeth, Dad and Mum slept in the Caravanette. Mum made our meals on its little gas stove and we sat on folding chairs round a folding table to eat our meals. We travelled all over the island, visiting Castletown, Peel and Ramsey, as well as Douglas. On Sunday, we went to the morning meeting at the Church in Douglas where Mr Bert Cain was the resident overseer. It was a small but welcoming assembly. They were always glad to have visitors. Mr and Mrs Cain invited us to their house for lunch. They lived in an upstairs flat, which had a splendid view of the front at Douglas. After lunch, Bert showed us photographs taken by Jonathan, the boyfriend of his daughter Elsie. He had been in Paris at the time of the student riots and took dramatic shots of the mayhem. I think he may have sold some to a newspaper. Later, when we moved to Galston, Alex McLuckie told the story of his holiday on the Isle of Man, and his visit to the church there. After the usual greetings, Mr Cain asked him to speak at the Gospel meeting in the evening. Alex accepted the invitation, but then Mr Cain said, "I hope you're not going to speak about the boy with the five loaves and two fishes?" When Alex asked why, Mr Cain said, "because that's what the last three visitors have spoken on!"

At the church, we also met Mr Southern, an older man who'd lost his wife only a few months earlier in a tragic car crash. He shed angry tears of grief as he told us how the driver of the other car had been racing round the TT course and had ploughed right into them. Elsie Sands (Mr and Mrs Cain's daughter) recently gave me the exact details of that awful event. She said: "It was a very well-known racer...Jeff Duke. He was coming round from Laxey on the Ramsey Road and was going too fast on a blind bend. Kathleen and her husband were coming from Ramsey and had to turn right into the lane for their house...right on the blind bend". It was sad to see how deeply the loss of his wife had affected him.

During that sunny week, we visited an outdoor pool somewhere. The shallow children's pool was full of children having a great time splashing about. Being about ten or eleven, I was admittedly a bit too old for the small pool. I was playing in it anyway, when a large, rather irate man dressed in nothing but swimming trunks came over and said, "You're not supposed to be in this pool." I ignored him. "Get out!" he said, and came rushing into the pool and pushed me under the water. As he exited the pool, James says I splashed him with water. Several adults sitting round the pool eating ice creams, muttered, "That's ridiculous that—a grown man—should be ashamed of himself!"

One year we had a two-week holiday in Marske, near Redcar, in the North East of England. Dad had heard of this holiday company called "The Holiday Fellowship," which ran activity holidays for families. We arrived at this impressive looking old mansion standing atop the sand dunes near the beach. Rita, the hostess, met us, a frumpy lady with a curly black perm and glasses. She took us to our rooms and showed us round. At night, there was a rota of parents to monitor the children, because they went to bed earlier than the adults, so that the adults could relax and have some time to themselves in the evening. One evening, one of the dads who was supervising looked in on our bedroom to make sure we were O.K. He was a friendly chap who showed us the secret of the 'take off your thumb' trick. He was really good at it and until he revealed the secret technique, we thought his thumb had actually come off and fallen under the edge of the carpet or into the empty cup from which he 'retrieved' it. I spent hours perfecting the thumb trick, till I could do it with ease. (It's the first thing my grand-children ask me to do whenever we visit!)

In the morning at breakfast, we met a Dutch girl who was working there as a waitress. She said "Vould you like more 'mill-ik?'", which we thought was very funny. We imitated her accent for the rest of the week. Since we were only a stone's throw from the beach, we spent a lot of time there. As well as beautiful white sand, there were lots of fossils in the stones, which intrigued me.

One day we went on an organised hike on the moors. We had the usual excellent packed lunch with us, made up for us by Rita. It was a scorching hot day, and we stopped beside a hillside stream. We were going to have a drink of water when one of the dads, who seemed very knowledgeable about these things, said, "Wait!" He bent down, scooped a handful of water and sniffed it, then gingerly tasted some. "Yup, it's fine to drink.'" He ex-plained that a dead sheep could have fallen into the water further upstream and contaminated the water. How he could discern the potability of the water with any cer-tainty, I have no idea, but we took him at his word and quenched our thirst with no adverse after effects.

In the evening, before we went to bed, Rita presided over the family games hour. There was no compulsion, but Rita made it clear that it would be a shame if people didn't support it for the sake of the children. So most folks felt obliged to join in. There were quizzes and party games. That was where I first became acquainted with: "You put your left leg in, you put your left leg out, — in out, in, out, shake it all about—Oh do the Hokey Cokey, that's what it's all about!" The most nonsensical song I'd ever heard (even more silly because most of the parents thought it was wonderful), but good fun, nevertheless.

James says he remembers one special evening at the get together when they divided us all into teams: England, Scotland, Wales, (and possibly Ireland.) Each team had a little party piece to sing whenever they won a game. They put James in the Welsh team to even up the numbers. They had to sing a little ditty which ended with "our dragon now has a tale". Eventually, after winning a few more games, a clever Welshman got them to sing: "our dragon now has two tails!"

One day, we visited the shops in Redcar. John, who was only six or seven, went missing. I don't remember the panic that must have ensued, but James remembered that John was found by a policeman and taken to the police station where, after more than an hour of searching the streets, Dad found him safe and sound.

On Sunday, we went to the Remembrance at the Church of God in Middlesbrough, where Dad and Mum made the acquaintance of Mr and Mrs Heary. They invited us to their house after the meeting and, in return, Dad invited them to visit us one evening at Marske. They brought their daughter Ruth and son David and went for a walk with Dad and Mum along the beach. Someone took a photo before they went home again.

Later that year, or maybe it was the year after, the Heary's came and stayed overnight with us in Greenock. David lay on the top bunk which one of us had vacated for him and gave us all nicknames in his north-east accent: "Jo Soap, James Bubble, Willie Flake and John Bristle!" We enjoyed his sense of humour.

Mum, Mrs Heary,
Ruth Heary, David
Heary, Dad

William helping Mum to peel potatoes while
Dad looks on outside the Pullman's holiday
coach in Carnoustie

One year we had a holiday at Carnoustie in a Pullman holiday coach, a luxury railway coach which had a dining area and sleeping compartments. It was parked in a quiet siding next to a disused platform near the station. It was a lovely sunny holiday, and we spent many hours on the beach.

At that time, there was a Church of God in Dundee. Jack and Olive Miller invited us to their house after the meeting. They had a large family, some of who were still at home. Claire was the same age as me and we spent ages talking with each other in the games room upstairs. I listened with great interest as she told me about some of the rather naughty exploits the girls in her boarding school had got up to. Just as she was conveying the details of the racy behaviour of one of her friends, Claire's dad opened the door and looked in to check that all was well. I hoped he hadn't overheard the conversation!

Another year we headed South for a few days' holiday near Manchester. I don't know why anyone would choose to go on holiday to Manchester and can only surmise that Dad had either a business reason or an academic reason for this excursion. We camped overnight in a place called Bury. On the way to the campsite, a horrible, sulphurous smell assaulted our nostrils. We objected vociferously. I guess it was from some sort of factory chimney. Anyway, as we approached the next town, James suddenly spotted the name of the place on a big street sign: It read 'Ramsbottom'. "Look!' said James, 'Ramsbottom!" We laughed ourselves silly at the irony of the name, given the noxious stink that pervaded the atmosphere.

After we pitched the tent at Bury we went for a walk near a small stream which ran along the bottom of a sort of gully. We met some English boys who were playing there. One of them went to pick up a stick. I decided to act tough. "Lea it alane" I said, in my fiercest Scottish accent. The aggression had the desired effect. He backed off and went away with his pals.

Another year we went to Loch Lomond with the tent and Caravanette but we were so badly tormented by midges[1] that Dad upped sticks and move to the East Coast. We ended up on the campsite in Crail in the East Neuk of Fife, where we pitched the tent once more. Thankfully, there were no midges in Crail, where we enjoyed a sun-filled week. Mum made friends with an epileptic woman in a one of the nearby caravans. This lady had the strange habit of regularly calling out the time of day. At eight in the morning, She shouted, "Eight o' clock and all's well!" At ten, "Ten 'o clock and all's well!" And so on throughout the day. Every morning an old man used to come round the campsite about 8.00 or 9.00 in the morning, shouting "Papers! Papers!" William made friends with a little blonde-haired girl and spent much of the holiday with her. She was a nice-looking girl, and I felt quite envious.

∾

26 TEENAGE YEARS

When I was twelve or thirteen, David and John Black and William (Bill) Kerr asked James and me and Willliam if we'd like to climb Ben Nevis with them and some of the other young folk in the church. We didn't need to be asked twice. We set off in Davy's Bedford Van around six in the morning while it was still dark, speeding along via Loch Lomond, across the wildness of Rannoch Moor, past the spectacular Buchaille Etive Mor, down through the brooding mountains of Glencoe and arrived at the parking area just outside the Glen Nevis Youth Hostel at the bottom of the Ben about nine o' clock.

The Blacks and William Kerr changed into their climbing boots. James and I had recently each got a pair of black leather 'Tuf' boots, which we thought were just the job. William was wearing his school gym-shoes! We set off across the Nevis bridge and up onto the hill. It was a long hard slog. The stony path wended its way up and around, looping back on itself over one false peak after another. After about three sweaty hours, we reached the upper rocky stretches of the mountain. The ice-cold air made us fasten our jackets. Then, near the top—snow! Next to the path, the mist drifted up from a ravine. I peered over the edge and saw a sheer drop falling away before me. It shook me to realise how easily someone could fall to their death if they weren't careful or if visibility was bad. The path opened onto a wide area of snow-covered rocks at the top of the mountain. We explored the old geological survey hut before the long hike back. On the way down, we took a shortcut over a couple of scree slopes in between the rocky path. We jumped in quick succession from one boulder to another. It was exhilarating. A young chap with a beard and a foreign accent saw us as we skipped past him and exclaimed, "You Scots are like mountain goats!" My patriotic young heart swelled with pride.

∾

MANY YEARS LATER, after I retired, I took David and Joel to climb the famous Ben. I got to the top alright but on the way down, I found it a real challenge to keep going as step after step, my leg muscles endured the relentless, repetitive flexing and bracing to maintain a controlled descent, until they continually trembled from the exertion. I just plodded on, one leaden foot after the other, determined to get to the bottom without collapsing! The intervening years had taken a bigger toll than I'd realised. We stopped and bought fish and chips in a cafe in Fort William on the way home. I was never so thankful to sit down as I was at the end of that day. It was the first inkling I had that something might be wrong.

∼

ANOTHER TIME, the Blacks arranged a ski-ing trip to Glencoe. I borrowed a 'How to Ski' booklet from Greenock library and read it avidly in the days leading up to the expedition. It seemed simple and straightforward in theory, and the illustrations clearly showed the position the skis should be in for each manoeuvre.

We enjoyed the excitement of catching the ski-tow, as it snaked around and scooped you up without stopping, the view from aloft as we looked down on walkers below, followed by the rapid ejection at the top. We stumbled into a winter wonderland of sparkling, snow-covered ski slopes. Excitedly, we strapped on our hired skis and boots and made our way up the nursery slope beside the wooden building that housed the cafe. We played around for a bit at the bottom of the slope, getting used to having two planks of wood attached to our boots, working out how to step up the hill without falling over. Eventually, I crab-stepped up to the top of the hill and got into position, crouching over, both skis perfectly parallel, ski sticks at the ready, hands through the straps exactly as it showed in the library book.

I pushed off on both sticks and whooshed down the hill, gathering speed at a terrific rate as I headed towards the solid wooden wall of the chalet at the bottom of the hill. Unfortunately, I hadn't paid the same attention to the 'How do I stop' section in the library book. Awkwardly, I tried to turn the skis to the right. I lost my balance and fell over, but my right boot twisted round at a grotesque angle with the ski still attached. 'Crack!' I felt something give way in my ankle as I collapsed in a heap on the snow. I later learned I'd broken my ankle. The immediate problem was how to get my foot out of the boot, which was now at right angles to my leg. The ski bindings attached to the boot had not released as they should, and James had to undo them for me. I carefully lifted my leg round, untied the bootlaces and eased my painful ankle and foot out of the boot. I knew I'd done serious damage. With difficulty, I hopped over to the Alpine style wooden cafe where I sat until James alerted some of our party to my predicament.

When the time came to return to the minibus, it was clear I wouldn't be able to go back down the chairlift, so John Bradley ('Brad') and Margaret Black put me between them with an arm round each of their shoulders and helped me down the steep mountain path to the bottom. Brad took me to Greenock Royal Infirmary where an X-Ray confirmed I had broken my ankle. I returned home with my leg in plaster up to the knee, which I had to keep on for the next six weeks. After a few weeks, the unwashed leg inside the plaster cast developed a rather interesting cheesy smell. I was glad when the day came to have the plaster cast cut off. To my horror, my lower leg looked like something out of a concentration camp. The muscles had wasted away through lack of use. From the knee down, my leg was just skin and bone. I had to use a walking stick at first. It took another couple of weeks before I could run without limping.

At school, as we approached the Christmas holidays, instead of P.E., we joined the girls in the gym to learn and practise the traditional Scottish Country dance steps which, back then (before disco's dumbed everything down), was still the main feature of the annual Christmas Party. Jimmy Lobban and the well-proportioned female P.E.Teacher—whose name I forget—demonstrated the dance steps and sequence: 'Heel, toe, heel toe, forward two, back two, one-two-three, two-two-three, three-two-three, four'. They showed us how to dance the 'pa de basque' (pronounced 'pah de bah'), the elegant 'dancing on the spot' step that is part of many dances, and is nicely demonstrated in the performances given by Highland dancers at every Highland Games. The girls picked it up quickly and soon became 'pas de basque' experts. I never got the co-ordination quite right. I was left-handed, and it seemed as if I also had two left feet.

Once we'd practiced the dances a few times, we were asked to choose a partner and line up in position for the start of the dance. The teacher placed the appropriate Scottish Country dance record on the turntable and away we went, whirling round the gym, swapping partners as we went through the dance sequences. It was actually quite good fun, but for me and I suspect for others, it was tempered by the annoying fact that, having plucked up the courage to ask a girl you quite liked for the next dance, in no time at all you had to let her move on to dance with the boy next to you, while you then danced with several other girls in succession, some of whom you'd never have chosen in a month of Sundays—and more than likely they'd never have chosen you either! It was a lesson in mutual tolerance.

For my thirteenth birthday, I asked for a new bike. Dad saw an advert in the Greenock Telegraph for a second-hand bike, which sounded ideal, and phoned the number. The address was a house in Blairmore Road near the area known as 'the Strone' in the East end of Greenock. Dad took me up in the car and after a trial ride up and down the street, he paid the money and I became the new owner of a blue 'seventeen incher', with proper sized bicycle wheels. It was a bit too big for me—my feet just reached the pedals and no more! But it was the most exhilarating ride home, following Dad's Vauxhall Victor down the hill to the bottom end of the Kilmacolm Road, along Ingleston Street, down the steep hill on Baker Street, past the permanent smell of burning bones from the glue factory, up the hill on Regent Street, past Terrace Road and on home to Bentinck Street. I spent many enjoyable hours on that bike, in Greenock and the surrounding countryside, before we said farewell to all that was familiar from childhood, and moved away to Ayrshire, where we had to start growing up fast in order to survive.

~

AUNT NETTE SOLD her lovely old bungalow in Observatory Road, Edinburgh. For the last two years of her life, she came to live with us in the house at John Knox Street in Galston. Dad and Mum moved out of their bedroom at the front of the house and converted Dad's study into a bedroom for themselves so that Aunt Nette had a comfortable room and space for some pieces of furniture she brought with her. She also brought her black Scottie dog 'Benjamin' with her.

Aunt Nette with Benjamin

We used to take Benjamin for a walk. Whenever he stopped to do his business, we dragged him by his leather leash across the pavement to the gutter. Benjamin wasn't comfortable with that treatment, but there was nothing the poor creature could do about it. He got a space for his basket in a corner of the dining room and most of the time stayed there and didn't make too many demands. Unfortunately, Aunt Nette's arrival came at a challenging time in our family life. James and I were well into our teenage years, and William wasn't far behind. We were each pushing the boundaries in various ways, typically only seeing things from a self-centred, adolescent point of view. Although we didn't say it outright, I think there was some resentment that Mum's attention was diverted from our needs to Aunt Nette's priorities.

Aunt Nette, Dad, me, William, Alex Breadon (a
family friend) having a meal in our house in
Galston

Around that time, I became interested in photography. I
had bought a Russian Zenith E SLR camera, and I
snapped the family sitting round the table with Aunt
Nette. I enjoyed learning how to develop my black and
white snaps in the photography club darkroom at
Loudoun Academy.

The house in John Knox Street was a bungalow, so Dad
had to convert the loft space into four rooms for the four
boys. (Elisabeth, being a girl, got one of the two downstairs bedrooms). He installed a Ramsay ladder, bought
timber and wood panelling, and together with some advice from Jimmy Barr, we knocked up the partitions.
Somehow, the project faltered and came to a halt in an
unfinished state. Either the money ran out or Dad's life
became busier than usual. We moved our beds and stuff
into the loft anyway, and made the best of it. In winter,
the condensation from my breath formed icicles on the
galvanised slate nails which poked through the timber
sarking[1] on the roof. Fortunately, we had plenty of Dad's
thick army blankets, to keep us warm. Perhaps this was

why, when our next-door neighbour Mrs Hynd, a widowed English woman in her 70s, offered the use of her spare bedroom, Dad agreed to that arrangement. James and I moved into Mrs Hynd's comfortable house where we enjoyed a bit more independence. I never got used to this arrangement. Although Dad had our best interests at heart, I felt pushed out of the family home. One perk was that Mrs Hynd allowed us to sit in her living room and watch TV, which was a novelty for us since up till then, Dad had resisted the pressure to buy one. James and I lived next door for about a year, eating our meals in our own house but sleeping in Mrs Hynd's. It wasn't the ideal arrangement. After Aunt Nette died, we moved back home under the same roof. All of us, including Dad, probably learned some lessons from this experience, although we never discussed it.

27 HOUSE MOVES

Dad became increasingly disillusioned with the challenge of teaching Maths and Arithmetic to the infamous 'third year leavers' at the Mount School in Greenock (a boys' secondary school). 'Third year leavers' were serving their final year of compulsory education and were desperate to leave and get a job. In their heads they were done with school, and took every opportunity to make mischief. John Bradley, who we first met at church, had himself attended 'The Mount'. 'Brad' amusingly used to call it "a finishing school for young gentlemen." It was anything but.

Dad decided to re-train as an R.E. (Religious Education) Teacher, believing he might have more opportunities to share his love of the Bible with young people. In the end, that didn't turn out to be so straightforward, but his switch to teaching R.E. was the catalyst that precipitated our move away from Greenock and all that was familiar and dear to our hearts.

Dad got his first appointment as an R.E. Teacher in Irvine Royal Academy, Ayrshire. He sold the flat in Greenock and instead of immediately buying another, rented a house in a new development called Pennyburn, on the outskirts of the Ayrshire village of Kilwinning. Pennyburn was a carefully planned maze of little squares surrounded on three sides by rows of boxy flats and small houses, each with their own communal landscaped area of grassy borders and shrubberies. Our square was named 'Lainshaw'. The name was about the only thing that differentiated it from all the rest. The four bedrooms at 15 Lainshaw, Pennyburn, were much smaller than those at 19 Bentinck Street, so we four boys doubled up and slept in bunk beds in two of the bedrooms so that Elisabeth had a room of her own. But Pennyburn was well placed for travelling between both Irvine and Kilmarnock, which was the nearest place where there was a Church of God.

Unfortunately for James, William and me, the nearest secondary school was Ravenspark Academy in Irvine. On our first morning there, Dad dropped us off on his way to work at Irvine Royal. We entered a very different world from the one we'd left at Greenock Academy. For a start, there were 1,200 pupils on the roll—exactly double the number of secondary pupils at Greenock Academy. Many pupils came from housing estates in Irvine, plus the outlying districts of Kilwinning, Dalry and other places round about. One of the first things we noticed was the difference in dress code. At Greenock, everyone wore a school uniform—maroon blazer, school tie, grey trousers, etc. At Ravenspark, only some pupils wore the regulation blue blazer and tie. The head-teacher and his staff didn't enforce the uniform policy, so differences between the less well-off and pupils from more affluent homes were more obvious. In fact, the alternative uniform, emulating the pop stars of the day and worn by many, was a pair of Doc Martin 'bovver boots', jeans, and braces. We quickly learned that bovver booted gang members ruled the playgrounds. They made it their job to challenge anyone who might threaten their dominance.

One dreadful incident is etched forever on my memory. It was lunchtime, and I was standing in the playground talking with a couple of classmates when suddenly the leader of the notorious gang known as the 'Winton Toi' appeared. He had a skinhead haircut and cut a striking figure in a pair of washed-out jeans held up with elastic braces—the effect of which was to pull up the bottom of the jeans to give full exposure to his giant, laced up, shiny black Doc Martin boots. He went straight up to a big lad with curly fair hair who was dressed in the Ravenspark school uniform. He began by saying, "you want a square go?"—pushing him backwards at the same time with both hands. The big chap was taken aback and made it obvious he didn't want any trouble, but the leader of the Winton Toi was after blood. Very quickly, the whole playground became alert to the situation. The cry went up: "A fight! A fight!" The crowd swarmed around, creating a circle with the skinhead and his victim in the middle. He gave the curly-haired boy a violent shove and began to throw punches at him. The boy bravely mustered a couple of defensive punches in return before the gang leader head-butted him and knocked him to the ground. Immediately, the gang leader and his cronies surrounded him like a pack of animals and began kicking him as hard as they could. I couldn't see him for the crowd, but heard the flurry of blows as their boots connected with his head and body. A be-gowned teacher hurried out into the playground, the crowd opened up and the ringleaders dispersed. The boy was helped up, dazed and wild-eyed. But the thing that shocked me most was the mass of bruises all over his face and head. He was covered in them. They had liter-ally 'kicked lumps out of him.' It left me shaken and angry that such wanton violence was allowed to happen, apparently with no meaningful retribution on the perpe-trators.

James got a paper round from the newsagent shop in the block of shops along the lane from our house in Penny-burn. The owner was a large bespectacled Englishman who wrote the names of all his customers on the papers for him, unlike the Greenock paper round, where we had to sort and write the names of the customers ourselves.

Mum made friends with a Mrs Dickinson who lived in a similar house in Pinmore Square, the next square along from ours. She invited her daughters Kathleen and Diane and their brother Bobby to come with us to the Sunday School at Kilmarnock. Kathleen was about the same age as me, a lovely, big-boned girl with an open, friendly per-sonality. She heard the gospel preached at Kilmarnock and put her trust in the Lord Jesus Christ as her Saviour. In due course, she asked to be baptised and, with her parents' blessing, was added to the Church.

Kathleen and Bobby came with us one weekend on a camping trip to Rothesay. Unfortunately, the weather was not good. That night, in the middle of a raging storm of wind and rain, the frame tent collapsed and almost blew away. We were all soaked and feeling miserable in the rain. Thankfully, Dad got some of us into a local bed-and-breakfast while the rest of us slept in the Volkswagen caravanette. Next day turned out sunny, and we went for a walk. I think Kathleen had taken a fancy to me and I liked her too. That morning she'd had a bath with Knights Castille soap at the B&B and she smelled delightful! She said to me, "Would you like to go for a walk, Jo?" I'm afraid I wasn't as sure of myself as she was, so I 'bottled it' and said I wanted to stay with the others. Who knows what might have transpired if I hadn't been so bashful!

It was while we lived at Pennyburn that Dad arranged for me to have piano accordion lessons from a professional accordionist whose name escapes me. He was a dapper little man with a clipped moustache, a trilby hat and a quick sense of humour. On his recommendation, for my birthday, Dad bought me a 120 Bass Clansman accordion, made in China by a company called Baille, which had a reputation for making good quality instruments at an affordable price. My accordion teacher came once a week over the course of a year and tutored me through two of 'The Sedlon Accordion Method' music books for beginners. He showed me how to use the counter bass to set up an interesting rhythm to accompany the right hand on the keyboard. I was making reasonable progress when our move from Pennyburn to Galston put paid to further lessons. But I had learned enough to play by ear and annoy the rest of the family with my incessant practicing.

Dad had banked the money he got when he sold 19 Bentinck Street but found it hard not to dip into savings whenever some extra expenditure came along. He decided to invest in bricks and mortar before it all disappeared. He looked at various properties and potential business ventures. Once he asked his cousin John Black to come and view a commercial site in Ardrossan with him. I remember walking around the place with them, but in the end, he decided against it. Around 1972, Dad heard that Jimmy Barr, the resident overseer of the Church in Galston, was thinking of selling his house and the adjoining gift shop in Henrietta Street, which he and his wife owned. Dad made him an offer, which Jimmy and Elsie gladly accepted, since it had the added benefit of almost doubling the numbers on the roll of the small church in Galston.

So, with no regrets, we said goodbye to Pennyburn, Kilwinning and Ravenspark Academy and moved to the Irvine Valley. There was a basement cellar in the house at Henrietta Street. It had no windows and was lit by a single electric lightbulb. Jimmy Barr had installed an ancient woodworking lathe which he left behind, thinking one of us boys might like to use it. He showed me how to turn wooden items on it which was quite an interesting way to pass an hour or two. One day I went into the cellar and flicked the light-switch too quickly. The bulb blew and plunged the cellar into inky blackness. I groped for an old chair and pulled it over to where I thought the light was, so that I could unscrew the dud bulb and replace it. I stood on the chair and reached up to where I thought the bulb should be. Instead, my hand hit bare wire and the most awful jolt of electricity knocked me off the chair onto the floor. The bulb had shattered when I threw the light switch and I had touched the still live lightfitting. I made sure I switched off the power at the mains before finding a torch to see what I was doing and safely removed the remains of the bulb.

Uncle Wille drove down from Greenock one Saturday in his big grey Rover to visit us in our new home. Two old sandstone steps at the back of the house had worn and crumbled away over the years, and Dad asked him to repair them. This was a simple job for Uncle Willie, who had trained as a joiner and builder. He came back a few days later dressed in his work overall, jacket and cap (He always wore a flat cap). I watched him take the folding wooden rule from his pocket, open it out and carefully measure, mark and cut the wooden batons with his crosscut saw to make the shuttering. Then, with a shovel, he mixed a sand, cement and aggregate mixture with water in a barrow and poured it in between the boards to form two new steps. Another day, he climbed the loft ladder to help Dad put up some partitions in the floored loft space, which he was converting into two attic bedrooms for James and me. Uncle Willie was in his early eighties and still very fit. Elsie Barr was visiting Mum that day and when she saw Uncle Willie at the top of the loft ladder, she exclaimed, "Oh my! At your age? Are you sure you should be doing that?" (Or words to that effect.) Uncle Willie's countenance fell. He took it as an affront and left in a less than communicative mood. Dad was really annoyed, because Uncle Willie had assumed that Dad had told Elsie Barr how old he was, which he was very private about. Elsie's remark was well-meant and she couldn't have known the effect it would have.

The shop, which Elsie had stocked with household gifts and ornaments, was actually the converted front room of the house. It had a door which opened onto the street and a 'back-shop' door giving access to the house. Dad's plan was to convert the shop into a small furniture showroom and create a mini 'Orrs House Furnishers', since he still had contacts in the trade from his time at

Terrace Road, not to mention his considerable business acumen and entrepreneurial skill.

Mum got the job of shopkeeper while Dad was at work teaching. They gradually reorganised the shop. Dad sold off the old 'giftware' stock and replaced it with three-piece suites, carpet samples, occasional tables, chairs, and so on. He placed adverts in the local papers, similar to the ones he had run for 'Orrs' in Greenock Telegraph. Business slowly picked up, but there wasn't the same footfall as there had been in a big town like Greenock. The final nail in the coffin of Dad's fledgling business was the opening of a large discount furniture warehouse just round the corner from our shop. Dad didn't have the capital to compete with the cut-throat prices and aggressive advertising of his rival. He decided to sell up and cut his losses. Not long after the property went on the market, Dad noticed a house for sale in a quiet cul-de-sac in Galston named John Knox Street (named in memory of the famous Scottish reformer, who preached at an ancient building in Galston called the Barr Castle). The John Knox Street house was a substantial red sandstone bungalow with a large garden. Even though Henrietta Street had not sold, he put in a bid for the bungalow, which was accepted. He then had to arrange a bridging loan with the bank and ended up paying two mortgages for several months until someone bought Henrietta Street. He was extremely thankful that this situation didn't go on any longer.

Posing beside someone else's Ford Capri,
Galston

The loft at John Knox street was 'L' shaped and the bit above the kitchen was where John kept his drum kit. He used to sit up in the loft, drumming away to tapes of Elvis Presley and other music. Sometimes I played some tunes on the accordion and we had a wee 'jam session' together.

Dad always had the notion that he'd like to keep some hens. The garden at John Knox Street was big enough to allow this, so he repurposed an old chest of drawers. He removed the inside sections from the drawers and re-placed the front of the drawers as a facade. Then he cre-ated a roosting area in the inside space and cut out a little door on one side, which had a wooden plank with blocks of wood nailed onto it as a stairway going up to the door. He put the hen house against the wall at the top of the garden beside the old brick outhouse for them to climb up at night. It was comical to watch them slowly going up the steps to bed every night as darkness fell.

They took a step or two, then stopped and looked around, making that low, long, drawn-out hen sound, before taking another few steps, and so on, until they hopped inside. They seemed to like to savour their last moments of freedom before settling down for the night. It was great to get fresh eggs, even though the price we paid for the privilege, was a back garden where every bit of greenery was pecked and scratched as the hens foraged for grubs and insects. John made a pet of one hen. He cradled it in his arm and stroked its feathers. It shut its eyes as he did so, lapping up the attention! Eventually, Dad got rid of the hens and the garden flourished again. I remember planting night scented stock in the raised bed just outside the kitchen. The fragrance on warm summer evenings was unforgettable.

~

28 THE CHURCH OF GOD IN GALSTON

The meeting place of the Church of God in Galston was a converted ground-floor flat in Church Lane near the river Irvine. As previously noted, the place had a utilitarian 1930s air about it and badly needed renovating. Dad was just the person to do it. As well as replacing the ancient seating with stacking chairs, he also refurbished the kitchen.

Jimmy and Elsie Barr had faithfully maintained the Sunday school for the few children who came along each week. When we arrived, Dad arranged for evangelist Willie Stewart to hold a series of children's meetings at the hall. Dad had leaflets printed to advertise the meetings, and we distributed these to most houses in the town. This resulted in an appreciable increase in the number of children attending the Sunday school.

Some years later, the church purchased the upstairs part of the building, previously a knitwear factory. Dad put out an appeal to our sister churches in the West of Scotland, asking for financial help with the refurbishment for the purpose of youth work. He gave me the job of choosing a colour scheme. I chose vibrant colours—purple for the main walls and orange for the two gable ends. We also hired a floor sander to clean up the old floorboards before giving them a fresh coat of varnish. When everything was ready, we invited friends from the Church in Kilmarnock to come over and see the transformation. I was proud of what we'd achieved and I asked one sister from Kilmarnock what she thought of the colour scheme. She replied with some feeling: "I think it's hideous!" Her remark reminds me of an amusing but very true saying, that my friend Martin Notman passed on to me recently:

> To dwell above with the saints we love,
> Wouldn't that be glory?
> But to dwell below with saints we know,
> That's a different story!

Whether or not my colour scheme was hideous, we attracted quite a number of teenagers to our youth night, held every Friday evening. We had table tennis, darts and other activities, followed by some chorus singing and a ten-minute talk from the Bible. While I was still at home, I used to accompany some choruses on the accordion. We invited the young folks to come to the gospel meeting on a Sunday evening. Those who did so often came up to the house for supper with us afterwards. When I went to Art School, I stayed in the halls of residence in Glasgow and only came home at weekends. James, William, John and Dad carried on the running of the Friday night class.

Jimmy Barr was a small, stocky man whose deep-set eyes and a jutting out chin reminded me of a chimpanzee. He had been the only overseer in Galston for many years and was used to getting things his own way. A joiner to trade, Jimmy was a 'can do' kind of guy who would tackle anything. He could turn his hand to most building jobs, although his wife Elsie sometimes shook her head in despair at him. Sometimes he went beyond his abilities and suffered the consequences. He just laughed when she mentioned some of those incidents.

When he was building dormer windows in the house he moved to in the town of Newmilns, just up the valley, he employed James, William and me to help him. We learned how to nail sarking boards across the roof joists, then nail slates to the sarking in an overlapping pattern, starting from the top of the roof and working down. Jimmy had a trait which we all thought extremely amusing and we used to imitate him when he wasn't present. Everything he owned was 'the best'. As he spoke, he cupped his raised hand and gestured with a slight movement of his hand—a sort of downward turn— for emphasis. For example, when he bought a new Hilman Avenger, he said: "Avengers are the best cars on the road"—(cupped hand gesture coinciding with the word 'best'.)

Alex McLuckie was another older brother in the church in Galston. He and his wife Celie lived in Darvel. Originally from Bathgate, Alex spent his working life as a baker until he retired. He had strong workmanlike hands. When he shook your hand, you knew he had kneaded dough for many years. Alex drove a light blue Ford Anglia. He often closed the remembrance in prayer on a Sunday morning, focusing his thoughts on the two disciples who met the Lord after his resurrection on the way to Emmaus. He never failed to be impressed by the Lord's words to them, "Behoved it not the Christ to suffer these things, and to enter into his glory?"—and their subsequent exclamation —"was not our hearts burning within us while he spake to us in the way?" I can still hear Alex saying these words with genuine feeling. Alex and Celie, Jimmy and Elsie were all at our house for supper after the gospel meeting one Sunday evening. Celie was on form as usual, with her vivacious personality, joining in with the conversation and repartee that night. Next morning Alex woke up to find her lying dead beside him.

～

29 LOUDOUN ACADEMY

To our relief, the local secondary school, Loudoun Academy, was much more welcoming than Ravenspark in Irvine. For a start, it wasn't such a big school, with only around 800 pupils. It also had a more even cross-section from its main catchment areas—the valley towns of Galston, Newmilns, and Darvel. There were also a few pupils from outlying villages such as Hurlford and (famously) Moscow! Being a rural area, there were quite a few sons and daughters of local farmers.

The school was about half a mile outside the town, on the road that wends it way uphill, past the entrance to Loudoun Castle, from which the school took its name.

I made a few friends at Loudoun, one of whom was Michael Anglin. He was a thin, serious boy with a mass of curly black hair and, although a natural introvert, had a quick sense of humour. His father died young and Michael, an only child, lived with his mother in the top flat of a block of red brick building in a small council estate near the outskirts of Galston. James used to think it

My school
photograph,
Loudoun Academy

funny when Michael came to the door and said "Is Jo in?"—bashfully dropping his head and looking down at his feet.

Michael was excellent at English and consistently got grades over ninety per cent. On the odd occasion his marks fell below that, he mentally beat himself up, thinking he was an abject failure. I tried to help him keep things in proportion by telling him I was pleased with my seventy-five per cent! He was widely read and had learned many passages from literature off-by-heart. One of his favourite quotes was from an anti-communist speech made by John F. Kennedy when he visited Berlin in 1963. Michael used to repeat it with feeling: "Ich bin ein Berliner!" (I am a Berliner). Perhaps because of his domestic circumstances or his 'working class' background, he was especially influenced by Marxist writings. Michael was an atheist, and we used to have many arguments about the Bible, Darwin's Theory of Evolution, and the existence of God. I tried hard to convince him, but although we remained good friends, he resolutely kept to his firmly held views. Michael went to Glasgow University to study English Literature. He got great marks in every one of his first-year exams but dropped out of university at the end of that year, because of the pressure he put himself under and his unfortunate perception of the other students on the course. When I asked him why he'd left after doing so well, he said in his broad Ayrshire accent, "They're a' middle cless". It was such a pity, because he had the potential to go far. Michael got a job as a postman in Galston and I lost touch with him when I moved away.

Iain Smith and Ronald Logan were the other two friends I made at Loudoun. They lived in Darvel. Iain was in the same Art class as me. He was always ready to see the funny side of things, especially if the joke was on him. Iain had shoulder length, straight black hair and was quite stocky and muscular. He invited me to his house in Darvel where he introduced me to his favourite rock groups: 'Free', 'Yes', 'Steeleye Span' and 'Bad Company'. He had LPs by all these groups and more, and played them to me on his father's record player. It was around this time that I grew my hair over my ears, '70s style. We went on the bus to a couple of concerts at the Apollo Theatre in Glasgow where the music was so loud, my ears rang for a long time afterwards. I suspect that may have been responsible for my hearing loss.

Iain got a job as an architect's technician and went to night classes in the Architecture department of Glasgow School of Art, eventually gaining his degree in architecture. We met up again many years later. To my amusement, he'd lost most of his hair. He married a lovely lady called Irene and now lives near Falkirk.

Ronald Logan was a tall, friendly, well-spoken, intelligent chap. He was good at Maths, wore glasses and played the piano accordion. He came to our house several times. As with Michael Anglin, Ronald engaged in friendly debate with me about evolution and the existence of God. I did my best to present the counter-arguments, but felt I was getting nowhere. I hoped and prayed my friends would get saved. One year, Dad invited Welsh evangelist Alan Toms to hold a series of meetings in Galston Hall. I

invited Ronald to come and hear him preach. At the end
of the meeting, Alan had a talk with Ronald and asked if
he'd like to put his trust in Jesus. To my amazement,
Ronald said he would. They got down on their knees and
prayed together. Ronald accepted Jesus as his Saviour. It
was an answer to prayer and a demonstration to me that
sometimes people put up an apparently impregnable
barrier to the gospel message, when all the time they're
not as sure about eternal matters as they'd have you believe. I'm also sure the Spirit of God was at work in his
heart. I believe God used Alan to bring Ronald to the
point of decision.

I was fortunate to have some good friends, but inevitably,
there were a few at this somewhat parochial school who
were not so friendly. In my metalwork class in fourth year,
there was a lanky, pale-faced boy with shoulder-length
blonde hair named Matthew. He and Murray, one of his
pals, a mousy-haired boy with a permanent scowl and
bloodshot eyes, took a dislike to me. Why, I had no idea.
One Friday afternoon, as I was turning a piece of metal
on the lathe, out of the corner of my eye, I noticed the
two of them sniggering to each other. Matthew sidled
past me as if he was going to another part of the workshop, but suddenly, while the teacher was busy helping
someone else, nipped my backside with a pair of pliers.
The two of them suppressed their laughter at my consternation. On the way home, as I was walking on the
pavement, back towards town, Matthew attacked me
from behind with a flying kick. His unprovoked attack
took me by surprise, and rather than face up to him and
his nasty sidekick, I went back to the school to seek
help. Most of the teachers had already escaped for the
day but the school Rector, Mr Jones, a bushy eye-

browed, red-faced man who always had an air of authority about him, was just about to get into his car. I told him what had happened. He hesitated for a moment, then asked if I'd like a lift into town. Gratefully, I accepted and, with some relief, was soon driving past the baddies. The Rector dropped me off and I walked the short distance to our house. Whether he spoke to the boys the following Monday, I don't know, but they never bothered me again, apart from the occasional sneer or obscene gesture.

There was a boy in my register class who lived in Newmilns (I forget his name) but he had the revolting habit of putting his fingers inside the back of his underpants and transferring bits of dried up 'doo-doo' to his mouth. One day he said he was selling a fishing basket and some tackle, which interested me, as I'd recently joined the Irvine Valley angling club. Club members could buy an annual fishing permit for the river, for a very reasonable fee. This gave us access to a well-stocked trout and salmon river. I offered to buy the fishing basket and was soon the proud owner of a vintage cane fishing basket, which had a carrying strap and leather buckles. Thankfully, it didn't smell of anything other than fish! The same boy used to collect local agate from the stones in 'The Burn Anne' (pronounced 'Burn-awn'), a tributary of the Irvine. He showed me the type of stones to look for. Occasionally, I walked up the stony bed of the burn, collecting little pieces of red agate.

One day I took my rod and started fishing the deep pool where the Burn Anne enters the Irvine, just below the bridge. Suddenly I got a good-sized trout on the line and played it into the side. I took it off the hook and placed it inside my basket. When I got home, I gutted it and Mum cooked it for my tea. Trout has a lovely fresh taste when cooked soon after being caught. The only thing that put me off (apart from scooping its innards out) was the sharp bones. I still have a phobia about fish bones after getting a bone stuck in my throat as a boy in Greenock. No amount of swallowing dry bread dislodged it, so I had to go to Dr Lyon's surgery in Greenock to have him re-move it with a pair of tweezers.

Mr McBain, my English teacher at Loudoun, was a tall man who always wore his flowing black teacher's gown. He was principal teacher of English and told me he ex-pected me to get an 'A' in the Higher English exam. I was always good at the Comprehension and Interpretation parts of the previous exam papers we practised but found the Literature paper more difficult, because it in-volved a race against the clock. We had to choose one question from a list, and answer the question by giving a critical analysis of a book, poem, or literary theme. To prepare myself for this, in the lead up to the exam, I memorised the whole of Lord Tennyson's poem 'Ulysses.' There was no certainty that I would find a question which would lend itself to the themes ad-dressed in the poem, but I thought I just might 'strike it lucky'. Fortunately, I found a question that enabled me to quote liberally from 'Ulysses' to illustrate my answer. I ended up with an 'A' as predicted by Mr McBain.

On moving from Greenock Academy to Loudoun Academy (via Ravenspark), I was very fortunate to come under the tutelage of David Longmuir, principal teacher of Art. He was an excellent teacher and a talented painter in his own right (although I've searched 'Google' in vain for even one of his paintings). He was passionate about his subject, and always went above and beyond the call of duty. Sometimes he took a few of us on drawing and painting expeditions around the Irvine valley. One time, he took us in his cream-coloured Saab 96, to draw the old Tolbooth Building in Newmilns. From the Art room window, he got me to paint the fields and trees which were visible from that side of the school. He would come alongside, mix the paint and paint some of my picture for me, demonstrating how to work in stages across the whole picture, painting an overall impression of the scene, without getting bogged down in detail. Mr Longmuir also set up still life exercises, lighted by lamps with different coloured filters, to show how the shadow areas took on the opposite (complementary) colour of the colour cast by the filtered light. He taught Art History with great enthusiasm and diligence, illustrating his talks with slides to take us through the main art movements and artists from Pre-Renaissance to the present day. I attribute to him the fact that I was able, over my last two years at school, to put together a portfolio that was good enough to get me into Glasgow School of Art.

~

30 GLASGOW SCHOOL OF ART

Under Mr Longmuir's excellent teaching and guidance, I submitted a folio which was good enough to secure me a place, in September 1975, on the first-year course at Glasgow School of Art. I remember Mr Longmuir looking through my artwork with me to select the pieces I should include in the folio. One of them was a demonstration painting that he himself had done, of fields and trees from the art room window. I was about to say "but that's the one you did"—instead, I kept my mouth shut. He hesitated slightly as he looked at it, and then said "Yes, put that one in". I sometimes wonder if I got in on the strength of Dickie Longmuir's painting, and not solely on the merits of my own work.

The first-year course was taught in a fine old sandstone building on the corner of Blythswood Square in Glasgow, which the Art school had leased. Danny Ferguson, one of the first-year tutors, told us with relish that an infamous murder suspect, Madeleine Smith, lived in the building during the 19th Century. Apparently, she had poisoned her lover with arsenic, but the trial jury returned a verdict of 'Not Proven' because no witnesses had seen them together prior to her victim's death.

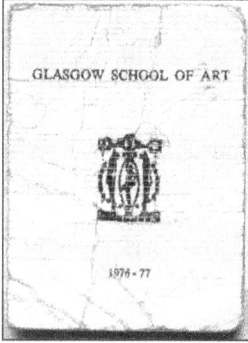

Matriculation card, Glasgow School of Art

Lawrence McClelland, one of the Auchenfoyle Camp leaders, worked in the building on the corner opposite and I saw him occasionally.

First year studies included attending Art History lectures in the famous Mackintosh lecture theatre, where we were immersed in the history of Western Art with a combination of slide talks, films, essays and lectures by Ted Odling, Director of First Year Studies, an extremely well-read Englishman with a

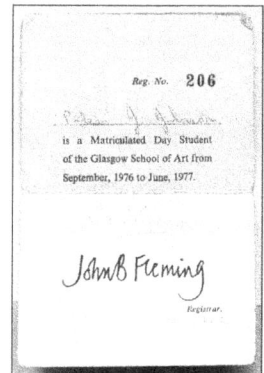

grey handlebar moustache and a comprehensive knowledge of the history of art from the Renaissance to Bridget Riley and the Op Art movement. I'm not sure he approved of some of the more modern stuff. My first-year tutors were Joan Tebbutt, Conrad McKenna, and Ken Mitchell. Joan was an amply endowed, well spoken, trendy lady in her 60s who sported a bowl haircut. She was a calligrapher to trade and encouraged an interest in lettering and the creative use of calligraphic shape and form. (According to salacious gossip among the students, she was a lesbian!) Joan introduced me to the work of Ben Shahn, a Jewish American Calligrapher and graphic designer. He designed some iconic posters during the '50s and '60s. I have a battered copy of one of the beautifully crafted books he produced.

Conrad McKenna was a well-fed bachelor about the same age as Joan. He always dressed in a smart sports jacket and tie. He wore a pair of black glasses, had straight black hair slicked over to one side, and spoke with a very proper, cultured accent. Some of the Glasgow students mimicked his accent behind his back and didn't take him seriously. I remember, though, that he showed me how to isolate part of my drawing using two 'L' shaped pieces of card. It was a lesson in how different parts of a drawing could provide more than one viable option for further creative development. Conrad and Joan represented the last generation of well educated, upper-middle class Scots who'd been in the driving seat at the Art School since the days of Charles Rennie Mackintosh, Fra. Newberry and their contemporaries.

Things had changed radically since those days and a much greater cross-section of lecturers replaced them. Some were recruited from the more 'progressive' Art colleges in England (it would never do for Scotland's flagship Art School to become a creative backwater.) One of those was the young twenty-something, moustachioed, jeans and leather-jacketed Ken Mitchell from Liverpool. With yellowish-brown nicotine fingers and beery breath, Ken was the epitome of everything that an aspiring avant-garde art student wanted to be. He drank with the students in the pub, giving them the benefit of his new and creative ideas, some of which were actually quite interesting. I liked Ken. He had an easy style and a great sense of humour. He enthused about the artistic merits of contemporary artists such as painters like Peter Blake, David Hockney, Roy Lichenstein, the sculptor Anthony

Caro and conceptual 'artists' such as Carl Andre and other artistic nonentities whose outrageous productions (thankfully) are already long forgotten by everyone, except, ironically, among the ivory towers of the art establishment.

Some of these new and exciting trends fascinated me. I was carried away with the buzz of those novel ideas for a time. With my first-year student grant, I bought a really 'with-it' blue cotton casual jacket with button down pockets. It was the nearest thing that I could afford, to the ultra-cool denim jackets worn by every self-respecting art student. One of our first-year projects was to do a series of self-portraits in different media. With enthusiastic encouragement from Ken Mitchell, I made a clay sculpture of my blue jacket and cast it in fiberglass. This turned out to be a valuable learning experience, even though the finished article was a bit rough around the edges. Ken said "you have an affinity with clay" and steered me towards the Sculpture Department, which, unknown to me, had recently fallen into the hands of some of his modernist pals from down South.

Going for a coffee with some art student
friends in Sauchiehall Street, Glasgow. L-R:
(?), Glen, Brian, Kenny

The other students in my year were mostly from Glasgow
and the surrounding area. One of them, named Kenny,
played for Celtic boys' team. Glen Coutts was another—
he completed his degree in the Murals department. After
Art School, Glen went into teaching and ended up as a
lecturer at Jordanhill teacher training college. Nice work if
you can get it.

Karen Cochrane was the daughter of a P.E. teacher in
Ardrossan. She was great fun—always upbeat—and
worked alongside my workstation in the studio. It was a
pleasant surprise to discover that one of my fellow students was Margaret Henderson, who I'd grown up with in
Greenock! She quickly became a favourite of Ken
Mitchell, because she was such a talented artist—or was
it because she was a really attractive girl? Probably both.
Her work had both flair and finesse. She just had that intuitive touch and a great eye for design. Ken knew that

whatever she did, it would turn out well. Another student who I made friends with was Donald McLeod. He was a big, friendly chap who wore glasses with very thick lenses. He came from the Yoker area of Glasgow and was full of the legendary fast-talking Glasgow 'patter' and was always entertaining to be with.

Before we broke up for the Christmas holidays, the first-year drawing competition was announced. We were to produce a drawing during the holidays based on the theme 'Inside/Outside'. The prize for five lucky winners was a three-day trip to the Art Galleries in London. The term ended with the first-year party, which was held in one of the upstairs studios in the Blythswood Square building. That was the only time I ever got drunk. I didn't intend to become inebriated but the peer pressure was such that, contrary to my resolve until then, not to drink alcoholic beverages (we'd been well warned), I per-suaded myself that I would just have one glass of wine, thinking I'd have the willpower to say "no" to any more. Inevitably, however, in the convivial atmosphere of fun and games and nonsense that ensued, one glass fol-lowed another, and before I knew it, my head was spin-ning and I felt as if I was on a ship rolling about in a storm. As the night wore on, I put my arm around Mar-garet Henderson, who was standing just inside the doorway listening to the music, watching her friends dancing. She just smiled, and I stood with my arm draped over her shoulder for quite a while before groggily making my way back to the Halls of Residence. I re-member waking up in the middle of the night after seeing little black, imp-like creatures screaming at me. When I told Karen Cochrane about this, she thought it extremely funny and said 'Wow! You saw the screaming Ab-Dabs, Jo!' It wasn't an experience I intended to repeat.

It was good to be home for Christmas. Even though the weather was cold, it wasn't raining or snowing, and I enjoyed several walks in the surrounding countryside. One day, I came across a rusty old car on the old railway line. It had been there for years. An ideal subject for the 'Inside/Outside' drawing competition, I thought. Back at the house, I looked out a large piece of cream coloured Ingres paper, which has a nice 'tooth' to it. I grabbed my drawing board, a folding stool and some red conte chalk pencils and went back to the railway line. The old car had the skeleton of a once comfy seat inside it. Its leather skin long gone, rusty springs were all that was left. I pulled the remains of the seat outside the car and rearranged it with other bits and pieces on the ground, so that they led the eye toward the car. By four o'clock, the cold was getting to me and I went home. Since I'd filled the sheet of Ingres paper with as much of the car as possible, I didn't have enough room to get all the foreground objects in, so I cut a strip from another sheet of Ingres paper and carefully taped it to the bottom of the drawing, making into a square. I went back next day and finished it.

My Conte Chalk drawing

I handed in my drawing along with twenty other drawings by fellow students. There was a fascinating variety of interpretations of the 'Inside/outside' theme. They were displayed in the exhibition area on the first floor at the top of the central stairs in the Mackintosh Building, and it wasn't long before the judges decided on the winners. I was one of them! There were five or six of us. Ken Mitchell organised the trip. He arranged for his wife and young son, who was only about two or three, to meet up with him in London.

We caught the overnight Glasgow to London Greyhound bus. When we arrived in London, we dumped our bags at the small hotel Ken had booked and started our tour of the galleries. We visited the Tate, the Hayward Gallery, the National Portrait Gallery and several others. We queued for ages outside the Tate to see the Constable exhibition, the biggest ever exhibition of the John Constable's work ever mounted. That was the one that most impressed and inspired me. I still have the exhibition catalogue.

One of the other winners of the 1976 drawing competition was Donald Williamson from Edinburgh. He was a friendly, studious looking chap. I first met him in the basement refectory just across the road from the Mackintosh building. Something about his demeanour made me suspect he was a Christian. He was. We got on well and it was good to have his company on the London trip. I met up with him briefly a few years ago when I attended a demonstration to support the Bodnariu family from Norway, outside the Norwegian Embassy in Glasgow. (They are evangelical believers like us and had their children removed by the authorities because someone reported them for daring to smack one of their children in contravention of Norwegian law. Eventually they escaped to Romania.) I promised Donald I'd keep in touch but unfortunately, became preoccupied with my health crisis. If God spares me, I hope to follow up on my promise.

In first year at Glasgow, I lived in Bilsland House, the student halls of residence in Hill Street. It was interesting getting to know the other students. There was a group of Chinese students who always made a group meal and ate it together in the communal kitchen. They were friendly and gregarious. Most of them were studying architecture or town planning. Then there were the two 'teuchters' from Inverness—one of them, a confident, opinionated town planner student called Ninian, who had a very loud way of laughing. A guffaw rather than a laugh. There were several other art students. One was a sculpture student named Douglas Haldane, an easy-going, friendly chap who was a keen hillwalker. There were two students from Dunoon, one a Graphic Design student and the other on the town planning course.

The town planner guy from Dunoon heard me practising my accordion one evening after visiting the pub with his friends, where he'd had quite a lot to drink. He knocked my door and said *"Can I have a wee shot of your accordion, Jo?"* I said *"Sure!"* and hand him the squeezebox. He put it on rather unsteadily, sat down on the edge of my bed, and adjusted the straps to his liking. He launched into a flawless, toe-tapping virtuoso performance of several Scottish country dance sets. I didn't know he was so good. It was a treat to listen to.

$\sim$

DURING MY SECOND YEAR , when I lived in the John D. Kelly halls of residence, on the opposite side of the road from Bilsland House, I made contact with Steve and Margaret Henderson, a married couple in the Church of God in Glasgow. They lived in Lansdowne Crescent and invited me to join a monthly class for young people which they held in their home. On Thursday nights, I also took the subway and went to the prayer meeting and Bible reading discussion at Hayburn Hall, Partick (the meeting place of one of the four companies of the Church of God in Glasgow.) There, I had the privilege of enjoying fellowship with men like Willie Archibald and his son Eric and Norman Miller-Miller (an accomplished artist and portrait painter). On one occasion, Norman visited the halls of residence and left me a note to say they'd cancelled the meeting that week. He had written it with a fountain pen, in exquisite calligraphic handwriting. It was a little work of art. I held on to it for many years until it got lost in the flitting.

~

ON ONE PARTICULAR night of the week, during my first year, all the students in Bilsland House used to pack the common room and gather round the colour TV to watch the new comedy show 'Fawlty Towers'. (One or two of them had a portable black and white TV in their rooms). John Cleese was in his element as Basil, the nutty hotel owner, ably foiled by his on-screen wife Sybil, played by Prunella Scales. But everyone agreed the real star of the show was Andrew Sachs, who played Manuel, the Spanish waiter. It was hilarious from start to finish. Ninian's guffaws could be heard above the rest.

One of the first-year students who was in a different tutorial group from me was Anthony, who'd come to Art School from St Aloysius College, the prestigious independent school at the bottom of Hill Street, un by Jesuits. Anthony was a tall, good-looking guy with jet black hair and a mischievous twinkle in his eye. He wore a long, heavy greatcoat which he left open most of the time, so that it swirled in his wake and made him look quite debonair. Like many Scottish Catholics, Anthony was a very sociable character and enjoyed nothing more than to sit around talking and exchanging gossip and banter, especially with the girls. He seemed to crave attention though, and went out of his way to be as outlandish and 'way out' as possible. One Friday morning we were sitting in the Mackintosh lecture theatre waiting for Ted Odling to arrive, when Anthony walked in minus his eyebrows. He had shaved them off. He sat down beside me in the back row, a knowing smirk playing on his lips. All the girls in the rows in front were turning round to look at him. He basked in the attention, enjoying every moment of the minor stir he'd caused.

At the end of first year, we had to decide which specialist area of Art we wanted to study for the remaining three years of the course. Ken Mitchell advised me to apply for a place in the Sculpture Department, which I did.

∾

31 SECOND YEAR SCULPTURE GSA

The Sculpture studios were in the basement of the Mackintosh building. I was allocated a space on a wooden balcony overlooking one of the main studios, along with two other students. Robin Tannock was a spindly, red-haired guy from Stewarton in Ayrshire, with an engaging, slightly nasal laugh. He wore thick glasses and spoke with a deep voice. I already knew him because we'd both attended the Ayrshire Schools summer art course at Culzean Castle. The other student was Robert, whose second name I forget. His carefully cultured accent marked him out as coming from one of the more affluent areas of Glasgow. He had shoulder-length blond hair, parted in the middle, and he wore a trendy brown corduroy jacket and a velvet waistcoat. He ostentatiously smoked a pipe, which gave him a distinctive air —not to mention polluting the air of the studio with a fragrant blue haze. His face seemed set in a permanent scowl. In conversation, a cynical or negative remark from Robert was virtually guaranteed. A 'glass half empty' sort of chap.

Opting to do sculpture at Glasgow was a disastrous choice. But not because I was incapable of learning. It appeared to me that the Sculpture lecturers—led by a recently appointed lecturer from Wales named Cliff Bowen —had little interest in teaching traditional techniques. Most of the time, they left us to our own devices. I floundered about, with no structured tuition, trying this and that, with no clear idea of what I should be doing. I felt that my tutor's main focus was the creation of their own masterpieces. On the odd occasion when they actually showed face, they made a bee-line for the most 'avant-garde' students, making approving comments about their latest conceptual art offering, and engaging them in earnest conversation about the 'meaning' of the piece. Robin Tannock spent his time painting, making slick, colourful abstract brush-marks on canvas. Robert swept dust and other bits of rubbish into neat little piles on the floor and sat for hours smoking his pipe, contemplating his handiwork. I began to wonder if I'd entered a parallel universe.

During that year, second and third year sculpture students went on a sketching trip to Morvich and Loch Duich. Cliff Bowen drove the Art School minibus and took us to a remote cottage in Kintail, owned by the Art School. It had bunk beds in two dormitories for the students and separate rooms for the lecturers.

I kept myself physically fit. I did fifty press-ups every morning. Cliff Bowen took up the challenge and impressed us by matching my record. The male students slept in one dorm and the girls in the other. When I brought out my Bible to read my usual chapter before going to sleep, Robert scornfully asked if I actually believed 'that rubbish', and savagely mocked me. I had an intense discussion with both him and Robin, who seemed more amused than anything. Robin was a 'live and let live' sort of chap. He shrugged his shoulders and preferred not to get too involved.

During the day, we went on various drawing and resource gathering expeditions. I tried to go some way towards a personal rapprochement with the glamorous new 'Conceptual Art'—a contradiction in terms when applied to sculpture, though held in high esteem by anyone who wished to be taken seriously by our dynamic young lecturers. I made some drawings of the mounds of seaweed draped over the rocks on the shores of Loch Duich.

Cliff Bowen brought his fishing rods and spent his days fishing for salmon on the nearby river. He looked at our sketchbooks in the evening and gave his opinion and suggestions for development work. Otherwise, we were free to do what we liked. One of the third-year students was a full-of-life chap called Macindoe. He kept us in good spirits by singing and cracking jokes as we drove along the single-track roads. Douglas Haldane and I had brought our climbing boots. One day, the two of us had an early breakfast and set off to climb the seven sisters of Kintail. We enjoyed a great day in the hills. At one craggy point, I climbed onto a rocky outcrop and Douglas took a photograph, which, unfortunately, I no longer possess.

Back in Glasgow, I tried to 'develop' my seaweed drawings into something three dimensional. I soaked strips of hessian scrim in Plaster of Paris and draped them over a plastic football to re-create the mounds of seaweed, then when I'd made several plaster mounds, I painted them a seaweedy greeny-brown. I couldn't quite convince myself, let alone the lecturers, that my seaweed installation had any artistic merit. The dreadful dishonesty inherent in much of what passed for art didn't sit comfortably with me. For example, in the Third Eye Centre on Sauchiehall street, where we used to go for a cheap mug of delicious filtered coffee, one exhibition featured a glass of water sitting on a little shelf which the 'artist' had placed on the wall. Beside it, neatly fixed to the wall, was a small white label, on which was neatly typed the words: "An Oak Tree". For me, this crystallised the monstrous deceit that so-called 'Conceptual Artists' foist upon a gullible public. "The bigger the lie, the more people will believe it." The magical 'oak tree'-come-glass of water was a case in point. In 2008, the Queen's composer, Sir Peter Maxwell Davies, said this about Damian Hirst's latest 'art piece'— a bull calf immersed in formaldehyde, which sold for £10.3 million—

'… all creative artists, in whatever branch of the arts they work, must ponder the implications of so much money scrambling after manufactured artifacts without content - with just a brand tag supposed to guarantee market value.'

'Manufactured artifacts without content' neatly sums it up. Thankfully, some folk still have the integrity to speak out against the degenerate culture in which we live.

In second year, I again lived in the Halls of Residence during the week, this time in the John D. Kelly building in Hill Street. One of the other resident students was Peter Howson, a friendly, well-spoken guy from Ayr. Donald McLeod was friendly with Peter and the two of them used to lift weights in the basement. I sometimes pumped iron with them there.

Before the end of the summer term, Peter was clearing out his room and, as he had no room at home for them (he said), he gave me two oil paintings, both painted on plywood. One was a large self portrait, the other a portrait of his grandfather in the style of Rousseau, with a cat looking in at the window. Later, while teaching at Ashcraig School, I sold the latter painting to finance the building of a large shed in my garden in Glasgow, thinking I might use it as a studio to kick-start my career as a sculptor. I abandoned that project when we moved to Fife. According to Norma, yet another of my 'great ideas'! I sold Peter's self-portrait several years later when we needed the money to do some work on the house in Fife.

Instead of continuing into third year at Glasgow, Donald and Peter did the fashionable thing and dropped out of Art school. Less fashionably, they joined the British Army. I kept in touch with Donald and got a hilarious couple of letters from him. Here's a sample of his zany sense of humour:

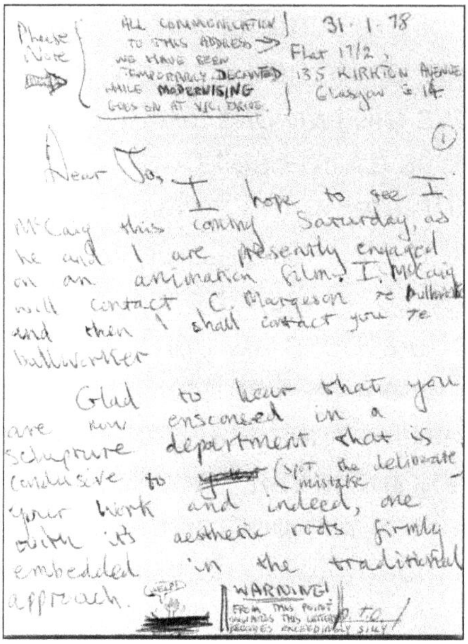

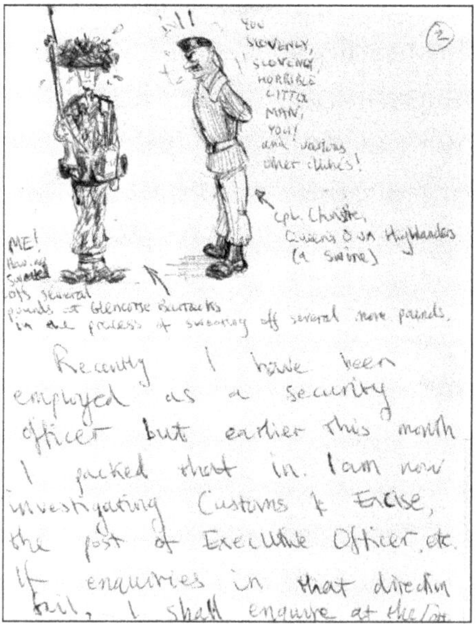

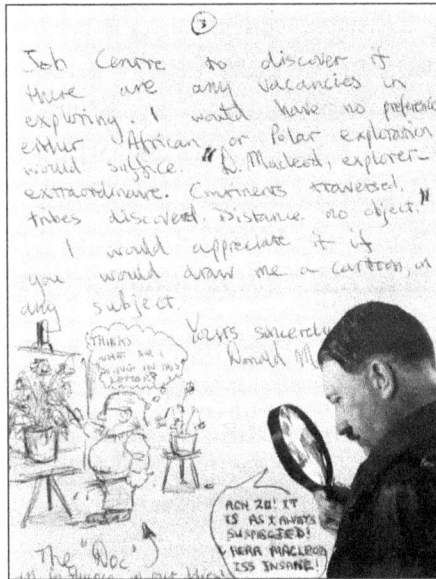

Donald became studio assistant to the now famous Peter Howson but also produced quirky paintings of his own in his studio in Glasgow. Sadly, I learned he passed away in December 2018.

~

DURING MY 'SOJOURN IN THE WILDERNESS' at the Sculpture Department at Glasgow, I became interested in Henry Moore and wanted to learn about traditional sculpting methods. I began working on a large, abstract clay sculpture in the style of Henry Moore. For no good reason that I could discern, they shunted me off to a windowless basement in the Haldane Building at the bottom of Hill Street. Occasionally, Cliff and one or two lecturers came and looked at it, poked it and asked me a few questions. As I recall, apart from some technical advice about how to construct a steel armature, that was the sum total of their involvement.

From the highly structured learning environment of secondary school and an equally tightly structured first year course, I was now supposed to 'self-direct' my learning. I groped about in the dark, trying various techniques, hopelessly searching for expert guidance. To my dismay, at the end of the summer term, my tutors returned the verdict that I'd failed to gain a pass in my studio work.

They set me a summer drawing project, which I conscientiously completed—I drew various scenes at Brownlees Woodyard in Kilmarnock, where I had a summer job. This still wasn't deemed good enough by those in charge at the Sculpture Department. Dad was extremely concerned. He wrote a letter to Mr Fleming, the GSA Registrar.

Meanwhile, I also applied to Duncan of Jordanstone College of Art in Dundee. Dad got a reply from Dugald Cameron, head of Product Design at Glasgow, offering me a place on the second year Product Design course, if I was willing to repeat second year. By that time, however, I'd received a reply from Duncan of Jordanstone, inviting me for an interview. Jake Kempsall, who'd taken over from Scotty Sutherland as Head of Sculpture there, offered me a place on the second-year sculpture course, which I readily accepted.

∾

32 DUNCAN OF JORDANSTONE COLLEGE OF ART

Thus it was that I found myself looking for a place to stay in Dundee. I took the bus to Dundee a few days prior to the start of term and stayed a bed-and-breakfast on Magdalen Yard Road, overlooking Magdalen Green. When I came down to breakfast, there were several men sitting eating. Most of them were lorry drivers or travelling salesmen. There was a friendly atmosphere, with some banter between the landlady and her husband and those who were obviously regulars. When the landlady found out I was looking for student 'digs', she suggested I try a house just along the road, on the corner of Magdalen Yard Road and Osborne Place. So off I went and knocked the door of this lovely old house with a conservatory, which looked ideal. Unfortunately, the lady who owned it said she was full up.

I went to the Art College administration offices on Perth Road, where I also met and had a chat with the student welfare officer. She pointed me in the direction of the college noticeboard, where I saw an advert for a rented flat not far from the college. I went to a call box and arranged to meet the owner of the flat at his office on the Perth Road. He was a Norwegian architect who had bought the flat to live in during his student years and was now letting it out.

He asked a solicitor to draw up a rental agreement, which also included instructions about who to contact in case of any problems, which I signed. The solicitor's secretary handed over the keys, and I moved into my new abode.

The flat was in Cleghorn Street, about twenty minutes' walk from the Art College, between Lochee Road and City Road, in a residential area of old tenement buildings near the hill that runs up towards Dundee Law.

It was a small two-roomed attic flat, comprising a bedroom with a dormer window overlooking the street, and a kitchen-cum-dining area fitted with a gas fire and a gas 'geyser' next to the sink, which heated the water. The kitchen window had a wonderful view over the city and the river Tay, with the rail bridge and the hills of Fife in the distance. Dad bought some second-hand furniture at an auction sale and brought them through on his trailer. It was great to have a place of my own.

At Duncan of Jordanstone, in marked contrast to Glasgow School of Art, the second-year sculpture course was carefully structured—with hands-on tuition—and introduced students to the entire range of sculpting techniques. I could hardly believe it—the lecturers actually spent time with us, demonstrating the techniques! What a relief and what a release of creative energy it gave me. I worked hard on all the set projects and progressed without difficulty into third year, which was a mixture of taught and self-directed projects. By then, I had a solid foundation on which to build, and a much clearer idea of what I wanted to do. Fourth year was devoted to completely self-directed projects under the supervision of our tutors.

Two of the lecturers, Alistair Smart and Alistair Ross, were figurative sculptors, creating portrait busts and figure sculptures in bronze and cold cast metal using traditional techniques. They had worked for many years alongside Scotty Sutherland, who had only recently retired as Head of Sculpture at Dundee. He created several national monuments around Scotland, including the famous 'Commando' memorial near Spean Bridge, just North of Fort William. At the start of term, the two Alistair's took us to meet him in his little workshop at the side of the Art College building. He was a small, unassuming, kindly old man. To each student, he gave a beautifully crafted little wooden spatula (for working with clay) which he'd made.

The two Alistair's were very different from each other. Alistair Smart was a real craftsman. He was more 'hands on' with the students and his practical, 'sleeves rolled up' approach, coupled with his quirky brand of humour immediately struck a chord. Alistair Ross was a virtuoso performer. Dundee University regularly invited him to give portrait demonstrations to their staff, and he used to relate some of those experiences to us. He usually chose a man with a beard and glasses to sit for him, because that made it easier to capture a likeness in the half-hour they gave him for the demo. On one occasion, he said, the sweat was pouring off him! Sometimes he got carried away with his anecdotes and spent less time giving constructive criticism about the piece you were working on.

But at least he showed up and showed an interest, which was more than I could say about his counterparts in Glasgow. The other lecturers were the Head of department Jake Kempsall and Gareth Fisher, a young English lecturer from the Lake District whose father was a well-known Cumbrian artist. Jake and Gareth were personally more committed to the development of abstract sculptural ideas but were happy to work within a well-established course framework where the hands-on teaching of sound technique was central to student development. From Jake, we learned how to carve stone and use oxy-acetylene gas to weld metal construction. Gareth introduced us to wood construction and casting in aluminium. In third year, they showed us how to cast in bronze, using the lost wax method, so we had a good grounding in all the basic techniques and processes involved in the making of sculpture, coupled with regular interactive discussion about the aesthetic qualities we were aiming for in our work.

Posing with one of my wood construction
Sculptures

Going to Dundee gave me the opportunity for a fresh
start in more ways than one. As well as having a second
chance to complete my art school education, I also had a
second chance to get my life on track spiritually.

Living on my own meant that there were fewer distractions than was the case when I lived in the halls of residence. I had also learned from first-hand experience that the soporific effect of alcohol, which seriously impaired my ability to think and act rationally, was not something I enjoyed—nor was the guilt I felt at letting the Lord down.

I established a daily routine of rising at seven, doing a fifteen-minute exercise programme (press-ups and sit-ups), then after getting washed and dressed, I had a quiet time of prayer and meditation on the Word of God before going into the studio.

After my morning's work in the studio, I usually got a cheap, substantial lunch in the college refectory. Dundee 'stovies'[1] were a special treat! I normally worked on until six before going home to make something to eat. There was an interesting second-hand bookshop on Polepark Road. I used to drop in there on my way home.

Dave Mach was a friendly third year student when I started at Dundee. He came from Methil. His family had emigrated from Poland to Scotland during the 2nd World War. Not long after I arrived in Dundee, I was walking back from town along the Perth Road and I met Dave coming towards me. He recognised me and said "Hi there!" I appreciated his out-going, friendly demeanour. He was a hard-working student who became Jake Kempsall's prodigy, producing large abstract constructions which won the approval of lecturers such as Jake and Gareth. They gave me the impression that they fancied themselves as pioneers of modern art. Dave got a scholarship to the Royal College of Art in London after graduating and became quite a celebrity, making disposable sculptures, such as a Polaris submarine constructed from tyres, created as a protest against nuclear weapons. This led on to many other projects, some more ridiculous than others, which somehow attracted vast sums from rich people or wealthy organisations with more money than sense. I think it says a lot about the moral and spiritual decay of our nation, that the art establishment supports many self-indulgent, crazy ideas and pretends they have artistic merit. It lends weight to the view that the creative output of societies throughout history acts as a mirror, revealing their spiritual and moral health.

Sometimes on a Friday evening after college, I used to stand inside the Nethergate shopping centre and give out gospel tracts to passers-by. I had some interesting conversations. One old man, a believer himself, often used to stop and chat. But one day, I was standing at the top of the stairs on the upper level of the shopping centre, when a woman took a tract, turned round, and asked me what it was about. I began to explain, it was about

God's love. That's as far as I got. Suddenly, I felt a crushing, oppressive, extremely powerful sensation of darkness descending upon me. I was powerless to resist the awful, malevolent force, which physically pressed down on my body. Suddenly, from within, a strong voice said 'NO!' The woman immediately turned round and walked away, leaving me trembling and shaking from the experience.

On my way back to the flat, I stopped at a call box and made my weekly phone-call home. In the course of conversation, I told Dad what had happened. I went home, made my tea, washed the dishes, then sat down and opened my Bible. It fell open at Isaiah 54. As I read down the chapter, verse seventeen leapt off the page:

"No weapon that is formed against thee shall prosper; and every tongue that shall rise against thee in judgment thou shalt condemn. This is the heritage of the servants of the LORD, and their righteousness which is of me, saith the LORD."

That promise gave me a wonderful reassurance that God was watching over me and had preserved me from being overcome by that evil entity.

About ten o'clock, just as I was thinking it was time for bed, someone knocked on the door of the flat. I was immediately apprehensive and called out, 'Who's there?' To my surprise, my father's voice answered. He had driven all the way from Galston to Dundee because he was so concerned about my welfare. I think he thought the woman had tried to hypnotise me. I showed him the verse which the Lord had given me in Isaiah and, after praying with me, we had a cup of tea before he drove all the way back home, a journey of at least two and a half hours. That's the man I was privileged to have for a father.

What was it that happened to me that day? I believe the woman was an instrument of Satan. Possibly possessed by a demon. It seemed to me then, and I still think so now, that an evil spirit tried to overpower me. I think the voice that came from within was the voice of the Holy Spirit saying, "No, this young man belongs to me. You can't come in here." How thankful I am that those who have trusted the Lord Jesus Christ as Saviour are "sealed with the Holy Spirit" (Ephesians 1:13).

Of course, educated people nowadays think such things are 'all in the mind' and try to explain them away as some sort of psychological or mental disturbance. But the Lord Jesus acknowledged the existence of evil spirits and encountered them when He was here on earth. Invisible to the human eye, but real. Thankfully, 'God is stronger than His foes' and I never experienced anything like that again, nor would I wish to. While I'm on the subject, I counsel anyone who thinks they can dabble with the paranormal to stay well away from it. My father often quoted Romans 16:19: be "wise unto that which is good, and simple unto that which is evil".

It was always good to get home for a visit, and I tried to do that as often as I could. Usually, I got the bus to Buchanan Street Bus Station in Glasgow or, if I could afford the train, took the train to Glasgow Queen Street. From there, I had to walk to Anderston Bus Station, where I caught a bus to Kilmarnock, then another bus from Kilmarnock home to Galston. One hot summer's day, I hitch-hiked from Galston to Dundee and saved on bus fares! I got a great lift that day from Dunblane to

Dundee from a man driving a souped-up Ford Capri. He asked me if I was an Army man on an exercise, which boosted my ego no end. People were quite used to picking up students and hitch-hikers in those days. All you had to do was write your destination on a piece of cardboard, or stick your thumb out, and eventually someone would stop.

It was during my time at Dundee that someone persuaded me to sign up as an Amway Distributor. They invited me to attend several Amway meetings where the presenters showed films of glamorous Americans who'd made a fortune selling soap. Various people at the meetings talked about the incredible successes they were having. All you need do was persuade your friends to sign up, then train them to do the same. The system gave those further up the line a larger share of the profits so, if you became a 'Diamond Distributor' for example, you were hitting the big time. The goal was to become a Platinum Distributor with endless groups of distributors attached to your group. You would hit the jackpot. The way the disciples of Amway talked about it made it seem that in no time at all you'd be a millionaire. I must admit, to begin with, I was sucked in by the hype and spent some of my student grant on a starter pack, which I touted around the houses in Cleghorn Street and one or two other places in Dundee in spare moments between College and Church commitments. I took some supposedly magic oven cleaner to a local Indian Restaurant and persuaded the owner to let me do a free demonstration on one of his cookers. He was so impressed he said, "I'll think about it." I sold some lipstick to a woman in a flat in Cleghorn Street, but it turned out to be a one-off sale. This business was harder than I thought. Eventually, it dawned on me—I wasn't cut out to be a salesman. But more than that, I couldn't shake off the nagging discomfort I felt as a disciple of Christ, with the ploy of making money by drawing up a list of family and friends who you then had to persuade to join the Amway religion. I sold some products to Dad and Mum. Dad agreed to become a distributor, but it wasn't long before he expressed the same misgivings. He wasn't at all comfortable with the suggestion that he write his financial goals on bits of paper beside his bed to look at first thing in the morning, or imagine circles on the ceiling of the ever-expanding groups of distributors he was going to command. It was all-consuming and spiritually damaging. When he spoke to Uncle Joe about it, asking his opinion, Uncle Joe wrote back, "If that's your bog, jump in." That clinched it for Dad. He packed it in and refocussed his attention on making an honest living. Technically, Amway wasn't a pyramid selling scheme. But it was pretty close.

My last year at Duncan of Jordanstone was a year of full-on, creative energy. Most days I was in the studio from nine o' clock in the morning till nine o' clock at night when the college janitors came round and threw me out. Producing several life-size figures in clay, then taking them through each stage of the casting process was time-consuming and physically demanding. It felt good to be firing on all four cylinders. Alongside the practical work, was History of Art and Sociology classes, with a dissertation to be handed in. I wrote my dissertation on the bronze sculptures of Ife and Benin in Nigeria.

Sitting in my studio at Duncan of Jordanstone

One of my fellow students whose company I enjoyed, was Ian Hughes. He came from Lesmahagow. I discovered that Malcolm McDonald, (who subsequently left teaching to become a full-time evangelist with the Churches of God) had been his Science teacher. Ian was a superb draughtsman. He was a student in the Drawing and Painting department. He was intensely creative and invested himself emotionally to a such an extent in his work that he found it difficult to part with a painting or a drawing.

One day, Ian visited the studio I shared with Keith Donnelly. When he saw the many terracotta maquettes I'd produced in developing my ideas, he exclaimed, "It's like Michelangelo's studio!"

Pastel drawing by Ian Hughes

I managed to persuade Ian to sell me one of his drawings—a beautiful pastel chalk drawing of the model sitting in a chair. He had made another drawing on the reverse, in sepia Conte chalk, of one of the male models. Every bit as accomplished as the one on the front, but in Ian's mind, I guess, just part of the learning process.

He was full of admiration for the work of Edgar Degas and I think it shows in his beautiful, subtle handling of colour in his pastel drawing. Ian continued to paint after graduation. He later took a job as an orderly in a Psychiatric Unit and was much affected by the inner life and emotional trauma of the patients. The Scottish National Portrait gallery in Edinburgh purchased some of his gigantic, visceral portraits. It saddened me when I learned that Ian had died suddenly in June 2014, aged fifty-five. I wished I'd had the chance to renew our acquaintance.

Plaster cast of my self-portrait bust

PROFESSOR BRYAN KNEALE from the Royal College of Art in London came to judge our Diploma show work. I'd never heard of him. Thankfully, he gave me a pass, and I was duly informed of this by Jake Kempsall. It was a great relief to have the professor validate my sculptural ability after the intense work of the final year.

Dad and Mum came to see me being awarded the Diploma in Art (Sculpture) at the end of the summer term in 1980. I also invited Neville and Helen Coomer, because they'd been so kind to me and had put me up every Saturday night during term time.

After the graduation ceremony, I took Dad and Mum for lunch at Raffles, a restaurant on the Perth Road near the University, which served a delicious Cannelloni pancake. Like many such eateries, it changed hands long ago. It no longer exists as it was then. I'm ashamed to say I wanted Dad and Mum to myself that day. Without spelling it out, I made it clear to Neville and Helen that I was going off now with Dad and Mum. They got the message and took themselves away. I've regretted that ever since, and wish I'd been more generous. I just wanted time on my own with

Clutching my 'Diploma in Art (Sculpture), Graduation day, Duncan of Jordanstone

Mum and Dad, whom I'd not seen since Easter and who had travelled from the other side of the country for the occasion. Thankfully, Neville and Helen were not the sort of people to hold a grudge. Much later, I applied for a job at Buckhaven High School, knowing full well that if successful, I'd be linked in fellowship with them at the Church of God in Buckhaven—and so it turned out to be. I hold them in the highest esteem.

33 WEEKEND VISITS TO HILTON AND METHIL

I spent three productive and enjoyable years as a student in Dundee. As I said, I got a good grounding in a variety of materials and techniques (welding, stone carving, clay modelling, mould-making, casting etc.), and, more importantly, developed the habit of regular reading and meditation on the Word of God, the mainstay of my life. There is nothing to compare with the preciousness of fresh thoughts which the Holy Spirit brings to mind when you "watch daily at the posts of wisdom's gate" (Prov. 8:34) I made it a priority to write down my thoughts each day in a reporter's notebook, so that by the end of the week I had honed in on some aspect of the person and work of the Lord Jesus, which I could bring to God in thanksgiving each Lord's Day morning at the Remembrance.

When I first made the journey from Dundee to Methil, Neville and Helen Coomer, who lived in a bungalow they'd built on their smallholding, invited me to come and stay overnight on Saturdays, so that I could more easily get to the meetings. For this, I will be forever grateful to them. Regular social contact with fellow saints was vital to my spiritual health. Neville and Helen had three children, Lorraine, Alistair and Lindsay. Lorraine and Alistair were also students at Galashiels and Paisley respectively, so Lindsay, who was a student at the local college, was the one I saw on my weekly visits and I got to know him well. Neville took full advantage of the availability of an extra brother with whom he could share church responsibilities. He wasn't slow to engage my services as a teacher in Sunday school, on the speaker's rota for gospel and ministry meetings, and taking my turn writing up the monthly Bible Studies paper. It was a good training ground.

Methil Sunday school. Robert and Robin on left.

Each Saturday afternoon or evening, I caught the train from Dundee to Ladybank, where either Helen or Lindsay picked me up in their white Ford Transit minibus, which was used to transport church friends and Sunday school children.

Lindsay was good at encouraging the older children who came to Sunday school. Now and then he used to organise Saturday afternoon trips to various places around Fife. Robin and Robert were two boys in their early teens who often came on those trips, as well as Robert's sister and some others. Sometimes I'd get an earlier train on Saturday so that I could go with them. On our way back, after dropping off the young folk, Lindsay often stopped at 'The Little Friar' fish and chip shop in Kennoway and bought a fish supper which we enjoyed when we got back to Hilton.

On one occasion, when Lorraine was home for the holidays, I invited her to bring the Sunday school children to my flat in Dundee, where I gave them their tea before taking them home again. There was lots of good humoured banter!

The church in Methil met in a building on Wellesley Road. They had converted the whole of the bottom floor into a meeting room. It wasn't quite 'through a close and up a stair' — 'you're sure to find the brethren there' — but it wasn't far off it. Many of our churches met in similar humble premises, which reflected the working-class origins of a large percentage of 'the brethren movement', so called. It also reflected the scriptural truth, that the church (Gk. Ecclesia) is the congregation, not the building.

The folks in the church in Methil were very welcoming. There was John Baird who lived in Leven, Andy McIlree senior and his wife Isa, originally from Glasgow, who lived in Glenrothes, John and Queenie Mackie from Markinch, Mrs Wilson from Freuchie, David and Winnie Reid from Buckhaven and Margaret Hamilton and Sandy Smith from Methil. On Sunday mornings, Neville always went to the hall early to open up and set the 'emblems' (the bread and wine) on the table while Helen took Lindsay and me in the minibus to pick up Mrs Wilson and the McIlree's.

After the Remembrance, we'd have a cup of tea and a biscuit in the hall before the Sunday School began and then go back to Hilton for Sunday dinner. Helen often served Brussels sprouts to accompany the main dish. I hated their bitter taste but was too polite to say I didn't like them, so whenever that generous helping of sprouts arrived on my plate, I reached for the HP sauce, smothered them with a generous squeeze and gulped them down as fast as I could. Only then was I able to enjoy the rest of my dinner. To my chagrin, Neville once remarked to Helen "I think he likes sprouts dear, give him some more"—to which I replied, "Oh no, I have more than enough, honestly—thanks all the same!" Helen also made the most delicious home-made ice cream, using a combination of condensed milk and other ingredients. That was a real treat and I wish I had asked her for the recipe.

After dinner, if it was dry, we'd go for a walk in the countryside around Hilton. Then we'd have another cup of tea before setting off again for the gospel meeting. In keeping with common practice in most other assemblies, we held a short prayer meeting in the hall before going out to a street corner or the back court of some houses, where we preached a fifteen-minute, open-air gospel message. We usually sang a gospel hymn, then a brother stepped forward, preached a short message and finishing with an invitation to anyone listening, to come back with us to the gospel meeting at the hall. We then walked back to the hall where either a local brother, or visitor from another assembly, preached the good news for half an hour.

We usually got back to Hilton about seven or seven thirty, where Helen made some 'supper'—often scrambled egg or beans on toast and a cup of tea. That was the one meal in the day when Neville finally seemed to relax. Supper-times were always full of good-humoured banter and teasing—especially between Neville and Lindsay. Then it was time for me to catch the train from Markinch back to Dundee via the Tay Rail bridge. As the train crossed the water, I always looked out at the remains of the original bridge which collapsed in 1879 when a train carrying ninety passengers made its way across the river during a winter storm. There were no survivors. McGonagall's excruciating masterpiece recorded the event for posterity:

> Beautiful Railway Bridge of the Silv'ry Tay!
> Alas! I am very sorry to say
> That ninety lives have been taken away
> On the last Sabbath day of 1879,
> Which will be remember'd for a very long time.
> ………
> So the train mov'd slowly along the Bridge of Tay,
> Until it was about midway,
> Then the central girders with a crash gave way,
> And down went the train and passengers into
>   the Tay!

WILLIAM MCGONAGALL

I'd arrive at the station around nine-thirty or ten, catch a bus going up the Lochee Road and walk to my flat from the bus stop at the bottom of Cleghorn Street. In the winter, the stairs of the close were in darkness and I was always apprehensive in case someone was lurking around the next corner as I climbed the six flights of stairs to my artist garret on the top landing. The family who lived in the flat below me were often 'out of their skulls', drunk. I used to hear them shouting and screaming at each other as I passed their door. There was always a strong smell of cooking fat, stale beer and one shudders to think what else, emanating from their flat.

There were occasions, especially in my final year, when the pressures of Art college work and Church commitments took their toll. Neville regularly asked me to take the gospel meeting. I used the little 'spare time' that I had in the two or three weeks prior to a speaking engagement, to do the thorough reading and preparation that was essential to do the subject justice. I told Dad how stressful I found this on top of the not insignificant time needed to keep on top of final essay preparation—plus the physically demanding studio work. He was very concerned and vigorously advised me: "You'll need to tell him, 'I've got too much college work on at the moment, I can't do it.'" But I struggled on, juggling all the commitments. On the one hand, as Lamentations 3:27 reminds us, "it is good that a man bear the yoke in his youth". I suppose it taught me to manage my time efficiently, so that each responsibility was fulfilled in the spirit, not just the letter. I think Dad had a point, though. Sometimes out of eagerness to please, an inexperienced or less assertive person (such as I was), can take on so much that they end up either doing nothing well, or giving themselves a nervous breakdown when they should just have said "No". A lesson well worth learning.

34 BAPTISM TRAGEDY

Galston's Friday night club continued during my years at Glasgow School of Art and Dundee. During that time, the youth work bore fruit. Several young people placed their trust in the Lord Jesus and three of them expressed a desire to follow Him in their lives by being baptised in accordance with Matthew 28:19. Wisely, Dad counselled them to ask their parents' permission. He arranged for Gilbert Williamson and Drew Ramage to be baptised on Sunday 6th May, 1979. By this time, I was completing my last term on the third year Sculpture course at Dundee.

I remember phoning home from the call-box in Cleghorn Street when I got back to Dundee from my usual weekend visit to the Church in Methil on Sunday night. James answered the phone. He sounded preoccupied with something, so we exchanged some brief remarks and said 'Cheerio'. I went home to bed, went into the studio next morning as usual and got on with the work.

On the Tuesday morning at break-time, I went down to the College Library and picked up a paper. The front-page splash headline was: BAPTISM HORROR. As I read the details, it suddenly dawned on me—this is about Gilbert Williamson. He'd been electrocuted by touching a metal heater fixed to the wall above the baptism tank in the hall in Church Lane, Galston. Dad had already baptised Drew, who exited the tank without incident. Gilbert was next. As he came up out of the water, Gilbert reached out and took hold of the tubular metal heater to steady himself. He gave a loud shout and collapsed. Dad, who was wearing rubber waders, felt a huge electrical 'thump' go through him. They lifted Gilbert out of the tank and someone in the congregation tried to resuscitate him, but it was no good. He was gone.

James was so stressed by this dreadful event and its aftermath that he wasn't thinking straight when I spoke to him from the call-box. Piecing things together later, Dad, who helped lift Gilbert out of the tank, escaped fatal injury because he was wearing rubber waders.

The reporting of the incident in certain newspapers was atrocious. One Daily Record reporter described the Churches of God as an extreme cult, suggesting that we belonged to a previously reported cultish group in Cumbernauld. The article made several lurid statements about us, which were completely wrong. If it wasn't meant to be malicious, it certainly felt like it. Brethren in the district wrote a letter of complaint to the newspaper, which elicited a tiny apology, printed several days later at the bottom of an inside page. Unfair or not, the sensational headlines were extremely damaging.

The electricity board sent an inspector to check the wiring on the heaters. They found that even though the heaters had been switched off, the protective plastic sleeve was missing from the earth wire inside the junction box. The earth had fused with the live wire, which meant that the metal heater was live, even when the switch was turned off at the wall.

Newspaper reporters descended on Galston, interviewing anyone willing to talk to them. Dad refused to comment, since the fatal accident inquiry and formal investigation by the Health and Safety Executive had begun and the Police had referred the matter to the Procurator Fiscal.

The verdict of the fatal accident inquiry in October '79 was 'death by electrocution'. Dad, Jimmy Barr and others who'd been present at the baptism, gave evidence. It was an extremely stressful time, not least for Gilbert's family, who would miss him for the rest of their lives. We all wished it had never happened.

Why did God allow it? Dad received many sympathetic letters at the time from other Christians. One of those was from a lady who wrote that perhaps Gilbert was taken because he was 'a beautiful spirit'. Dad appreciated the sympathetic tone but thought it was going beyond scripture to say such a thing. As far as he was concerned, it was an accident that should never have happened. He prayed God would comfort Gilbert's parents and family.

Dad laboured on in Galston, distributing tracts, preaching and inviting people to the meetings. Sadly, it became clear that there was no future for the church there. He made one last effort to reach out to local people with the Gospel. He prepared a series of meetings on the subject of 'The Call of God' and had invitation leaflets printed. I helped distribute them. At one house, I posted the leaflet through the letterbox. As I turned to go back down the path, the door opened and a man appeared, holding the invitation in his hand. "Are you from that church where the wee boy was killed?" he asked. "Yes" I said. "Well, take this, I want nothing to do with it" he said. He handed me the leaflet and slammed the door. It summed up the lasting damage that had been done.

Dad had to face up to this grim reality and took the hard decision to close the doors. Several brethren and sisters from the district, including Jack Ferguson, Willie Kerr, John Black and others, attended the final Remembrance at Galston. At the end of the meeting, someone gave out PHSS number 147, "Amen, one lasting long Amen…" I never sing that lovely hymn now, without being reminded of the finality of that sad occasion.

> Amen, one lasting long Amen-
> Blest anthem of eternal days;
> The fulness of the rapturous song
> To Christ the Saviour's endless praise.
>
> Amen, one lasting long Amen-
> Heaven's blissful cadence, deep and loud,
> While every heart before the throne
> In holy, solemn awe is bowed.
>
> Amen, Amen, it rolls along,
> Re-echoing from the throne again;
> Be ours to mingle with the throng
> In that eternal, loud Amen.

Dad and Mum, and the other saints from Galston, transferred to the Church of God in Kilmarnock. They travelled fifteen miles there and back again each Sunday, to re-member the Lord. Some years later, Dad sold the house at John Knox Street and moved with Mum to the village of Dunlop, where they spent the rest of their lives. Dad died on 15th October 2008, Mum on 13th January 2021.

~

35 CAMP 1979, TENT THIRTEEN

At the first week of Auchenfoyle Camp in July 1979, I was monitor to a group of boys from Hamilton. They were John and Paul Carruthers, the two Hardman brothers from Meikle Earnock, Derek and Alistair (who was nicknamed 'Dod'), and John Walker. One of their friends was John Hunter's boy Andrew, from Airdrie—his nickname was 'Spock' on account of his pointed ears. He was in another tent, but he spent a lot of time with the Hamilton boys.

Friday night beanfeast with tent 13. L-R: Jock Kerr, (gatecrasher), Derek Hardman, John Carruthers, Alistair Hardman, John Walker and Yours Truly.

As usual, we spent the Friday afternoon shopping in Greenock for presents to take home as well as buying goodies for our Friday night 'Beanfeast'. Unknown to me, the boys had clubbed together and bought me a present —a retractable 'Stanley' measuring tape. I still have it as a reminder of the comradeship we enjoyed in 'Tent 13'.

I corresponded with the boys for a month or two after Camp and still have the letters they sent in reply to mine. I reproduce them here for my nostalgic enjoyment of the camaraderie and fun of those carefree days.

Almada Tower
Hamilton
30/7/79

Hi Jo,

I have just recieved (sic) your letter. I am writing so quickly to tell you that we are going our holidays on the 11th August. We are going to Arran for one week and when we come back we start school on the Monday. So there is not much chance for Paul and I to get to Galston before the end of the summer holidays. I do not know Spocks address but I'll find out for the next time I write.

Both Paul and I have given thought to your idea about daily reading of the BIBLE and we both read every night. I read from the revised version and Paul reads from Good News BIBLE.

Iain Gardiner has not started the Bible Studie project up yet but I'll let you know when he does.

P.S. I am writing for both Paul and I because I have all the brains and I know what to say. Paul is adding his bits in. Yours in the Lord,

Paul and John

~

Meikle Earnock
Hamilton
31/7/79

DEAR JO,

Thanks for your letter and your postcard.

I met the two Carruthers and John Walker and they all received theirs, Mum wasn't too pleased about Dod's jeans although there was no spanking I'm afraid. Pity?

Are you back at the Art College yet. If so I hope you are enjoying it. I was shocked to hear of the theft at the camp. But God knows who done it and he will punish them in due time.

I received my first Bible worksheet from Iain Gardiner and after completing it I felt that I knew and understood the passage better.

I am looking forward to our day-trip to Galston if it's possible, although if it's a Saturday I may not be able to come if the boss at the shop where I work does not let me away. Do you have Spocks address? I did have but I lost it. The Carruthers have it I think, if you ask them to send it to you. Hope the photos in your camera have developed allright although I fear Dods face may have smudged the film.

I have just finished reading my Bible for Ians worksheet. Hope very much that you will be able to come to camp next year D.V. and we can all be in the same tent. Hope this letter reaches you at the Dundee address. Till I hear from you,

Yours

Derek and Alistair Hardman

P.S. can you still play our silly song on the accordion? I hope so.

See you Jo!

~

Strathaven Road,
Hamilton
STRATHCLYDE

DEAR JO

Thank you for your letter.

I had a great holiday. It was raining most of the time but it only lasted for 10 min. During the day we went into the town and walked around the tower, castle and round the old golf course. At night Andy (Spock) and I went fishing but we never caught anything. I am sorry to say that I have not got the photos ready but the next time I write to you I will have the photos ready and I will send them through.

Ian Gardiner has sent the Bible searchings through to me. It is very good they are 18 questions and it is about the time Jesus spent with his disciples in the upper room. The first study is in John chapter 13v1-17 where Jesus washes his disciples feet. Better finish for now. I am looking forward to your reply.

Bye for now.

In Jesus name,

John

PS

Andrew Hunters (Spock) address is Craighead Street, Clarkston. Airdrie

Almada Tower

Hamilton
20/8/79

Hi Joe,

How are you? All right I hope. We enjoyed our Arran trip very much. We did not climb Goat-Fell though. My dad was too lazy.

Paul and I cycled round half the Island. From Brodick to Machrie via Lochranza then back to Brodick by the Blackwaterfoot main road. During this we had to push the bikes up a couple of big hills but it was great whizzing down the other side.

About the weekend at Methil any week except the first week would suit us fine. There has been a fishing trip arranged for the 8th of September.

Iain has sent us the second worksheet. He was telling us too, about your attempt at Goat-Fell.

When we were there it rained every day but it would only rain for about a couple of hours then it would brighten up. We caught about 40 mackerel 1 codling and 1 pol-lock I think it was a pollock but I am not quite sure.

Chow

for now

Yours in the Lord

John and Paul

~

Meikle Earnock

Hamilton
31/7/79

DEAR JO,

Thanks for the letter. Hope you are all right and having a good time at Art College. I have started back at school. and am getting on okay.

I have asked my boss about the trip to Methil and I will (and Dod) be able to come the SEPTEMBER WEEKEND if that is ok with you. If we go that weekend it will not be so much of a rush when we come home to get ready to go to school.

So if you could arrange I would be glad to come through. Will you be there? I hope so.

I have just sent Ian Gardiners second worksheet back (this time even more interesting) and he said both Dod and I done very well which isn't too bad, is it?

Anyway hope to hear from you soon Joe

so I'll finish now.

Bye for now

Derek and Alistair H.

On the underside of the envelope flap Derek had written:

"Unlucky 13?

No chance, Tent 13 Rule OK?? (& Spock!!!)

～

Craighead St
Clarkston.
Airdrie

DEAR JO,

How are you. Hope you and your family are Keeping well mine are. Sorry I haven't wrote any earlier as my Dad's motor engine in his car was cracked and I had to help him and also Ian Gardeners Bible Study sheet came in and I have been busy with that.

About going to Methil I think it is a very good Idea and I would gladly go.

I hope you enjoyed the Second week at camp I enjoyed it at St Andrews I thing John Walker enjoyed it as well. I am going through to his house sometime, I am looking forward to seeing his Mum and Dad, they are very kind people and I think if you met them you would like them as well. his dads a bit crazy but he's a good laugh.

Your faithfully

Andrew Hunter

STRATHAVEN Road
Hamilton
STRATHCLYDE

Dear Jo thank you for the letter. Sorry I have not written sooner because Ian Gardiner has sent through the other worksheet and he will be sending the third one through sometime.

About the trip I think it is a good idea and so does Derek, Dod and Spock.

Spock has been phoning me up and he is coming up to my house some Saturday to visit me.

About the photos, I am glad to say that I got the photos back and there is only one good one out of the lot of them and that is you and Spock. I will be sending the photos through to you. That's all for now as I have nothing else to say.

Hear from you soon.

In Jesus name, John

Tent 13, Auchenfoyle Camp, 1979 - L-R:
Derek, 'Dod', me, Paul C [front], John W,
Spock and [unknown].

36 SUMMER JOB, DUNDEE

My student grant ran out as usual, at the end of the summer term. It was my first year living away from home in Dundee and I didn't want to lose the flat in Cleghorn Street. I had to find a way of paying the rent over the summer. So I stayed on and looked for a summer job. I'd heard that the Waste Management department took on students, so I walked to the depot on Harefield Road. The office was in a building that looked like a house just along from the depot. The manager was a cheerful chap who told me there were no 'bin lorry' vacancies left (bin-men were paid the most money), but if I was interested, there was a vacancy on one of the street sweeping teams. He signed me up there and then. I duly reported to the foreman at the depot at eight o'clock sharp next Monday morning. For part of the week, I joined a team comprising the driver of an electric dustcart and two 'sweepers'. I was a sweeper. The other days, they sent me out with another man pushing a hand propelled 'car-tie'—a long barrow with bicycle wheels on either side and two empty bins screwed onto it. Dundee folk have a habit of putting 'ie' on the end of certain words, somehow making the object in question seem more homely. A 'cartie' sounds much more appealing than a cart. Our brushes were wooden handled brushes with stiff natural bristles and we carried a couple of shovels on the cartie as well as a supply of black plastic bin-liners.

I loved being in the open air all day, soaking up the sunshine—but working in the rain wasn't so hot. The driver of our electric cartie was a sharp-featured, swarthy man of medium build with a neatly clipped moustache and fierce eyes. I forget his name, but he had the deepest chip on his shoulder of anyone I've ever met, so I'll call him 'Scowling Face'. The least thing annoyed him. Invariably, there was something in the newspaper to get angry about. When he found out I went to church on Sundays, he told me he didn't believe any of that rubbish. One day, he started mouthing off about how ridiculous it was that Jehovah's Witnesses refused to accept blood transfusions. Then he turned his attention to the Mormons. "How come there's no black people in their churches?" he asked. "They can't be Christian if they don't accept black people." Apparently, he had discovered that Mormons had a very prejudiced view of black people. To be fair, I believe they've changed their views on this since then, although I certainly wouldn't call them Christians either.

The other sweeper on the electric dustcart was Willy (or 'Wullie', as 'Scowling Face' called him). He was a soft-spoken man originally from Aberdeen, who walked with a pronounced limp. When we arrived at the area we had to sweep, he and I took our brushes, went to opposite sides of the street and started sweeping. You pushed it in front of you with a rhythmic motion as you walked along the

gutter: "Shhh, Shhh, Shhh"—"Shhh, Shhh, Shhh"—
"Shhh, Shhh, Shhh."

It was a welcome relief to stop for lunch, open our
packed lunches, have a drink of tea from our flasks and
read the paper for a wee while before going on with the
work.

Wullie and I swept the dust and debris in the gutter into
little piles as we moved along and 'Scowling Face' came
behind us in the dustcart, picking up the piles of rubbish
with a shovel and throwing them into the bins on the
back of the cart. At the end of the day, sometimes on the
way back to the depot, 'Scowling Face' thoughtfully
made a detour in order to drop Wullie near his house. He
wasn't so nasty that he didn't look after his team. Wullie's
house was in Loons Road[1]—which, for a man from
'Aiberdeen', was very apt!

On the 'hand-cartie' days, my partner in crime was a man
called Tommy. He was about six inches smaller than me
and had a furtive, shifty, hangdog look about him. His jet-
black, oily hair was slicked back from his receding hair-
line and his lined face and hands were leathery brown
from long exposure to the weather. He only had a few
teeth, and his mouth always hung slightly open, which
made him look rather vacant. Besides his 'Rizla' cigarette
paper, lighter and tin of tobacco, he always carried a
packet of Beecham's Powders in his pocket.

The day usually began by pushing the cartie over to the
council estate across the road, which was lined with rows
of 1950s flats, four in a block with a communal entrance,
or 'closie'. There was a grassed area in front of each flat.
We parked the 'cartie' at one end of the street, but instead of each of us sweeping opposite sides, Tommy in-

sisted I walk to the end of the block and brush back towards him on the same side of the road. We would start brushing and meet in the middle, so that there wasn't so far to go to fetch the 'cartie' when we started shovelling up the piles of dirt. There may have been some method in his madness, but I soon discovered that Tommy either had no stamina — or — a self-imposed policy of doing as little as possible so long as possible. Or both. Anyway, instead of keeping going till the usual mid-morning break, Tommy worked a couple of streets, then parked the cartie outside a block of flats. He walked up to the entrance of the 'closie' and stood just inside the doorway. Then he rolled a cigarette, licked the paper, struck a Swan Vesta[2] iin his cupped hand and lit up with a sharp sucking intake of air through his pencil thin roll-up. He stood there, nervously smoking, keeping a weather eye out for the foreman, who occasionally came to check up on the street sweeper teams. If Tommy saw the foreman in the distance, he quickly stubbed out his fag, hurried back to the 'cartie', grabbed his brush, and started sweeping industriously.

I hated standing about idle and usually tried to keep working while Tommy took his unofficial breaks. At around five or ten to eleven each morning, no matter which part of the estate we had reached, Tommy downed tools and wheeled the cartie to the back of the housing scheme into a small industrial estate, where at eleven o'clock he rendezvous'd with one of the other sweeper teams in the doorway of a large factory. The chief attraction was the big metal vending machine just inside the door, which, in return for a few coins, dispensed hot tea, coffee and hot chocolate into cream-coloured plastic cups. Tommy always bought himself a drink and stood holding it in his shaking hand while staring straight ahead. Sometimes he took out his packet of Beecham's Powder, extracted a sachet and with trembling hands, carefully opened the folded paper. Then with a quick tilt back of his head, he poured the white powder onto his tongue. I asked him once why he was taking them. He said, "To steady my nerves."

Eddie was a sweeper on one of the other hand-cart teams. We regularly met up with him at the vending machine. He was older than Tommy and wore glasses and peered at you through very thick lenses. He was also extremely deaf, despite wearing two hearing aids. Anytime you spoke to him, Eddie cupped his hand to his 'good' ear, turned his head towards you and leaned into your personal space, shouting "EH?"

On Friday afternoons we got away early, so I used to take the bus down to the Olympia swimming pool, which was knocked down a few years ago to make way for the new waterfront development. To get there, I walked across the walkway above the road between the Leisure Centre and the high-rise block known as Tayside House, which housed the council offices. At the Olympia, I booked an hourly session in one of the private bathrooms. These were downstairs in the basement, along the corridor from the Turkish baths. For a couple of pounds, they provided you with a fresh white bath towel, a bar of soap and a sachet of shampoo. It was great to luxuriate in a hot bath filled to the brim after a week of tramping around the streets, pushing a brush.

I didn't have a washing machine in the flat, so every Saturday morning I used to stuff my weeks' washing into my sports bag and take the bus from Blackness Road at the bottom of Cleghorn Street to the Laundrette in Lochee. Lochee was, and to some extent still is, a little self-contained 'village' within the city. There was a genuine community feeling about the place back then. All the shopkeepers knew each other and passed the time of day with locals and with the taxi drivers who lined the pavement just along from the Laundrette. I sat and read a book in the Laundrette while waiting for my washing to finish. Sometimes I went for a walk around Lochee High Street or had a haircut in the Barbers Shop on the corner. When the clothes were dry, I walked or caught the bus back to the flat and had some lunch before heading to the train station to catch the train for Ladybank and my overnight stay at Hilton of Forthar.

∾

37 ADVENTURES IN LONDON

In my final year at Dundee, with thoughts turning to the practicalities of getting a job, I applied for teacher training at Dundee College of Education in Broughty Ferry. The head of the Education Department at Gardyne College interviewed me. From the way he conducted the interview, I got the distinct impression he'd already decided I wasn't teacher material. To my great disappointment, a letter followed in the post telling me I had been "unsuccessful on this occasion."

Like Dick Whittington, I went to seek my fortune in London. Why they didn't make me Lord Mayor, I have no idea, but I eventually had to admit that my enterprising foray into Sassenach country had been a bit of a wild goose chase. On the positive side, I gained vital experience in the school of life, so the episode wasn't entirely wasted. Sometimes we learn more from the dead-ends, failures and challenging events in life, than we do when everything goes swimmingly.

I got off the train at Kings Cross Station in London, without having a place to sleep for the night. Not wishing to impose myself on friends in the church, I went looking for accommodation. The few places I tried in the limited time I had to find a bed for the night, were too expensive or full up, so in desperation, I booked myself into a Salvation Army hostel where several unkempt, odd looking characters were sitting or standing about outside. The only good thing about it was that it was cheap. In exchange for less than a fiver, I got a worn but clean pillowcase and duvet cover and was allocated the top bunk of a bed in the dormitory. During the night, wild cries and shouts emanated from the poor soul in the bunk below me. His nightmare seemed to last all night. I hardly slept a wink. It was a great relief to check out next morning with my few belongings intact.

I found a phone box and rang Madame Tussaud's to ask if there were any vacancies for figurative sculptors. I imagined myself sculpting portrait busts of famous people for their waxwork museum. Unfortunately, they didn't have any vacancies. Helpfully though, they suggested I try 'Gems Wax Models', a rival waxwork company based in North Kensington who supplied various wax museums in Britain and abroad. I made my way there, post-haste. John Bates, the managing director at 'Gems' informed me they already had two freelance sculptors who did most of their work, but if I was interested, he could give me a temporary job in their factory, which manufactured fiberglass mannequins for shop windows. I saw this as my opportunity to get a foot in the door and gladly accepted.

I found a (so called) 'B&B' within walking distance of North Kensington. Unfortunately, the price was extortionate, and I could only afford it for a few nights. It was a house in which they had partitioned off every room, creating two or three narrow cells, each with a bed, a door that locked and just about enough space for a shelf on which was placed the 'Continental Breakfast'. This consisted of a plate with a tiny plastic wrapped croissant, a kettle and cup with a tea bag and a small plastic pot of long-life milk. Talk about being 'ripped off'. I was not sorry when I handed back the keys.

Fortunately, Stef Freeman, a Canadian girl who worked in the Wax Models department at Gems, heard I was looking for digs and offered me a room in her flat in Chiswick until I got myself sorted out. I was very grateful for the 'breathing space' this gave me.

When I went to the meeting at Wembley on the Sunday morning, Graham Smith found out where I'd been spending the previous few nights and scolded me for not getting in touch. Graham was from Innerleithen and his father and mother knew my parents well, since Mum's paternal aunts lived in nearby Walkerburn. They were in the Church of God in Innerleithen. Graham worked for a Graphic Design firm. It so happened he was moving out of his digs near Ealing Broadway and was looking for a place nearer his work. Stef's flat in Chiswick was a better location for him, so we did a swap and I moved into the bedsit in the attic space of the house he vacated. It was a decent enough house with a path leading up the garden to the front door. It was owned by a Roman Catholic Polish family who lived in the lower part of the house. The lady of the house was a force to be reckoned with. The best word I can think of to describe her is haughty. She was a small, buxom woman with greying hair neatly tied back in a bun. On the few occasions when I had to interact with her, she appeared to regard me with a mixture of disdain and suspicion. She had a strong Polish accent and whenever she referred to the previous occupant of my flat, she pronounced his name as 'Grah-ham'. This always brought a smirk to my mouth, but it made her regard me with even more suspicion! One day, she saw me going out to church with my Bible in hand. She drew herself up to her full five feet and said archly: "We are Cat-o-leek!" She reminded me of Manuel, in 'Fawlty Towers': ("I know no-theeng! I am from Barcelona!")

The Gems factory was a rambling old building, several streets away from the smart offices and wax technician's workshop. Entry was via a narrow lane near the famous Portobello Road. Entering the building, the first thing one noticed was the overpowering chemical smell of fiber-glass resin. Industrial sized electric fans on each window, clogged with thick grimy dust, added a constant background hum. Despite this, the fumes were all pervasive.

Fiberglass technician at GEMS Wax Models,
London

The company was dissolved in 1999, and I wasn't able to find the address of the factory when I searched online. I think it was in Dunworth Mews near Notting Hill. Anyway, most of the workers were West Indians who jabbered away to each other in the Creole Patois dialect. I hardly understood a word they said. 'Issy' was the foreman. A big, confident West Indian from Grenada, he had a shiny bald head and sported a moustache and a pair of black-rimmed glasses. Issy showed me how to prepare a re-usable fiberglass mould so that they could refill it with sil-icone rubber, from which the legs, arms torso and heads of the fiberglass mannequins were produced. First, I cleaned off all the encrusted fiberglass gel-coat that had seeped out of the joints, and wiped over the moulds with acetone. Next, I applied red wax 'Mansion Polish' with a brush, then brushed a layer of pink liquid over it, which dried to a papery thickness to form a separation layer. I rubbed on another layer of wax. Then I brushed the resin gel coat on, taking care to avoid air bubbles. While the gel-coat was setting but still tacky, I added chopped strand fiberglass squares overlapping them for extra strength, and brushed on a thinner type of resin called 'lay-up' resin. The fiberglass outer sections were screwed together with wing-nuts while the resin was still tacky. I poured a final mixture of catalysed resin in and rolled it around the mould to ensure the seams were sealed. It was messy, sticky, smelly work.

Issy spent most of his time casting the wax hands and heads, using plaster and silicone moulds. He was a real craftsman. In the same workshop but in an adjacent room, was the little Cockney man who made silicone moulds. He took infinite care, surrounding the original piece to be cast with a layer of plasticine before casting a fiberglass mould surround for each half, then pouring the turquoise-coloured liquid silicone into the space between the fiberglass and the original piece, which he had sealed with a protective coating of wax or vaseline. They made the outer fiberglass moulds with flanges around the edge of each half, so that they easily fitted onto their counter-part. The flanges were drilled and fitted with wing nuts to hold them together.

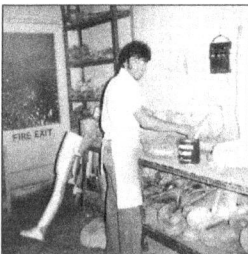

Sammy, at his bench in GEMs fibreglass workshop

I worked at a bench alongside a boy named Sammy from Cork in the Irish republic. He had rosy cheeks, jet black hair and Elvis style sideburns. When I asked where he was from, he said "Carck". ("Where?" — "Carck!") Eventually, I worked out what he meant. Sammy was always happy and sang along with the radio as he worked. One day he asked if I'd ever read the 'Bhagavad Gita'? I said "no". I'd no idea what he was talking about, but from his description, I guessed it involved explicit information about sexual matters. On checking online, I think he probably meant the Kama Sutra, since the Bhagavad Gita has more to do with Hindu philosophy than anything of that nature. Most likely he'd heard about it from his Indian friend (who also worked in the factory and took on house painting jobs at the weekend). The two of them used to go out on the town on Friday nights and, by all accounts, had a wild time drinking and womanising.

The West Indian workers were nice guys. Everyone wore white overalls provided by the company. There was Winston, a big, strong, smiling faced man who operated a power tool with a small circular blade on it. He used this to trim the fiberglass moulds and smooth off the excess gel coat from the joins.

An older, slightly built man with greying hair, glasses and a neatly trimmed moustache was more reserved. I learned he was a Seventh Day Adventist. He maintained a more aloof attitude towards me, although always polite. He was a careful, scrupulously tidy man.

Winston, preparing to cast a waxwork head, GEMs workshop. (Notice the wax hands hanging up!

Every Friday afternoon, work finished earlier than usual. Around four o'clock, all the workers gathered to drink a few cans of beer in the kitchen area upstairs before going home. They swapped stories and chatted away in their Creole dialect, laughing and enjoying the chance to relax together after a hard-working week.

On Sundays after the Remembrance at Wembley, I was usually invited to one or other of the saints' houses for Sunday lunch. In those days, when the church was more numerous, there was an evening Gospel meeting as well as the morning meeting. One of those generous saints was a little old Welsh lady who lived on the ground floor of a block of luxury flats. Before she retired, she had operated a bed-and-breakfast in London (a proper one, not the rip off variety). Her name was Mrs Avon-Jones, but everyone called her 'Auntie Muff'.

The first time I visited Auntie Muff, she asked where I was from. I said "from Greenock—my father is John Johnson", naively assuming Dad's fame had spread far and wide. I've never forgotten her reply. She said in her direct, down-to-earth Welsh accent: "Oh, so you've a good pedigree!" It taught me the folly of trying to bask in reflected glory. Auntie Muff loved having young people round to the house, and the young teenagers and singles often ended up there on Sunday afternoons. There was quite a crowd. Alistair Coomer (Neville and Helen's son) had come to London after graduating at Paisley University and was a sales executive with a company called Pioneer Mortars. Phil Ashman, nicknamed 'Flashman' (what else?), was a young Welshman a few years older than me. He was a manager with MFI, the flat-pack furniture and kitchen unit company. Alistair used to tease him rotten about the questionable quality of MFI products. Flashman took it all in good fun and enjoyed the repartee.

Graham Smith was a Christian gentleman. He had a great care for others and a concern for sharing the gospel. Every December, Graham made beautiful, handmade, quirky little Christmas cards, thoughtfully presenting the wonder of the incarnation.

Penny Luck and Peter Gault were 'an item'. She had come to London from Leicester. Pete, originally from Scotland, worked as an air-traffic controller. His father was Jack Gault, an able speaker and writer in the Fellowship[1]. Penny was a vivacious, good-looking girl with dark wavy hair, a great figure and a warm personality. She sometimes played Auntie Muff's piano. I envied her ability to play 'The Moonlight Sonata' from the music. Actually, Penny was the daughter of a Scottish lady from Greenock, whose maiden name was Nancy McKinnon. According to Dad, Nancy was a very attractive girl. He told me that as young men, both he and Uncle Joe had 'had a notion' for Nancy. Her younger brother George was just a boy. Uncle Joe bought a pet rabbit for George and used that as his excuse to visit the McKinnon's house and chat up Nancy whenever he got the chance. In the end, neither of them got her, and she married David Luck from Leicester. 'All's fair in love and war'!

On one occasion, I invited all the young folks to my flat. I made a big pot of pasta and, when it was ready, I held the pot lid firmly on, to stop the pasta falling out as I poured out the boiling water. Graham had come in to the kitchenette to help me get things ready. Suddenly—disaster! The lid slipped and all the pasta fell into the sink. Panic stations! Thankfully Graham saved the day. With a reassuring chuckle he said, "don't worry, we'll spoon it back into the pot". My reputation as a cook was intact.

After some time working in the factory, John Bates asked me to transfer to the wax department, where Stef

Freeman was responsible for making wax heads look like real people. For me, this was a step up from working in the factory. I enjoyed the more creative aspects of this work. Stef showed me how to apply thin layers of oil paint to build up the correct facial complexion—how to paint subtle bluish veins onto the wax hands—how to attach real human hair (from China!) one strand at a time, into a wax head with a needle, and how to set glass eyes into the eyeball sockets. To do that, you had to cut away the wax eyeball and then, from the inside of the hollow wax head, stick the glass eye in behind the eyelids with molten wax. Stef was excellent at what she did and gave me expert tuition. She had long tresses of fragrant blonde hair which, on one occasion, accidentally fell across my face as she demonstrated a painting technique. One day she asked if I'd like to share her lunch—she had made a delicious dish with a mixture of brown rice and fried egg.

Two older men looked after the wardrobe department for the wax dummies. One was a tall, thin, white-faced character, who barely spoke a word. He glided silently about the place. One day, I got the uncomfortable feeling that he was watching me from behind the door. The other man was a flamboyant, talkative man, very entertaining and obviously 'gay'. He told me he'd been brought up in a religious family—his father had been an Anglican Priest. His favourite place was San Francisco. He made it quite clear his reason for going there was to meet other like-minded men. He often consulted with Stef about which clothes were appropriate for this or that wax figure. They shipped the finished pieces to wax museums in Britain and across the world. For example, while I was there, Stef organised a significant display for the Edinburgh Wax Museum.

I enjoyed the regular social life among the saints in Wembley, and my work at Gems Wax Models Ltd., was not unpleasant. After the best part of six months, however, during which I had (in my spare time) sculpted a head in clay as a sample for John Bates, I questioned whether my future lay there. The work was interesting enough, but living in London was very expensive and there seemed little opportunity for promotion.

I followed up on my original intention and applied for teacher training in England. I went for an interview at Liverpool Polytechnic and was accepted for the 1981/82 Art teacher training course. Around the same time, the Churches of God launched the 'LSV' (Lord's Servants Volunteer) scheme, to encourage young people to take a year out and accompany some of our full-time evangelists, assisting with various outreach efforts among the Churches. I thought this was a better way of spending my time between January and August '81 when the teacher training course started. So, I applied and became the first volunteer on the scheme. I packed in my job, informed the landlady that her flat would again be vacant, said cheerio to my good friends in Wembley and took the train home to Scotland.

~

38 SHETLAND, WITH HARRY KING AND JOHN BLACK

My first assignment on the LSV scheme was to accompany Harry King and John Black senior on a month-long visit to Shetland, to encourage the small Church of God in Lerwick and reach out with the gospel to the local community. Harry had his prophetic chart with him since he planned to deliver a series of meetings on Bible prophecy.

We took the train from Glasgow to Aberdeen, where John Thomson met us. He took us to his house for a cup of tea before going on to Peterculter to stay overnight with Leonard and Hilda Ross.

Leonard and Hilda's youngest son Roger was a cocky wee chap of about eight or nine. We were sitting in the lounge talking when suddenly Roger said to me in his round Aberdeen accent: "You smell!"

Back then, I was still rather shy in company and Roger's remark focussed the company's unwelcome attention on me for a moment of sheer embarrassment. Perhaps I'd been sweating a lot that day, I don't know, but wrongly or rightly, I assumed he was referring to the smell of my breath. Of course, like all good boys, I brushed my teeth twice a day—except that back then we'd never heard of dental floss, so I probably had lots of decaying particles lodged in various cavities between my teeth. Also, since having my adenoids removed as a boy, I occasionally coughed up creamy little blobs from the back of my throat, which stank like a drain. Whatever the cause, I cleaned my teeth with extra vigour and double the amount of toothpaste that night.

Next day, we had a few hours to kill before the ship left for Shetland, so Leonard dropped off Harry, John and me beside some high-rise flats not far from the Aberdeen shoreline. I disappeared into the lift of one block while Harry and John went into the next high-rise block. When I reached the bottom flat, a plump young mother with several young children invited me in for a chat. I took this as an opportunity to share the gospel with her. After about half an hour, I realised it was time I caught up with Harry and John, so I thanked her for the cup of tea she'd made and said "Cheerio."

Outside, it was drizzling with rain, and Harry and John were nowhere to be seen. Suddenly, I spied Harry in the distance and shouted over to him. He didn't look too pleased. When I caught up with him, John appeared from the entrance to an adjoining block of flats. They demanded to know where I'd been. I told them a lady had invited me in, and so forth.

It gradually dawned on me that they'd been frantic with worry, searching for me, thinking something awful had happened—and all the time I was sipping tea, chatting to an Aberdeen 'wifie'. As far as they were concerned, I'd vanished. I fully deserved the telling off. It was an early lesson in the importance of communication within teams, making sure everyone is aware of each other's movements.

~

WE BOARDED the good ship 'St Clair' in Aberdeen harbour, a sea-going vessel with passenger berths below deck. I had a cabin to myself and John and Harry shared a cabin further down the corridor.

There was a report of some incoming bad weather, but the captain set sail, hoping to cross the notorious stretch of the North Sea between Orkney and Shetland before the storm hit. There was an interesting mix of passengers. One of them was a tall, well-spoken Englishman, a Roman Catholic priest on his way to Shetland for the first time. After several hours' sailing, the sea gradually became rougher until the ship began to roll and heave from side to side as it plunged on through the waves. This went on into the night. Both Harry and John felt seasick and went to lie down in their cabin.

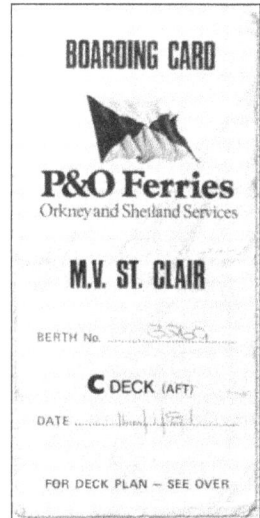

BOARDING CARD

P&O Ferries
Orkney and Shetland Services

M.V. ST. CLAIR

BERTH No. 335

C DECK (AFT)

DATE ....

FOR DECK PLAN – SEE OVER

Boarding Pass, St Clair

Around eleven o'clock, I went downstairs to my cabin after looking at the night sky on the upper deck. As I was walking along the narrow corridor, the whole ship suddenly shuddered and keeled over to the left. In front of me, a ship's steward shifted his feet over to the edge the corridor floor to keep his balance. Instead of his body being parallel with the walls as he walked along, he was now in a diagonal position, between the bottom corner of the corridor and the opposite corner on the ceiling above. I turned round and went back upstairs to find out what was going on. When I passed the galley, I saw a pile of broken china plates and cups strewn all over the floor. As I emerged on the upper deck, a man opened the side door of the wheelhouse, and walked along the deck above me. His head and face was covered in blood. The ship heaved up, and then down, as it sank into, and emerged from the gigantic waves crashing over the bows. I looked up at the stars and noticed they were in a different position in the sky. "We must have changed course," I thought. By this time, I was tired of running around the ship like an excited schoolboy. I decided that the warmth of a bunk below decks was the best place to be on a night like this.

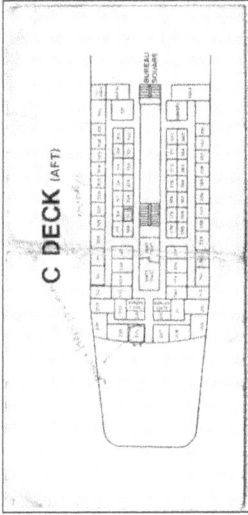

C Deck Plan, St Clair

I woke to the sun shining through the cabin porthole. I got washed and dressed—cleaned my teeth thoroughly (thank you Roger Ross)—and went to the dining area for breakfast with Harry and John. Just then, one of the ship's officers informed us, that a freak wave had hit the ship during the storm the previous night. It had smashed the wheelhouse window and damaged the radar equipment. The ship had turned round and we were back in Aberdeen!

Harry enjoyed telling the folks in Lerwick, how in the morning, when he looked out the cabin window and saw modern, high-rise buildings, he said to John Black, "My, my, Lerwick's changed!" They gave all the passengers free meals while we waited for the repairs to be done before setting sail once more.

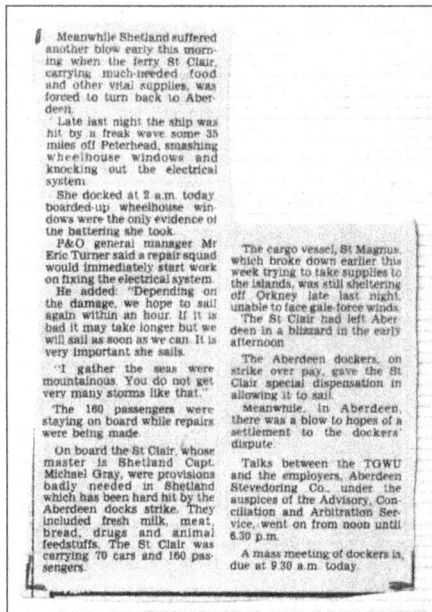

Meanwhile Shetland suffered another blow early this morning when the ferry St Clair, carrying much-needed food and other vital supplies, was forced to turn back to Aberdeen.

Late last night the ship was hit by a freak wave some 35 miles off Peterhead, smashing wheelhouse windows and knocking out the electrical system.

She docked at 2 a.m. today boarded-up wheelhouse windows were the only evidence of the battering she took.

P&O general manager Mr Eric Turner said a repair squad would immediately start work on fixing the electrical system.

He added: "Depending on the damage, we hope to sail again within an hour. If it is bad it may take longer but we will sail as soon as we can. It is very important she sails.

"I gather the seas were mountainous. You do not get very many storms like that."

The 160 passengers were staying on board while repairs were being made.

On board the St Clair, whose master is Shetland Capt. Michael Gray, were provisions badly needed in Shetland which has been hard hit by the Aberdeen docks strike. They included fresh milk, meat, bread, drugs and animal feedstuffs. The St Clair was carrying 70 cars and 160 passengers.

The cargo vessel, St Magnus, which broke down earlier this week trying to take supplies to the islands, was still sheltering off Orkney late last night, unable to face gale-force winds.

The St Clair had left Aberdeen in a blizzard in the early afternoon.

The Aberdeen dockers, on strike over pay, gave the St Clair special dispensation in allowing it to sail.

Meanwhile, in Aberdeen, there was a blow to hopes of a settlement to the dockers' dispute.

Talks between the TGWU and the employers, Aberdeen Stevedoring Co., under the auspices of the Advisory, Conciliation and Arbitration Service, went on from noon until 6.30 p.m.

A mass meeting of dockers is due at 9.30 a.m. today.

Cutting from Aberdeen Press and Journal

When we finally arrived in Lerwick, Graham Nicol met us at the pier when we disembarked. He took us in his car to his grandparents' house, where we stayed for the duration of our trip. Walter and Evelyn Briggs, Graham's grandparents, had moved from Yorkshire to live near their daughter, Joan, who had married Sandy Nicol, a Shetlander. Tragically, Sandy had died suddenly around 1978. He was out fishing in a small boat with his youngest son Lindsay when he had a heart attack and died.

Walter was a typical Yorkshireman, a larger-than-life character who happily offered his opinions in a forthright way, whether you wanted to hear them or not!

He'd worked on the railways in the North of England and had a collection of postcards of famous locomotives.

Walter and Evelyn lived in a whitewashed house at number 17 Twageos Road, on the other side of a hill in Lerwick, looking across to the Island of Bressay. The name 'Twageos' comes from the proximity of two (twa) 'geos', or linear clefts in a cliff beside the sea, where the rocks have been eroded or a cave has collapsed. So it was a bracing place to live—perhaps not too different from the Briggs ancestral homeland in North-East of England. Evelyn Briggs was an excellent cook. For Sunday lunch, she made each of us a large Yorkshire pudding, which she served on a plate on its own with gravy, as a starter to the meal. Delicious!

I usually spent the mornings distributing gospel leaflets and invitations to Harry's meetings. Later on, when I'd been round all the streets in Lerwick, I took the ferry to Bressay, and leafleted all the houses there.

The Church of God in Lerwick met (and still does) in a little wood-panelled hall about three quarters of the way up a steep hill, accessible only by a pedestrian path. David Smith, one of the overseers, met us at the door, and shook hands warmly. He and his wife Margaret had been born and brought up in Lerwick. They had a daughter named Yvonne. David was the manager of a furniture shop in town and they lived in a substantial, stone-built upstairs flat, near the town centre.

Like several Shetlanders, they also owned a small country cottage which had a peat bog included in the title deeds. Every Shetlander had the right to dig their own peats and dry them out for use as fuel to heat their homes.

Playing Scrabble with Harry King and Walter and Evelyn Briggs

During the winter in Shetland, the hours of daylight are very short and it gets dark around four o'clock. So the work had to be done while it was day, just as the Lord said, 'the night comes, when no man can work'. This was true in a literal sense in Shetland. We spent our evenings visiting local saints or relaxing with the Briggs. Walter and Evelyn enjoyed playing Scrabble, and we spent a fair bit of time doing that. I had brought my accordion and our friends in Shetland enjoyed listening to me bashing out a few hymn tunes.

Chart illustrating Bible prophecy, on the wall
of Myrtle Hall, Lerwick. painted by Jackie
Forbes of Kirkintilloch

Harry hung his Bible prophecy chart on the wood-panelled wall in Myrtle Hall and spent several nights giving a
detailed presentation of the future events foretold in the
Bible. Harry was a riveting speaker who spoke, not just
with the authority of a man who knew his subject, but
with great force of character and spiritual power. Several
folk from other evangelical churches in the town attended
the meetings, and also a few people who'd previously
been in the Church of God there.

Stewart Nicol was a big, strong, twenty-something man.
He worked at Sullom Voe Oil terminal and drove a BMW.
Recently, he'd become friendly with a Glasgow girl who
was working in Shetland. He brought her to Harry's meetings. I'm not sure whether their friendship lasted. His
brother Angus was going steady with a girl called Wendy
who worked in the Lerwick branch of the Royal Bank of
Scotland. She was a friendly, outgoing girl. John Black
discovered that her father kept his caravan at Newmains
Farm, which was a remarkable coincidence. I only met
Angus briefly at the beginning of our visit because he
was preparing to leave for a work placement in Canada.
It was great to make his acquaintance properly a few

years ago, when he visited the church in Buckhaven when he came down to attend his daughter's graduation ceremony at St Andrews University.

Graham Nicol was a motor engineer at a local garage. He was extremely generous with his free time at weekends and took us all over Shetland in his car. All the Nicol boys were mad keen on birdwatching. Graham was also building a boat in a large shed near the beach. He took us to see it. The scale of it impressed me.

I wrote home, telling Dad and Mum and the family about my experiences. I kept the draft copy I'd made of that letter, which I've transcribed at the end of this chapter, along with the transcription of a letter I received from Walter Briggs later in the year.

Harry was well known by many people in Shetland, having visited frequently over the years. Shetland had a special place in his heart and the saints held him in high regard.

Lerwick Schoolchildren enjoying Up Helly AA

During our visit, the annual 'Up Helly AA' festival took place. This is the winter fire festival which celebrates the

Norse and Viking origins of the Shetland people. Every year, the townspeople form an Up Helly AA committee, assigning jobs to various individuals, groups, school-children, teachers, parents and businesses. This includes the making of Viking costumes and swords as well as learning a variety of rousing songs, written for the occasion by a local musician during the 19th Century. The most important job by far, though, is the building of a giant wooden replica of a Viking longboat, which transports the 'Guiser Yarl' and his team of men, all of whom dress up like Viking warriors. They parade the impressive wooden ship through the streets while a team of bearded warriors sit in the boat. Together with the other 'Viking' teams accompanying them on foot, they sing their manly songs and wend their way through the town. The procession ends at the harbour, where the Viking warriors jump out, set the longboat on fire, and launch it into the sea.

On the night of the procession, David and Margaret Smith invited us to their house. After a lovely meal, we put on coats, hats and scarves—David gave me a deer-stalker to wear—and we sallied out into the cold night air to watch the procession. It was an unforgettable sight. The longboat was huge! All the men on it, as well as the cohorts of Vikings walking on either side, were holding huge burning torches, which cast a fiery orange glow as they passed. The singing was tremendously rousing stuff, and made the hairs on the back of your neck stand up. I took some photos in the dark with my very basic camera, but the results, when they came back from the chemist shop, were just a blur of orangey yellow against a smoky black background.

Harry wasn't looking forward to the return sea journey to Aberdeen. He was relieved when Leonard Ross arranged for him and me to fly back. John Black had left a week earlier as he had business to attend to back home. Graham Nicol drove us down to Sumburgh Airport, passing through the hamlet of Dunrossness where we had visited an old brother called Jimmy Bairnson earlier in the week. He was just over 80 in 1981. His wife, Ellen had written several poems which he compiled and got the local newspaper to print several copies of the booklet after she died on 27th August 1975, aged 72. Jimmy gave me a copy of her little book of poems, entitled *'In Praise of the Saviour'*. I've reproduced three of her poems in the Appendix.

We boarded the twin-engined British Airways plane and took our seats. It was only the second time I'd flown and the excitement factor was high. The pilot taxied out to the end of the exposed runway beside the sea. He turned the plane round and, without stopping, gave it full throttle. A momentary lurch to the left, then full tilt towards the waves which lapped the beach at the end of the runway —and suddenly we were airborne! It was a beautiful day, and I snapped away with my camera as I looked out the window and watched the islands below disappear into the distance.

~

TRANSCRIPTION **of the letter I wrote to Dad and Mum, in January 1981**

Dear folks,

We are having quite a good time up here in Shetland. Glad to say Mrs Briggs seems to be a good bit better now.

About four or five believers not in Fellowship have been attending the meetings, but apparently two or three of them just go anywhere.

The biggest family in the church in Lerwick is the Nicol boys whose father died suddenly about two years ago. The three oldest, Stewart, Graham and Angus are working and Lindsey is still at school. Stewart and Angus have brought two girls along to the meetings. One of them—Wendy, works in the Bank and comes from Bishopton and her father has a caravan on Newmains Farm!! Quite a surprising coincidence for John Black when he found out.

We have been out with tracts most afternoons (I've been stamping tracts in the mornings while John and Harry have been writing letters etc.), then in the evenings, it's either visiting people or meetings. On Saturday Graham Nicol took us away out to Ollaberry (where there used to be a church) and we visited two older ladies who used to be with us. Maisie Ratter and Jean Peterson (I think). They live on a 'peerie' croft (peerie is the Shetland word for 'wee') with an old peat fire with a chain hanging down to heat the kettle on. There was a short power-cut, so they put on a Tilley lamp — it was like taking a trip into the past. They hand knit Shetland jumpers and will take orders. (John Black ordered one for himself —price £26.) They're real old fashioned characters, beautiful speakers ('chon' instead of John and such like).

We also visited another old character — Jesse, in Lerwick, who's over 83 and plays a piano and a wee (peerie) kind of harp thing. We had a musical evening with my accordion and Harry on his mouth organ. She made us sausage and egg and as many oatcakes as we liked. (But her tea was like tar—I couldn't go to sleep that night, it was so strong!) Aye, she's a tough yin!

On Sunday afternoon Graham took us a one hundred mile run up the west side of Shetland and back. We saw the huge Atlantic waves and also the island of Foula (pronounced 'Foola') in the distance.

Tonight John Black is showing his slides of India to the children before the meeting. Tomorrow is Up Helly AA (burning of the Viking boat and procession) so that should be interesting. Have the photos I took of the church come out?

Well that's all for now,

Yours Jo

Transcription of Walter Briggs' letter to me:

2nd May 1981
17 Twagoes road,
Lerwick
Shetland
ZE1 OBB

Dear Joe,

I have meant to write to you since I first received your card from Swindon with the Great Western train pictured on it. Your card with the locomotive making so much smoke also gave rise to much thought. Yes you are right, I have not a one similar to that one but it evoked many memories, naturally, working on the 'line' I have seen many locomotives emitting steam and smoke as the engine driver pushed over the regulator to allow steam to enter the cylinder. If the fireman was replenishing fire at the same time, then also a fair amount of smoke came out of the funnel. I was on the Old North Eastern Railway which had a line from Leeds to Stockton passing through Harrogate and there were notices in Our Books of Regulations that great care had to be taken at Harrogate to keep smoke to a minimum. So, in or near Harrogate, the fireman kept off stoking up. Well so much for that.

When you were over at Swindon you would or will contact Robert Hawthorne, who really hails from Middlesbrough and is a helpful brother. We have learnt that his girlfriend is Margaret Black which is a very interesting thing to us.

I have heard from Harry King since he arrived in Australasia and have been able to pass on to him good news which I now send to you, Caroline Smith nee Gifford, has attended meetings regularly since you and Harry went home, sitting behind at the Remembrance with the very evident reason that she desired to be restored and we were glad to give her the right hand of welcome and Fellowship last Lords Day morning. So one of the family is back after so long a time due to prayer and Harry's visitings. So pray on for the rest of the family. Charlie and wife Winnie attend the gospel meeting only so far.

What I suppose has startled you is the news of the proposed departure of the Smith family to the mainland, the reason given that it was upon the transfer of Yvonne to Ayrshire. Kilmarnock was the town name David gave to me but Ayr is the place and the assembly there is the one they have chosen though their home will be in Alloway. Well though we are to be reduced in number we are not downhearted and look to the Lord to meet all our needs. So far, the Smiths are still here. Though they have sold their Country and town houses, the strange feature is that David has no job to go to but he told Tony Mitchell, the Lord will provide. I'm not happy about this aspect. Jessie went to Woodend Hospital, Aberdeen to have eye operations and since then has been in a convalescent Home but she is due back to Shetland shortly.

I have been pleased to see your name in intelligence and bits about your activities since you left us. Now I see that you hope God willing to help with the Gospel Van Work. It is a good worthwhile work and I'm sure that you will enjoy it. I look back with pleasure to my times with the England and Wales Van, both in Middlesbrough and South Wales when I spent a fortnight with Arthur Jones. So, as the time comes along we will think of you and pray for you also. I do not know if you know my son-in-law Jim Mitchell (Macduff). His mother died suddenly last Monday, his father did the same a little while ago, it makes for a good measure of sadness.

Now I trust that you keep well Joe. We often recall your helpful visit here. Give our warm regards to your parents.

I close with love in the Lord. My wife joins me in this.

Walter

Walter's wife added this note at the bottom:

We had Pamela for a week, in April, Rita my daughter from Florida last week, Margaret, Heather and two babies hoping to come next week from Macduff, Walter's sister from Scarborough and her daughter and granddaughter first 2 weeks in June. So I have had a rather busy time. Hope you keep well. Love to all friends, Evelyn.

39 GOSPEL VAN WORK, ENGLAND AND SCOTLAND

After Shetland, my next assignment took me down to Swindon, in Wiltshire, to work on the English Gospel Van with Brian Tugwell, one of the younger, full-time evangelists. The little church in Barrow-in-Furness, on the edge of the English Lake District in North West England, had invited him to assist with outreach. Brian and his wife, Elsie, had three little boys: Matthew, Paul and baby Andrew. They were a lovely, happy family. I enjoyed Brian's blend of seriousness and humour. Brian subsequently spent many years going back and forth to India, supporting and teaching the growing number of churches of God in that land.

I spent a few days giving out tracts in Swindon and met the saints in the assembly on Lord's Day. Joe Wannop was the local overseer—a friendly man who enjoyed a laugh. At that time, Bob Hawthorne was also living in Swindon. He was 'going steady' with Margaret Black, who he later married. One day, before we took the van to Barrow on Furness, Brian and Elsie took me to see the famous Uffington white horse—the 'prehistoric', 3000-year-old white horse carved into a chalk hillside close to Swindon. I'd seen photographs of it in books but it's enormous scale amazed me as we walked across the hill.

Elsie's brother Donald Doel, from Maidstone in Kent, joined us a couple of days later. Donald, (affectionately known as 'Doonie'), was a freckle faced, gap toothed, slightly balding chap of about twenty-eight. He walked with a limp because of a nasty accident—someone had knocked him off his moped and he ended up with a badly smashed hip and pelvis. It left him with one leg shorter than the other, and he couldn't walk more than a few miles before the pain became too much. Doonie had trained as a horticulturist and knew all about pruning apple trees and rearing young plants. He spoke with a droll, Kentish accent and was always ready to see the funny side of life.

When Doonie arrived, we set off for Manchester, where we picked up George Prasher, an uncle of Elsie and Doonie, also a full-time evangelist. When we arrived at Barrow, we met Trevor Sands, a brother in the church there. He kindly lent us the use of his static caravan on a lovely spot, overlooking one of the nearby lakes. We spent the week distributing tracts and knocking doors in Barrow, inviting people to the special meetings being held by George Prasher.

Back at the caravan each night, we'd sometimes re-hearse the answers to some of the common questions people might ask. Doonie had been researching the Mor-mons, who he jokingly called 'the morons'—because ap-parently, the Book of Mormon actually contained a section called 'The Book of Moroni'. (One wonders if

George Prasher, Brian Tugwell, Tom Meally, 'Doonie' (Donald) Doel

Joseph Smith was playing a secret joke on his gullible followers). One day, Doonie and I knocked on a woman's door in Barrow. We chatted with her for a while. Then she said: "You know these people that come round the doors? — Oh...what's their name... I've just forgotten... you know them people that come round all the time..." and with a mischievous twinkle in his eye, Doonie said "Is it the Morons?" Immediately the woman said "Yeah, that's it, the Morons"—and continued her story without a pause. Doonie kept a straight face, but I'm afraid I had to turn away to hide my suppressed laughter. As soon as we were clear, we both burst out laughing at the definite way she picked up Doonie's deliberate misnomer: "Yeah, that's it, the Morons!"

After Barrow, Brian and I said farewell to Doonie and George and we motored on to Nottingham, where we spent a week with a crowd of young people, helping them with their Easter holiday club for children at Glaisdale Hall. This involved lots of energetic storytelling activities and interactive drama productions.

Back in Scotland, after a week or two at home, Willy Horne, a brother in the church in Ashgill, arranged for me to go on the Scottish Gospel Van with evangelist Willie Stewart and the Irish preacher, David Rea, a retired brother from the church in Belfast. I had met David a few years prior to this, when I went over to help at the Northern Ireland Camp near Cookstown. (Willy Horne was the administrator for the LSV scheme, and reimbursed the expenses I incurred, as a volunteer.)

Willie Stewart was a kindhearted, godly man who looked and sounded very unassuming. He had a winning smile and was an expert in personal soul-winning. Willie had a comprehensive knowledge of the scriptures and spent an hour with me every morning, methodically going through the subject of the kingdom of God in scripture. I still have the notes I took during those sessions.

At Bathgate, Willie conducted special children's meetings, which were well attended. He had a gift for communicating with children, with lots of anecdotes and interesting illustrations to hold their attention. David preached the gospel each evening for two or three nights over that week. On a one-to-one basis, David had a softly spoken way with him and was easy to talk to. He was very particular about eating healthy food and told me that, in a recent survey, they had identified Weetabix as one of the most nutritious cereals one could eat. David's method of preparing his gospel addresses was to spend an hour or two each day reading his Bible, looking up the meanings of words in his large and weighty 'Young's Concordance', which he'd brought with him in his suitcase from Ireland. He preferred Young's because it makes it easy to follow the occurrences of the same Hebrew or Greek word throughout the scriptures. On the platform, David only used headings as prompts to bring back the 'meat' of what he'd gleaned in his study sessions. He was a powerful speaker and put everything he had into his delivery—so much so that he often took his white cotton handkerchief out of his pocket as he was speaking, to wipe the sweat from his brow.

From Bathgate we moved on to Cowdenbeath, where we slept on camp beds in the back room of the hall in Bridge Street, where, unless one of the saints invited us out, we made our own meals in the hall kitchen. Willie was a dab hand at mince and tatties! We visited Martin and Evelyn Notman during that visit. Ten years or so before our visit, Martin had become very ill with a rare autoimmune disorder called 'Good Pastures Disease'. He was given a life-saving kidney transplant in 1971. During our visit, while Evelyn was in the kitchen, Martin lay down on the living room floor and showed us a noticeable bulge in his lower abdomen, where the donor kidney was connected to his system. At the time of writing, despite many setbacks, Martin is still going strong with a fifty-year-old kidney from someone else's body. Without doubt, a living testimony to the amazing achievements of modern medicine; but more than that—a living testimony to the keeping power of God.

Evangelist Bernard French, 100 not out, Welsh Camp, 1981

That summer, just prior to starting my teacher training year at Liverpool Polytechnic, I spent several busy weeks going round three of the six youth camps run by the Churches—in Scotland, South Wales and the North West of England. The only camps I didn't spend time at that year were the camps at Killymoon in Northern Ireland, Cromer in Norfolk, and Shoreham in the South East of England.

40 LIVERPOOL

In September 1981, I travelled by train to Liverpool to start my Art teacher training course. I found digs in a terraced house in Errol Street, Aigburth. It was a quiet area on the South-West side of Liverpool, close to the river Mersey. The house was owned by Mary, a small, neatly dressed thirty-something lady who worked as a nurse. She had two rooms which she let out to students. My room was in the attic and below me, a Geography student from Holland called Jan (pronounced "Yan") who was working on his PhD. Jan was tall and studious, with a mop of fair hair. He spent most of his time in his room writing his thesis. Occasionally, I got a peek inside his room as I went up the narrow staircase to my attic bedsit. He had a big dot-matrix printer hooked up to a BBC Microcomputer, on which he plotted graphs and printed out complicated diagrams.

Mary saw me coming and going to church, with a Bible under my arm on Sundays. One day as I was having a cup of tea in the kitchen after college, she sat on a stool and told me she'd been brought up a Catholic but had become disillusioned and lost her faith. Why? Because, only an hour or two after her mother died, the priest came knocking and asked for money to say a prayer for her mother. He had no words of comfort. Mercenary motives instead of mercy. She was very bitter.

From Aigburth it was actually easier to get to Birkenhead than take the Sunday morning bus service across the city to the Church of God in Liverpool. So, every Sunday morning, I caught a train to Birkenhead. It rattled along beside the docks, took a deep dive into the bowels of the earth, through the tunnel under the Mersey, then into the light again at Birkenhead station. The Church of God in Birkenhead met at Atherton Hall, a lovely new building with plenty of windows and warm cedar wood panelling inside. There were around forty or fifty saints in the church, and they gave me a warm welcome. Three families regularly invited me to spend the day with them. Roland and Margaret Williams, Richard and Margaret Halpin and Alan and Joan Hyland. Roland and Margaret had four children: Felicity, Neil, Rosemary and Jonathan. Felicity was away at University most of the time while I was there, so I only met her once or twice. I got on well with Rosemary and Neil, who were in their final years at school. Jonathan was about ten or eleven and even then, had a precocious talent for drawing. He was in my Sunday School class. Jonathan later went to Edinburgh School of Art and made a name for himself as a Graphic Designer. (After I retired, I asked him to design the cover for my one and only colouring book, which, through no fault of his good work, ended up as a spectacular flop. But that's another story.)

Roland was a Pharmacist and Margaret a Primary teacher in a local Church of England School. Grey bearded Roland had a wise way with him, but was always ready to see the funny side of things. Margaret was full of life and very down to earth. Her mother, Mrs Balcombe, was an aunt of Helen Coomer's. I believe she and Willy Archibald in Glasgow were twins. She was a kindly old lady. Roland's mother, Granny Williams—a diminutive woman with a keen eye and a sharp tongue—usually came for lunch on Sundays. She was very deaf and sometimes didn't catch what people said, much to the amusement of Rosemary, Neil and Jonathan. Brian Johnston, who later went out full time in the Lord's work, was working as a Government Scientist in the North of England and was going steady with Rosemary. He used to visit her at weekends and they became engaged during my year in Liverpool and Birkenhead.

When I heard the news, I wrote the following poem. I was going to give it to them for their wedding, but never got around to sharing it until much later. I emailed it to them a few years ago. For me, these lines recapture the enjoyable times I spent with the Williams family in Birkenhead.

> For Brian and Rosemary's Wedding
> To Birkenhead came Brian J.,
> And met a lot of people,
> But when he saw "Her Loveliness",
> He thought "My, there's a bonny lass!"
> Her name was Williams – Rosemary,
> And to her house he went for tea;
> Her mother said "Sit down in here and make your-
>   self at home",

And so he did, upon the couch, inside the living
  room.
Then she came in!
His hands began to quiver,
And when she sat right down beside him,
His spine went all a'shiver!
He managed to compose himself, however,
And so they chatted for a while, together,
'Till Neil her brother came to say,
"Okay folks, it's time for tea."
They filed into the dining room,
Where father allocated seats – to guests, and then
  to family—
Imagine Brian's delight when placed,
Beside the lovely Rosemary!
When all were seated quietly,
The Sunday roast was laid upon the table,
Then all heads bowed respectfully,
As Father gave thanks for the meal.
"Amen", said everyone together,
And instantly the air with friendly clamour filled —
But Mother's voice rose strong above the rest—
"It's stretch or starve now,—help yourselves!"
Accordingly they all dived in,
With pleasant rumblings in each belly,
First the ladies then the men,
Scoffed meat, potatoes, peas and gravy!
So after tea with waistlines tight,
(not one could eat another bite),
They all retired into the lounge;
Then Granny thought she'd Brian question:
"What's your name young man" she said,
"If you do not mind me askin'?"
He tried to speak but only croaked,

"Ma'am, if you please, it's Brian".
"What did 'ee say?" Said Gran to 'Mosey,
And 'Mosey with a shout said "BRIAN!"
He looked at her a bit bemused –
To hear her shout he was not used.
The moment passed;
They settled down to conversation,
The clock struck seven; eight; then ten,
– TIME FOR BRIAN TO GO HOME!
His car outside was cold,
His heart inside was warm – he quickly drew her
    close,
And "SMACK!"
He kissed on the lips!
Then jumped into his Ford,
And make post-haste for home
Before the blushing girl had time,
To realise what happened!
Transfixed with joy was Rosemary,
She stood there on cloud nine,
Until her father shouted "Hoi!"
It's after half-past ten!"
So off she went to sleep and dream,
Of future days with Brian,
He, driving home was realising,
That he'd really started something!
Well since that day their friendship's grown,
At last he popped the question,
She answered "Yes," they got engaged,
And now as man and wife they're joined.
Your dreams at last come true!
And all the best we wish to you,
May God be with you all your days,
And love, and happiness.

∼

MARGARET AND RICHARD HALPIN had two primary aged girls, Joanne and Lindsey. Richard held a Bible class in their home on a Sunday afternoon once a month and they usually invited me for lunch on those days. Richard's nephew attended St Anselm's College and usually came along to the Bible class. One weekend, Margaret invited me to stay overnight with them. Richard met me after his work in Liverpool and I enjoyed the novelty of crossing the Mersey on the ferry with him.

Alan and Joan Hyland's daughter Susan was a brilliant student. She was in her final year at school before going '*up to*' Oxford, as they say in England. In Scotland, we just '*go*' to university—no metaphysical hill climbing. The other member of their household was a grumpy wee dog called 'Benjy'. He was quite old and had arthritis and various lumps on his body, so he probably had good cause to be grumpy.

Birkenhead Sunday school was a big Sunday School. Many of the children came from poor homes in a run-down council estate nearby. One regular was was a young man called John, who, as they say in Scotland, 'wisnae the full shilling'. Despite that, he had an exuberant character and gave us many a laugh. Rosemary and Neil made friends with several Chinese students who lived in Birkenhead. They used to come to the gospel meetings and then come up to the Williams' house afterwards. Being very family oriented, they highly valued this friendship.

My Art teacher training at Liverpool comprised of lectures, essays and projects, combined with blocks of teaching practice. One lecturer, named Eric, was a veteran of the Second World War. He had been a POW in a Japanese internment camp in the Far East and had good reason to be prejudiced toward 'the Japs' (as he called them). Many of his comrades had not survived. Eric taught a very useful class, which was optional, called 'The Voice', which I signed up for. The aim was to help trainee teachers use their voice effectively in the classroom without straining. He took us through a variety of exercises to make us aware of pitch, tone and volume, etc. One of the key things he taught us was to increase the volume while keeping the pitch low. This puts less strain on the vocal chords and also gives one's voice more authority. The thing to avoid at all costs was to increase the volume at a high pitch, which not only results in screaming but is more likely to damage the vocal chords. This advice was extremely helpful, not only when I started teaching, but also as a preacher and speaker at Church.

For my first teaching practice assignment, they sent me to St Anthony of Padua's Roman Catholic Primary school with another student, an opinionated, self-confident girl, whose name I forget. She and I used to meet beside a bus stop near Sefton Park and walk up to the school. She had been taught by Nuns at a convent school in London. The headmistress met us when we arrived on our first day. She made us welcome and handed us over to her Depute Head, an energetic, friendly man who had an excellent rapport with the children. Every morning, they started with school assembly and prayers. The Depute Head usually told a Bible story or a tale with a moral lesson. We enjoyed delivering our art lessons to the children in various classes. All too soon, however, our teaching practice ended there, and it was back to lectures, taking notes and writing essays for several weeks. After the Christmas holidays, we all had an extended teaching practice placement in the Art departments of various Secondary Schools throughout the city. They sent me to The Liverpool Bluecoat School, an independent, all boys Grammar school in the leafy suburb of Wavertree. Just before we began our secondary teaching practice, we had a very entertaining talk from an Art teacher in one of the local comprehensives. He imitated the way young adolescent boys of fifteen or sixteen shouted across the corridor at the tops of their newly broken voices instead of talking in normal tones.

I arrived at the grand, red-brick Bluecoat school, with its imposing sandstone entrance, and reported to the school office. I was shown into a plush, wood panelled room to meet the headmaster, Mr Peter Arnold-Craft. A brisk, efficient Englishman, he exchanged the usual pleasantries and instructed his secretary to call the Art master, Mr Jamieson.

Mr Jamieson, 'Head of Art and Craft', was a fat, balding man of about fifty. His world-weary expression gave the impression that he'd seen it all, and even if a bomb fell on him, would emerge as if nothing had happened. He wore a rumpled grey suit and spoke with a slightly careless, upper class drawl.

I followed Mr Jamieson through the building to the Art department, where he introduced me to his assistant, a younger man who spent most of his time in the pottery room teaching pupils to make hand-built ceramics. Mr

Jamieson's art room was a mess. There were mountains of paper and books stacked untidily on tables in every part of the room except the middle, where a few tables were arranged in a square for pupils to sit at. This was to be my main area of operations for three days of each week over the next few months. Mr Jamieson drew up a timetable for me, working between his room and the pottery room. At first, I did my best to deliver my lessons amidst Mr Jamieson's bomb-site of a room, but eventually I couldn't stand it any longer and tidied up during non-teaching periods and in the afternoon when the pupils had gone home. I suspected Mr Jamieson was suffering from depression. Whatever the reason, I don't know—he was a very reserved man and talked little. It seemed as if he'd allowed things to pile up for so long that the effort of doing something about it was now too much to face. It took a fair bit of work, but it was worth it for my sanity. He was grateful for my help and gave me a good reference when I left.

I had lunch at the staff table in the school dining room of the Bluecoat School. That was where I met their school chaplain, Stuart Olyott, the evangelical pastor of Belvidere Road Church. He had a great desire to reach others with the gospel and we had much in common. It was good to make his acquaintance. I later discovered he'd written a very accessible commentary on the book of Romans, which I still have in my library.

Back at the Polytechnic, we all looked forward to the informative and entertaining lectures given by a very experienced Scotsman by the name of Hamish McDonald (or was it McKay?) He was the senior lecturer in the Education department. He had qualifications in Educational and Clinical Psychology and had previously run a private child psychology clinic. One story he told us was about a little boy who was an elective mute and hadn't spoken to anyone for over a year. Hamish worked with him and his mother for several weeks, to no avail. By chance, he discovered the boy's mother was taking him to a party immediately after one of his therapy sessions. With the mother's permission, he said to the boy: "You're not leaving this room until you speak to me." An hour passed with no response. Finally, the boy turned to him and said: "I hate you!". Hamish punched the air as he told us this and said "Hurrah!' — it worked!"

In one of his lectures, talking to us about the relative value of the various subject disciplines in the educational development of children and young people, with characteristically flamboyant gesture, Hamish waved his outstretched arm at us with pointed finger and said: "You are the creme de la creme"! On another occasion, he used the same gesture to drive home the startling but true assertion: "Most learning takes place by copying." He was an excellent teacher.

One of the female tutors on the course was a very sincere Christian lady. She told me she was a Baptist. One day, she asked if she could pray with me. Inwardly, I wasn't keen on her doing that at all, but she was in a position of authority above me as my tutor, so I agreed. In her prayer she said "Lord, make Jo a **GOOD** Art teacher," which was very nice of her I suppose, but made me wonder — did she say that because I wasn't very good? On balance, looking back, I think her prayer was answered!

During my sojourn in Birkenhead, Bob Armstrong from the Church of God in Vancouver, another of our full-time evangelists, visited the Churches in Britain and Northern Ireland. With Jack Ferguson, he had recently co-authored an excellent primer on Bible Prophecy called *'The Finger of Prophecy'*. The church in Birkenhead invited him to give a series of meetings on the subject. They advertised the meetings locally and generated considerable interest. He was an electrifying and powerful speaker, who had a way of saying things that captured the imagination— some people thought he was too 'sensational'—but his use of language was never irresponsible and was always used to communicate scriptural truth in a direct and memorable way. For example, speaking about the coming again of the Lord Jesus to the air recorded for us in 1 Thessalonians chapter four, he said "millions will go to heaven in a giant airlift" and, talking about the immi- nence of the end times foretold in the Bible, "we're living on the thin edge of these end times." At the time of writ- ing, his addresses are available on SoundCloud by searching for 'theymaybeone Bob Armstrong'.

At the end of my teacher training, I scoured the Times Educational supplement for Art Teacher vacancies. I ap- plied for several and, to my surprise, was shortlisted for an interview on the Isle of Man. The Isle of Man Educa- tion Department paid my airfare and overnight stay on the Manx island. On the plane, an attractive-looking girl sat down beside me. To my surprise, she was also on the shortlist for the same job. Imagine my even greater sur- prise when I discovered she was a Bible believing Chris- tian from the South of England, associated with a Brethren church there. Her name was Petrina, and by the end of the flight, we had both agreed, that whatever the outcome, God's will would be done. We wished each other well in the interview. Our meeting was no coincidence. It was all overruled by our Father in heaven, who guides and directs his children according to His perfect will and purposes and makes no mistakes.

Before the interview, we toured the school with the Head of Art. He told us a small cottage was available for rent by the successful candidate. It sounded idyllic and raised the stakes considerably.

The interview took place in a large boardroom at the longest table I've ever seen, around which were seated about twenty solemn looking faces. Councillors, education officials, the headteacher of the school and who knows who else—all staring at you, analysing your answers. One of them was an old Scotsman, which made me feel a little better. I did my best to answer all their questions, but I knew I was up against a formidable candidate in Petrina. I think she knew it too, and so it turned out. She swept all before her and got the job.

A few years ago, I searched Google for 'Petrina, The Isle of Man'. Lo-and-behold, a website link for 'Petrina Kent' appeared, which took me to her online art gallery. She had left teaching and started painting full time. I dropped her an email and got a nice reply. It was good to make contact after all those years.

The other school with an art teacher vacancy which I applied to and visited was a Secure Unit in a residential school for emotionally disturbed young people in St Helens. The teacher who showed me round, locked the steel reinforced doors behind us as we moved from one part of the school to the other. He told me the students could become extremely violent without warning. On the way back to Liverpool, I tried to convince myself I could cope in such a challenging environment. It came as a relief when the letter arrived thanking me for my interest, but on this occasion, they'd not be inviting me back for interview. I decided not to give them another occasion. I turned my sights homeward and caught the train for Scotland.

∼

41 TEACHING ART, AYRSHIRE AND GLASGOW

I came back home to John Knox Street and started applying for Art Teacher vacancies. In 1982, the Scottish Education department had overestimated the number of student teachers needed, which meant there were too many newly qualified teachers competing for the same few jobs. The Education authorities adopted a policy of short-term temporary contracts which were not automatically renewed. They hired probationer teachers at the beginning of the school year and fired them at the end of the summer term—so that they didn't have to pay them during the summer holiday. But, because probationer teachers had no security of income, the banks wouldn't give them a mortgage. The teaching unions took the authorities to task and forced them to give new teachers a permanent contract after they'd been working a set number of months.

My first two jobs were temporary contracts, covering maternity leave positions. The first post was in the Art Department at St Andrews Roman Catholic Academy in

Saltcoats, on the Ayrshire coast. I wasn't at all sure what teaching in a Catholic school would be like once they found out I was a 'Protestant'—but since it was the only way to get my foot in the door and start my career, I was glad of the opportunity. The head of department was Jim Butler, a fierce-eyed, straight-talking guy with a clipped moustache and a military bearing. He'd been a Regimental Sergeant Major with the Army Cadet Force and was a talented bagpiper. The other two Art teachers were Chick McGeechan and Hugh McKay. At weekends, Jim Butler played in a local pipe band. He used to practise in the Art Department at lunchtimes, walking up and down the corridor playing the full set of pipes. Maybe that's why Chick and Hugh went home for lunch most days.

Since I lived in the Irvine Valley, a good twenty miles inland, some teachers from further up the valley who worked at the school offered me a lift. We usually picked up one of the Depute Heads in Kilmarnock, an older chap called Danny. He came from Cumnock and was quite a talker. Every Wednesday he said: *"Well, that's the back of the week broken!"* Danny had a sizeable chip on his shoulder about the way those in authority had treated him and other Catholics while growing up. When he discovered I was an evangelical Christian, he wasn't slow to let me know it was the Protestant majority who had acted in a discriminatory way towards the Catholics in the town.

I enjoyed my year at St. Andrews Academy. The pupils were a lively bunch. One time, I took a class of boys outside to sketch an area at the back of the school. I had an old 8mm cine camera with me and shot one or two clips while we were there. I asked a boy to take a shot, with me in the frame, which he did. Unfortunately, he also turned the camera on one of his pals who'd climbed a tree. This guy started playing to the gallery when he realised he was being filmed. Eventually I got the camera back and restored order. It's funny to watch now, but it was just as well the Head Teacher didn't put in an appearance, otherwise my contract might have ended sooner than expected.

I took various snapshots of the pupils and their artwork. Looking back through my photo archives recently, I found a shot of some 3rd year leavers lolling about in the art room at St Andrews, some with their feet on the table— being creative in every other way except making art.

3rd Year leavers, Art Class, St Andrews Academy, Saltcoats

Against my better judgement, I introduced that class to hand-built pottery techniques. I'm afraid I had to cut short their education in the finer points of ceramics, because they spent more time chucking blobs of wet clay at each other instead of making pots. At the end of that day, it took me quite a while to clean the splodges of clay off the walls and windows. As a famous author once said, "When one teaches, two learn."

Chick McGeechan had studied drawing and painting at Duncan of Jordanstone College of Art. He was an excellent painter and a charismatic character with a witty sense of humour. All the pupils loved him, especially the girls. Hugh McKay was also a talented artist. He lived in Maybole, further down the Ayrshire coast. He and Chick were both skilled guitarists. They sometimes had a 'jam' session during lunchtimes in the Art Department staff base, where I ate my packed lunch. One day, they played and sang the Jim Reeves song 'He'll have to go'. They gave it the full treatment and their combined harmonies sounded terrific.

After my year at St Andrews, I had a few months in the Art Department at Grange Academy, Kilmarnock. There were no separate art rooms there. The entire department was an open-plan teaching space, with partitions between the teaching areas, which were set up for specific art activities. I spent most of my time in the 3D area, getting pupils to make three-dimensional models with wire, clay or plaster of Paris. I enjoyed working there and was sorry when the lady whose classes I'd been covering returned.

I spent a few weeks applying for jobs before I bagged the next temporary vacancy, at Craigbank Secondary, near Pollok in Glasgow. The Principal Teacher of Art was a big, red-bearded, full of life character who regaled me with lots of stories about his time at Glasgow School of Art and the characters he'd known there. There were four more art teachers besides me and Mr red beard. Two older male art teachers worked in their own rooms and two younger female teachers shared a large classroom. Their names were Carol and Jennifer, and they often combined their classes and worked together as a team. They had a huge, elaborate still life area which ran the full length of the room, around which their pupils sat. They were expert at coaching pupils to produce lively, colourful work and worked with enormous enthusiasm. Without being too 'sexist' (well, maybe just a little), I think their approach and subject matter—lots of sparkly sequins, beads etc.,—appealed more to girls than it did to boys. Carol gave me a book on Ceramics for Christmas, which I didn't expect and was very kind of her.

❧

AROUND THIS TIME, Elisabeth, who was studying Librarianship at Robert Gordon's University, invited a friend home from Aberdeen for a few days. Her friend was the sixteen-year-old Joan Philips. One day, James asked Joan if she'd like to go for a walk. That was the start of the romance which culminated in their marriage. James moved to Aberdeen, and then to Bridge of Don, where their family—Bethany, Robert, and Joe—were born and brought up.

Best Man at James' wedding, Aberdeen

❧

42 APPLICATION FOR FULL-TIME SERVICE

As a boy, the preaching of various full-time evangelists (known as 'Lord's Servants') impressed me. Men like John Mawhinney from Ireland, and Harry King in Scotland inspired me. George Millar's Uncle George visited us one day when I was about seven or eight and asked me what I'd like to be when I grew up. I said "I want to be a Lord's Servant, like Harry King". He laughed and repeated this to Mum.

That early interest in full-time service was further strengthened when I later worked alongside such men of God on the LSV scheme. Not long after starting work as an Art teacher, I spoke to Dad about it. He advised me to write to the brethren in the district. Jack Ferguson invited me to his house for tea and a chat. He gave me helpful advice about how to study and prepare a Bible message. Jack said they had kept Bob Armstrong waiting ten years before before they accepted him as a full-time servant in Canada. He said "Brethren in the district will want to hear you speak so that they can recommend you when your

name comes up at the [annual] conference of overseers".
After a few months, during which they invited me to
preach and speak at various churches in the district,
three overseers representing the district interviewed me. I
felt strongly that my principal field of service lay in Scotland and I made this clear to them. This was a problem
for them, because, as they explained, my funding would
come from churches across the world, therefore I should
be prepared to go wherever I was invited. They took my
answer back to the district, and they declined my application for that reason. Perhaps I should have been more
flexible, but that's the way I saw it.

It was a time of spiritual crisis. I had felt a definite desire
to serve the Lord in a full-time capacity. After much
heart-searching, I decided to concentrate on my career in
teaching and be the best I could be for the Lord in that
sphere of service. Looking back, I think I had an inflated
notion of my own importance. I ought to have had more
humility and been more willing to compromise. I have no
doubts, though, about the need for Spirit-led gospel
workers in Scotland. Life takes unexpected twists and
turns. One thing I learned: no-one is indispensable to
God. He has men and women in every walk of life and He
can raise up and equip those He calls to serve Him in
whatever capacity or sphere, whether full-time as a
Lord's servant or in full-time Christian service within the
work environment. Prominence as a speaker—or one's
position in any form of service for the Lord—is of far less
importance than faithfulness in His service. It took me a
long time to learn that lesson.

∾

43 MARRIAGE AND FAMILY

In 1987, I was invited to the wedding of Lorraine Coomer and Ian Strachan. They were married in the Church of God Hall in Randolph Street, Buckhaven and all the guests were invited to the reception at a hotel in Kirk-caldy. That's where I bumped into two attractive young ladies from Northern Ireland: Norma McNair and her sister, Lorraine McIlree.

Norma was having difficulty loading a roll of film into her camera and asked me if I could help. Being the gallant chap that I am, I was pleased to assist! We got talking and although Norma thought no more about the encounter; I did. Somehow, I found out her address in Belfast and wrote to her.

Courting couple, with Mum and Dad at
Dunlop.

She wrote back; I wrote back, and our relationship developed. Norma was chief cashier at Kingsberrys in Belfast, a firm that bought and sold coal and fuel oil. She flew over to Glasgow with Loganair as often as possible. I picked her up and took her to stay with Dad and Mum at Dunlop. We enjoyed days out together, as well as spending time with Dad and Mum. I also flew to Belfast, where I enjoyed getting to know Norma's sisters and her mum. We spent our courting days going on car trips with a picnic, either to Loch Lomond and the Arrochar Alps when Norma visited me, or the mountains of Mourne and other local places of interest when I visited her.

On one of my visits to Ireland, we went out to a nice little restaurant for a meal. We both chose salmon for the main course. What I didn't know until much later was that Norma had never eaten salmon before and only chose it because she wanted to make a good impression! Fortunately, she acquired the taste and salmon has been a regular dish on our table for many years.

I popped the question fairly early on. I knew I'd found a girl who shared the same spiritual and moral values and whose company I really enjoyed. Norma took longer to be sure I was right for her. That made me pray about it more earnestly. I was so thankful when she eventually said "yes!" Years later, she told me the reason for her apparent reluctance was that her mother found it extremely difficult to let her go. Eventually, she came round and accepted that she couldn't stand in the way of Norma's happiness.

We went shopping for an engagement ring in Belfast. Norma chose a lovely ring studded with sapphires and diamonds. I had to use my credit card to buy it! Dad laughingly told me "You'll never have any money again!" —which in one way was very true—all my income from then on went towards the joint interests of home and family. Then again, Norma's numerical expertise quickly brought a disciplined approach to our finances!

We became officially engaged when I stopped the car beside the river Bann, on the way to visit William and Edith in Armagh. We walked along the river bank and I slipped the ring on her finger. It didn't take Edith long to spot the ring! The secret was out.

We married in Belfast on 2nd August 1988 and spent our honeymoon in the Lake District before coming back to set up home in the flat in Millerston, which I'd bought a year or two before.

Watercolour of Ennerdale Water, painted on
our honeymoon. Norma sat patiently and
waited while I finished it!

Norma got herself a job with an insurance company in
Glasgow and settled into life in Scotland. Each Sunday
morning, we drove across the city to remember the Lord
at Brisbane Hall, one of the two remaining companies of
the Church of God in Glasgow. There used to be four
companies—Partick, Parkhead, Cathcart Road and Go-
van. We usually stayed in the hall to help with the Sunday
School before coming home for something to eat.

Norma and I used to go for a walk on a Sunday afternoon. One day we walked across the fields behind Millerston, to a recent development of bungalows and semi-
detached houses, built by Barratts, at Robroyston. The
show house in Saughs Gate was for sale, which we really
liked. We bought it on the strength of our joint income
and moved there in 1989. Victoria was born the following
year, David a couple of years later, and Joel arrived on
Christmas Day, 1993.

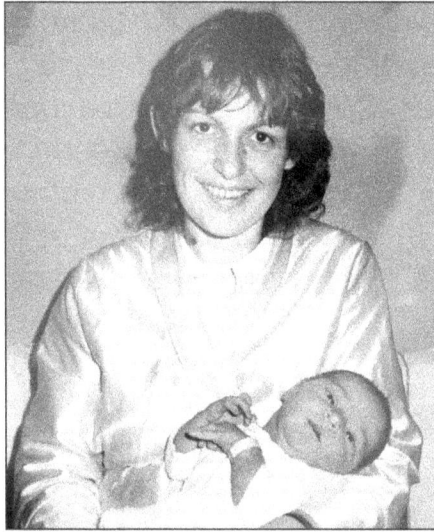

Norma with baby Victoria

Both Victoria and David were sociable children. They thrived on each other's company and made friends easily at nursery and school. Joel engaged with others on his own terms and preferred his own company much of the time. But he always enjoyed visits from family and cousins and enthusiastically joined in with the general fun and games and friendly banter.

Joel's Nursery School photo

When we moved to Fife, it was especially hard for Victoria and David, who had already started attending Lenzie Primary. Suddenly, they had to learn to fit into a little country school, and make friends all over again, with children who'd already established their own circles of friends. In contrast to Lenzie—at Coaltown Primary School, there was a marked social divide between the children from the bottom of the village, where most of the Council houses are located and the children from privately owned houses further up the village. Added to that, they were incomers from Glasgow—and they came from a home where the Bible was revered and their parents took them to church every week. So, one can imagine the challenges they had to deal with before being accepted in a community where that was not the norm. I also think the parochial mentality of most of their small-town peers meant they were never fully accepted. It wasn't easy for them and I regret that my move to Fife made life more difficult for them socially than it might have been if we'd stayed in Glasgow. Joel had a slightly easier passage through Primary since he started school along with the other children of his own age in Coaltown.

Victoria and David,
Coaltown of Balgonie
Primary School
photograph

Our family's secondary school years at Auchmuty High School were challenging years in more ways than one and both Norma and I were thankful when each of them emerged from the difficulties of their teenage years and made their own way in the world.

After a false start at Watt College in Greenock, Victoria studied beauty therapy at Elmwood College, Cupar. After her graduation, she got a job at the Old Course Hotel in St Andrews, where she gave beauty treatments and back massages to golfers and other tourists who came to stay at the hotel—including the British entertainer Bruce Forsyth and various wealthy Americans.

Victoria and James with David, Heidi and Hannah

Victoria is now happily married to husband James, who runs a profitable window-cleaning business. They live in Stockport, Manchester, with their three children, Heidi, Hannah and David. They serve God in a local evangelical church there.

David took various courses at Fife College in Glenrothes and Kirkcaldy, including an outdoor pursuits course and a painting and decorating course. He began his working life with a Lithuanian painter and decorator named Tomas Siminatrovitch who lived in Dalgety Bay and was always busy. He has several amusing stories to tell from those days, which he may well write about in due time.

David and Roslyn Smith, Philippa and David,
me and Norma

He then trained as a paramedic and went to work in England, where he met and married Philippa, daughter of David and Roslyn Smith, a hardworking farming couple in County Durham. They have two lovely children, Harry and Blair.

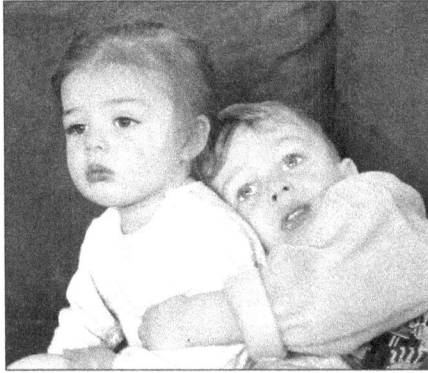

David and Philippa's children, Blair and Harry

Joel studied catering at Glenrothes College. He works for a restaurant business in St Andrews. They own several restaurants in the town and although based at 'Mitchells' most of the time, he helps out in any of their establishments when needed.

Joel, with Norma and me

At the time of writing, Joel has resumed work after a second, three-month 'Lockdown furlough'. The incredibly damaging behaviour of politicians astonishes me. They seem hopelessly out of touch with the devastating economic reality that their recent over-reactions to the COVID-19 virus have had on ordinary people.

The ongoing 'lockdowns' imposed by national leaders have also disrupted our contact with both Victoria and David and their families. Will they ever grant us the freedom of movement to visit our loved ones whenever we like again?

Despite all that, I give God thanks for our children and grandchildren. We pray for them every day, that each of them will come to know the Lord Jesus as their Lord and Saviour. In the last analysis, that's the only thing that really matters.

∾

44 FROM GLASGOW TO FIFE

My contract at Craigbank Secondary ended in the summer of 1984. Just before the term ended, Marion Mitchell, the glamorous, well-spoken, energetic Art Adviser for Glasgow City, asked if I'd be interested in a vacancy at Ashcraig, a secondary special school for physically disabled pupils. I've always taken the view that 'a bird in the hand is worth two in the bush', so I happily accepted, even though I wasn't sure what to expect.

Ashcraig was led by Agnes Allan, a strong, self-confident Head Teacher. She was proud of the fact she'd worked at the top-secret, code-breaking centre at Bletchley Park during the second world war. An 'old school' educated Scot, she entered the teaching profession after the war. She noticed that children who were physically disabled and academically able were being short-changed in the education system, mainly because of a lack of access infrastructure such as ramps, lifts in multi-storey buildings and so on. There was also a general tendency, among many, to underestimate the educational abilities of wheelchair users. Agnes and other like-minded colleagues lobbied the education department until they were granted the use of a building on the South side of Glasgow, which was named Summerton School. She and her colleagues demonstrated by the results attained by the first 'guinea pig' pupils at Summerton, that when physical barriers to learning and unconscious bias were removed, those pupils flourished. The City Council eventually built Ashcraig School, a purpose-built, modern special school on the banks of Hogganfield Loch.

I had a brief chat with Mrs Allan, who welcomed me to the school. She looked me up and down and said, "I run a tight ship here, you know." She handed me over to her Depute, John Doran, a long-haired, chain-smoking, Chemistry and Maths graduate who was father to a large family of eleven children. (A good Catholic!) His wife was an intelligent, good-looking lady who was always very pleasant to me when she visited the school. John showed me round, introduced me to the staff and gave me my timetable before dropping me off at the Art Room, where I later met the other Art teacher.

Catherine McCallum had recently retired as Principal Teacher of Art, and was the reason this vacancy fell open for me. She pioneered the teaching of Art at Summerton and Ashcraig. She was a dedicated professional and contributed several articles to educational journals. For her, no disability was so severe it couldn't be overcome. She even taught visually impaired pupils how to draw and looked for ways to make art accessible to everyone. She was a determined and inspirational teacher, and her pupils loved her. A hard act to follow.

I didn't fully understand why Catherine wanted to continue her attachment to the school after she retired. It wasn't until I'd worked in 'Special Ed' for years that I appreciated the strength of connection she had developed. I too, came to discover that teaching at Ashcraig and subsequently Kingspark in Dundee, was an immersive experience—it wasn't just a feeling of being part of a school community; it was a vocation.

Not long after I started work at Ashcraig, I received an invitation from Catherine to go to her house for a meal with her husband and son. Her husband, also a teacher, originally from the Isle of Lewis, was a flamboyant, cultured man with his own brand of humour. He referred to himself as Catherine's 'slave'. He had spent the afternoon cooking a special fish pie delicacy—which was never my favourite meal, but I pretended to enjoy it so as not to offend. Their son was a railway enthusiast and could talk at length about the famous, and not so famous, locomotives he had spotted.

It was clear Catherine wanted an ongoing association with Ashcraig. She visited the school from time to time and created a monetary Art prize—to be awarded by herself in person—at the annual school prize-giving. When Agnes Allan retired however, the new head teacher was less inclined to encourage Catherine's involvement. Catherine was dropped from the list of invitees to the prizegivings, and 'the McCallum Prize' was presented in her absence.

The other Art teacher had worked alongside Catherine McCallum for many years. Her name was Maureen Mc-Cracken, a mature, slightly stooped lady in her 60s with a

'Kelvinside' accent. She lived in the leafy suburb of New-lands on the South side of Glasgow.

John Lafferty was a small, rotund English teacher from Barrhead. He had Brylcreemed hair and black plastic glasses and used to sit in his Nissan Sunny at lunchtime and smoke cigars. One day I was sitting with John in the staffroom, when he nodded his head towards Maureen who was sitting opposite us talking to one her colleagues and said,"she's only here for the 'pin money'." John was a staunch Roman Catholic. He got very angry with me during one lunchtime discussion, when I pointed out that Mary, the mother of Jesus, wasn't a virgin after His birth, since it's recorded in the gospels that he had brothers and sisters in Nazareth.

The Art Department consisted of one large Art Room and a small pottery room. Maureen was part-time. She worked on Mondays and Tuesdays and finished at lunchtime on Wednesdays. The Art room was arranged with a set of tables and chairs on each side of the room so that we each had a separate teaching area. I inherited the lovely big executive desk, made with veneered ma-hogany, which Catherine McCallum had vacated. By con-trast, Maureen had a standard issue, plain beechwood teacher's desk on her side of the room. John Doran, the school timetabler, had arranged the Art classes so that I usually had a non-teaching period when Maureen's classes were in the room and vice versa. I never quite got used to the distraction of having another class in the room while I was preparing for the next class—but it gave me an insight into Maureen's teaching style. Invariably, she started with a demonstration of what she wanted the pupils to do. She often became so engrossed in creating her demonstration piece, that what should have been a

five-minute demo, morphed into fifteen or twenty minutes, and her pupils began to fidget and whisper or do
stuff behind her back. Now and then she'd look over her
glasses at them and bellow "PAY ATTENTION!" It sometimes took several "PAY ATTENTIONs" to restore order.

One day, Maureen showed me some watercolour paintings she'd done. She'd painted one of them while on holiday, at the back of the Taynuilt Hotel near Oban. I
admired it and asked if she would sell it. She named her
price—£50, which I happily accepted, wrote her a
cheque, took the painting home and framed it. Several
months later, Maureen said "Thet painting I sold you—I'd
like to bey it beck from you." I said "Sorry, I don't want to
sell it Maureen." Instead of shrugging her shoulders and
accepting the situation, she continued to argue about it,
implying that because she'd painted it, I was honour
bound to relinquish my claim to it. I told her that was
faulty logic. She had sold it to me, therefore it now belonged to me—and anyway, I had spent money getting it
framed. Her face imploded into an angry scowl. She
spluttered something unintelligible and stormed over to
her beechwood desk where she sat and glowered like a
spoilt child. It was a relief when the bell went for morning
interval. We both sought refuge on opposite sides of the
staffroom. It was quite some time before Maureen cooled
down and could speak civilly to me.

I always enjoyed friendly conversation with other
teachers in the staff room. There was a constant, friendly
hubbub. Mrs Allan occasionally interrupted the staffroom
bonhomie by pressing the intercom button on her desk in
the Head Teacher's office to make a tannoy announce-
ment. Loudspeakers were built into the ceiling in every
room of the building. One day at morning break in the

staffroom, we were sitting chatting away as usual when the "ding-dong" of the tannoy caused a momentary hush. Mrs Allan's plummy voice boomed out: "I'm ready for you now, John!' The staffroom erupted with loud hoots of laughter and I'm sure Agnes Allan must have heard it in her office, which was only two doors along the corridor!

Back then, computers were only beginning to find their way into schools. At first, the only departments for which they were deemed appropriate were Maths, English, Business Studies and Science. BBC Micro's with their floppy disks were the order of the day. Gradually, they appeared in other departments. When the opportunity arose I went on a Computer Graphics course in Glasgow with some Art teacher colleagues because I saw their potential as a creative tool.

One of the Computing advisers asked if I'd like to try out the latest model in the Art Department—a small, square-screened Apple Mac. He brought it to the school and left it in the Art Room. I enjoyed finding out how the thing worked. It made little whirring noises as it accessed the data on its neat little magnetic disk. As the whirring stopped, I pressed the release button and pulled out the disk. As I did so, the machine suddenly started up again —I felt a grinding vibration through the disk. "That didn't sound good," I said to myself. When I switched the computer off and on again and put the disk in, it was unreadable. So I had to confess my sins to the Computing Adviser when he came back to collect it. He put on a pained expression and took it away, cradling it in his arms, as if I had injured one of his children. How was I to know the wretched thing would start up again without warning? Fortunately, this experience only whetted my appetite, and I eventually ended up with two Amiga Computers in the Art room, which were great for Computer Graphics.

I raised the money for these machines by doing pencil portraits of pupils and staff at lunchtime, for £1.00 per drawing. I also, wrote to several charitable trusts, asking for funding to develop digital art as a way of providing disabled pupils with an alternative means of creative ex-

The Amiga Computer

pression. This netted several thousand pounds, which I invested in the necessary equipment and software. One visually impaired boy took to it like a duck to water. He pressed his nose up against the screen and enlarged the image until it was pixillated beyond recognition. He produced amazing work, holding the entire image in his mind while working at such huge magnification. Another boy, born with practically non-existent arms, dextrously used his mouth and lips to shove the mouse around and create professional quality graphics. When he left school, he landed a job in the Graphic Design department at Glasgow City Council.

Ashcraig had advantages and disadvantages. Thankfully, there were no major pupil discipline problems. Most of the pupils loved coming to school and, even more-so than their peers in mainstream, depended on the social interactions they enjoyed with friends at school. But I had only just completed the two probationary years required to become a fully qualified teacher of art, so I was still learning on the job. In Ayrshire, and at Craigbank in Glasgow, I had benefitted from working alongside more experienced art teachers. Now, here I was, the only full-time art teacher in a Special School, responsible for delivering the Art curriculum at all levels, from first year pupils right through to Secondary 6. In addition, I had to learn how to adapt the lessons to meet the needs of pupils who were physically (and often developmentally) more challenged than their mainstream counterparts. The Bible says 'it is good for a man that he bear the yoke in his youth'[1], but even with support from the Art Adviser and taking time out to visit and talk to Art teachers in the other Glasgow Special schools, for those first few years I struggled to become the 'good' art teacher my old tutor at Liverpool had prayed I would become. Eventually, I got my act together and achieved some modest successes, presenting pupils for Standard Grade and Higher Art qualifications. Later, I was promoted to Senior Teacher within the school. My main remit was to develop an Induction programme to help new staff become acquainted with the way the school ran and to organise talks from teachers and other professionals based in the school who worked with the pupils, including the Visual Impairment specialist, Speech and Language Therapist, Physiotherapist, and so on. I enjoyed working with staff in this capacity and decided that rather than continuing to plough a lone furrow as an Art teacher, I would set my sights on moving further up the promotion ladder. I applied for various posts within Glasgow but had a feeling, which was also shared by other 'Non-Catholic' teachers, that there was a virtual monopoly in favour of Catholic candidates when applying for promoted posts in the Education Department of Glasgow City Council. I remember remarking to an education official at the time that the term 'Non-Catholic', printed on Education department documents, was actually very discriminatory. He just shrugged. I read everything I could on how to interview well, and honed my ability to answer the typical questions that came up.

I applied for a postgraduate study course at Strathclyde University, to gain further qualifications. Anyone who wanted promotion in a Special school, had to complete the two-year Diploma in Special Education.

Several Assistant Principal teacher posts came up in and around Glasgow. I applied for every vacancy where I thought I had a chance, but they always went to other people. One of my colleagues, an ambitious young man called Colin Crawford, one of the science teachers, applied for and was appointed as Head of a local school for autistic children. Before he left, I sat down with him and picked his brains about the type of questions they'd asked him, and what he said in his answers. That was a useful exercise—it gave me an idea of the topics likely to come up. Since Education officials in Glasgow apparently favoured those who 'kicked with the left foot' (a euphemistic term among West of Scotland Protestants for our Catholic colleagues), I cast my net wider and applied for posts in any town within travelling distance of a Church of God. I was short leeted for several without success. Then, out of the blue, an interview came up in Fife. I visited the school prior to interview. One of the candidates was already working in the school.

On the tour of the department given by the Special Education Adviser for the county of Fife, I chatted away and learned that the DSE catered for a high number of young people with social, emotional and behavioural difficulties and for that reason there was a higher than usual staff/pupil ratio. I also learned that the previous PT had been very popular. Fife Council had recently appointed a new Head Teacher at the school, so I thought I was in with a chance, and took particular care in my preparations for this interview. I prepared a list of questions and typed out comprehensive answers, which I then bullet pointed on A4 sheets. At Ashcraig, I had developed several 'Scotvec' units on basic video production techniques —so I borrowed the VHS video camera and tripod and videoed myself answering the model questions I'd put together, using my A4 bullet points as prompts. I also recorded the soundtrack to this video on tape and listened to that in the car everywhere I went, in the lead up to the interview. In the interview, I drew on my stock answers and spoke with confidence in front of the interview panel. Finally, my perseverance paid off. I was elevated to the illustrious position of Principal Teacher in the Department of Special Education (DSE) at Buckhaven High School on the East Coast of Scotland.

∿

45   FIFE TO DUNDEE

Norma and I put our house in Robroyston on the market and began taking trips to Fife every weekend to search for a suitable new home. Looking back, it wasn't the ideal time to leave Glasgow. David and Victoria had started at Lenzie Primary and had made friends with some classmates. I was going to uproot them, and they'd have to start all over again. The start date for my new job arrived and we still hadn't found a house in Fife. Dougie McKay, a brother in the Church in Kirkintilloch, offered me the use of his caravan—which he brought all the way from Queenzieburn where he lived and parked it beside a cottage belonging to Ken, a farm manager with the Wemyss Estate, who gave me permission to park the caravan there. It was just next to Wells Green golfing range, a mile or two outside Buckhaven. Ken and his wife Alison had a little toddler. Alison was studying art at the local college. When she learned I'd been an art teacher in a former life, she asked my opinion on some of her work, which I was glad to give. Once we eventually found a house, Norma and I invited Ken and Alison and their little one for a meal. I was extremely grateful for the kindness they had showed me when I needed it.

On my last day at Ashcraig School in Glasgow, Norma dropped me off with my suitcase. As she drove off, David, who was only five, turned round in his seat and looked out the back window of our Nissan Bluebird. The image of his solemn wee face looking at me through the window as they drove away is forever imprinted on my memory. I realised the irreversible actions I'd set in motion. I left Norma with the job of packing everything up. Dad and Mum came and helped her. During the week, I lived on pot noodles and cups of tinned soup in the caravan at Wells Green. I'd brought my bike with me, so I cycled to work each morning. On Fridays, I packed a suitcase and caught a bus home to Glasgow so that we could drive back to Fife on the Saturday to continue our house hunting! It was an exhausting time. Eventually, we settled for a newly built house beside a farmer's field in the little village of Coaltown of Balgonie. We didn't see it as our ideal choice, but we had to put an end to all the travelling back and forth. Over time, however, we came to appreciate the benefits of living on the edge of a village, with plenty of healthy country walks on our doorstep.

In many ways, Coaltown was a good place to bring up a family—in other ways, not so much. I was never convinced that the move was a good one, educationally or socially for our children. Spiritually, although we took them to Camp each summer, we had removed them from regular contact with the Christian young folks they'd known in the West.

Group photograph of the Church of God in
Buckhaven some years ago.

Naturally, the adults in the Church at Buckhaven were
very pleased to have a young family to swell their numbers, but there were no other young folk there to keep
them company. With hindsight, I regret that the most.
Such are the decisions one makes in life. We may learn
from our mistakes, but we have to live with the consequences.

Unfortunately, an unexpected obstacle surfaced in my
new post at Buckhaven High. Working with some (very
difficult to manage) children and young people, required
extremely effective communication between staff. It was
essential that everyone followed a consistent approach
so that pupils knew exactly where the boundaries lay and
what would happen when they made unwise choices in
their interactions with each other and with staff. One of
my colleagues was less than cooperative with me and it
began to have a negative impact on the consistency of
our approach with the children. I tried to build bridges to
no avail. As they say, 'it takes two to tango'. It seemed to
me I was the only one dancing.

The situation worsened and the stress of constantly
trying to work with someone who didn't want to work

with me, became intolerable. Fife used to be a coal mining area. I began to dread the drive to work. Every day, it felt like I was entering a dark and inhospitable coal mine. Eventually, I sat down with the Special Education Advisor and discussed the situation. She told me about her grandfather, who, like me, had moved his family to Fife from Glasgow. She recalled that her grandfather used to say, "the only guid thing aboot Fife is the road ootay' it!"[1]

I realised the only solution to my predicament and the only salvation for my mental health was to use the Buckhaven job as a stepping stone to a fresh start somewhere else.

The PT's of the four or five DSEs in Fife used to meet for a meal from time to time. All female except one, they were a friendly bunch. They invited me to join them for their annual Christmas dinner at the Sandford House hotel, near Newport in Fife. That's where I met Steve Johnston, formerly Principal Teacher of Special Education, at Balwearie High School, Kirkcaldy. He had recently left Fife to become Head Teacher at Kingspark School in Dundee, about thirty miles North of Glenrothes.

Steve mentioned that an Assistant Head post was coming up at Kingspark. I submitted an application form and was grateful to be placed on the 'short-leet'. I spent the weeks leading up to the interview, refining and going over my questions and answers besides putting together a 'set piece', given to each of the candidates—a PowerPoint presentation on the subject of 'Motivation'. The interview was held in the Education Department headquarters, several floors up within Tayside House, the high-rise council building that used to stand opposite the old Olympia Swimming pool. The place where I'd had a bath each Friday night as a student!

Even if I say it myself, my presentation went over well. I'd had plenty of public-speaking practice at church over the years, so a set piece like that was a gift. It was a cause for thanksgiving, when I got the phone-call telling me I'd been successful at interview and asking me to confirm my acceptance of the post in writing.

The verse which came to mind at the time was:

There hath no temptation taken you but such as man can bear: but God is faithful, who will not suffer you to be tempted above that ye are able; but will with the temptation make also the way of escape, that ye may be able to endure it.' (1 Corinthians 10:13)

I'm certain God answered my prayers at just the right time, providing a way of escape from what, for me as well as the staff at Buckhaven High, was an impossible situation.

For the next fifteen years, I commuted from Coaltown to Kingspark School in Dundee, where, even though the job was not without its challenges, I finally found my niche among a friendly, supportive and hard-working staff, most of whom were there for the benefit of the children in their care.

∾

46 KINGSPARK SCHOOL

I took up the post of Assistant Head Teacher at Kingspark School, Dundee, around 1999. The school was purpose built during the 1970s and brought several previously separate special schools and units under one roof. As Assistant Head of Practical and Aesthetic subjects (Art, Music, Drama, Craft, Design and Technology) my job was to support the teachers of those subjects and lead a weekly Department meeting. I also had some 'whole-school' responsibilities. There were four other departments: Secondary, Primary, The Enhanced Support Area (known as 'ESA' for short) and 'The Unit', each led by a member of the Senior Management Team. There was also an NHS department with accommodation and offices for medical and nursing staff, physiotherapists, speech and language and occupational therapists.

What a difference it made to my sanity, moving from the disunity and occasionally stormy staff relations at Buckhaven, to the positive and supportive atmosphere that prevailed at Kingspark! I emerged from a dark and hostile 'coalface' in Fife to a sunlit world of friendly Dundonians, all keen to work together for the benefit of the children. Of course, there were some staff (as always) who were more difficult to get along with, but mostly, they were positive and supportive. Did I mention that it was a happy working environment? It was a HAPPY working environment! Something I never again took for granted.

Pupils at Kingspark were taught the core subjects (Maths, English, Science, Social Subjects etc.,) by their class teachers and they came to the P&A department for Art, Music, Drama and CDT (Craft, Design and Technology). When they came to P&A, their class teacher got non-teaching time for lesson preparation and administrative classroom work. Each class had two, and sometimes three, care-assistants who accompanied the class when they came to P&A subjects.

Pupils in the three departments of Primary, Secondary and ESA, were all mobile enough to come along the corridor to the P&A classrooms—but, since pupils in the Unit were wheelchair users, the Art, Music and Drama staff worked a system of wheeling a trolley, filled with the tools of their trade, to one of the four Unit classes, where they conducted their lesson. It was quite a logistical exercise, making sure you had all your paintbrushes, paints, bits of paper, and other resources needed to deliver the lesson.

Not long after arriving at Kingspark, a care-assistant knocked my door and said 'the Art teacher needs your help'. Louise Laing was covering Beth McDonough's Art classes, while Beth was on maternity leave. She was teaching a secondary class that day, when one boy, who had severe epilepsy, became agitated and increasingly uncooperative. When I entered the art room, he was jumping from one table top to another. Suddenly, he ran out and jumped onto a table outside the Art room. He refused to come down. I did my best to coax him, without success. Eventually, we sent for his class teacher and he went back with her to the secondary classroom. It was an incident that remained vivid in both Louise's mind and mine, since it happened when we were both new to the school. Louise was an excellent Art Teacher. She lived in Cupar and came from a Scots-Italian family. Although only about five feet tall, she made up in personality what she lacked in stature. She eventually went back to college and took a postgraduate course in the education of visually impaired children.

Maggie McGregor was Principal teacher of Physical Education and ran the PE department and swimming pool, along with her colleague Jane Tyler. Maggie was an easy-going, friendly woman who lived with her husband Gordon in Enochdhu, in the foothills of the Cairngorms, where he worked as a Ghillie on a Highland estate. She had contacts among the farming community there and brought ponies to school each summer during our annual 'activities' week—a highlight of the school year. Maggie, Gordon and their helpers used to give the children pony rides around the school grounds, an experience they always enjoyed.

Malcolm Gracie was the Technical teacher, a larger than life, jovial Dundonian with a full grey beard and a belly to match. Nothing was ever too much trouble for Malcolm. He was one of the most helpful people you could ever wish to meet. Over time, the pupil population changed. Able-bodied young people were now being taught in mainstream schools and, because medical science was more successful at saving the lives of newborn children with life-threatening conditions, we saw an increased number of children with severe and complex educational needs coming to Kingspark. This meant less demand for Malcolm's artisan skills because fewer and fewer pupils could safely use tools such as bandsaws, hammers and chisels. Malcolm then became the school's computer expert—which meant he was never idle! When he finally retired, the technical department was broken up.

Seonaid Birse (first name pronounced 'Shonnie')was the music teacher. Several other music teachers came and went, but Seonaid was always there. A tall, flaxen-haired, immensely talented girl, she played the Clarsach (Scottish Harp) in her spare time. She was also a brilliant pianist. She hosted the school choir in her classroom at lunchtimes. In the lead up to Christmas concerts and Summer prizegivings, Seonaid and the choir were always centre-stage. When drama teacher Marion Heredia taught at the school, there were also pantomimes and shows to prepare for. Seonaid played a major role in the success of those productions. Nothing ever phased Seonaid. At least not visibly. She always appeared serenely in control and I think her calm demeanour helped some of the more anxious pupils to stay calm, too. After I retired, business manager Allison Paterson sometimes called me in to provide cover for the other music teacher who was off on maternity leave. Seonaid made sure I had everything I needed to cope with the music lessons. Between us, we worked out a system of me playing some simple songs on piano or piano accordion—with pupils playing along on drums, cymbals and other instruments. When I ran out of ideas, there was always YouTube, which, in the new school, was available on a giant whiteboard on the wall, via computer and overhead projector. I thoroughly enjoyed my stint as a supply teacher in the music department!

Steve Johnston was a big man in every way. He was over six feet tall and must have been at least sixteen stone. His physical presence exuded authority. He had a formidable intellect and didn't suffer fools gladly. Fortunately, I got on well with Steve and always found him willing to listen and advise on the best course of action when various challenges arose in my department. He had an easy-going side to his nature and introduced a 'bacon roll' rota to the weekly Senior Management Team (SMT) meeting, an enjoyable tradition which I missed after he retired. The predominantly female SMT that followed, were more interested in watching their figures, so the bacon rolls were voted out!

Steve used to compile the annual school timetable, which in a complex special school like Kingspark, where NHS staff had also to be included in the timetable for Physio and other therapy sessions, was not easy. It was a 'Gordian Knot' exercise, necessitating several drafts and extensive consultation. To my surprise and private consternation, Steve asked me to take over the remit of school timetabler. He was an expert in the art of delegation. I had never put together a school timetable in my life and hardly knew where to start. I took copious notes from Steve on his method of addressing the priorities as he worked through the list of things and people to be included and consulted. Fortunately, several software solutions for scheduling were now available. I trialled most of them and finally came across a versatile application created by a Finnish PhD graduate called Vesa Saario. He named his app MIMOSA. It was infinitely configurable, and could easily process the copious amounts of data required to produce workable timetables for both colleges and schools. Once I had configured it to fit our requirements—all it needed was the input of data to combine classes, teachers, rooms, etc., and produce the required balance of subjects and activities. It was just the tool I needed to master my brief. It enabled me to produce an annual timetable which kept the school running smoothly for the next fifteen years. Looking back, the most important thing about the annual timetabling exercise, was not so much the computational logistics—which the software took care of—it was the lengthy consultation process with staff which ensured we arrived at the optimum version. Abraham Lincoln's famous adage is particularly apt: 'You can please all of the people some of the time and some of the people all of the time, but you can't please all of the people all of the time!' The law of diminishing returns inevitably meant that a line had to be drawn once we achieved the highest priorities. The more boxes we ticked, the less room there was for manoeuvre. Some teachers inevitably had to draw the short straw. Predictably, certain individuals turned up at my door to complain about this or that decision and to do their utmost to persuade me to change the timetable in their favour. Where it was possible, I met them half-way. If they didn't always get what they wanted, at least they'd been part of the conversation. Most of them accepted that, in the grand scheme of things, I'd done my best and pulled out all the stops to make it work as well as possible.

When Steve Johnston retired, I applied for his job along with the assistant head in charge of the secondary department. For legal reasons, (with apologies to Muriel Spark), I shall call her "Miss Jean Brodie".

There was an agonising moment following the interviews, when neither of us knew who had been successful and all the staff were obsequiously friendly to both of us! Jean got the call and staff finally knew who they needed to curry favour with!

Jean Brodie was an excellent Headteacher. Comparisons are odious, and everyone puts their personal stamp on the job. Not everyone saw eye-to-eye with Steve. Edna Morris summed him up well, when we reflected on his life following his funeral on 1st November this year. His death came as a shock to us all. Edna said, "He did things by the book". Steve was meticulous in his preparation for his annual meeting with Education officers where he had to argue his case for the high level of staffing we needed each year. Steve was a strong leader and a man of absolute integrity. The world is the poorer for his passing.

Scottish Qualification for Headship, (SQH) Graduation Photo

Jean had a different approach and usually won people over to her point of view. She always listened carefully and took pains to explain the reasons for her decisions, so that people would understand where she was coming from. Like Steve, she was passionate about wanting the best experiences for the children and communicated that passion to the staff not just through what she said but by the actions she took. For example, where there were very challenging children in a class group, she fought tenaciously for additional staffing, just as Steve had done before her, in the annual meeting she had with Education officials. Both Steve and Jean were more than equal to the challenge.

Jean worked closely with Education and NHS colleagues, to take forward plans for a new, purpose-built school building, in the grounds of St John's High School. After two years of intense planning and endless meetings, we finally moved to the new building. Allison Torano (now Paterson), was appointed as Business Manager. The daughter of a well-known coal merchant, Allison became a great asset to the school. Always smiling, she took everything in her stride. She and Edna worked together to support staff who returned to work after absence. Certain individuals appeared to be expert at 'playing the system', returning to work just in time to ensure their pay didn't take a hit. But Edna and Allison made sure anyone who wasn't absent for genuine reasons was held to account.

Edna, Depute Head in charge of Primary and ESA, was full of fun. She had the happy knack of seeing the funny side of any topic, even when serious issues had to be addressed. All the staff loved her and in school pantomimes, or shows, Edna was always a star turn. Not long after I arrived, Edna noticed I had a Psion electronic organiser, which I kept in a leather pouch on my belt. (I was always an early adopter of new technology). Whenever I took out the Psion to consult my electronic diary, she jokingly pretended to draw an imaginary gun. Edna allowed no one to get 'above themselves'. Every year, one of the care-staff used to organise a special ceremony outside her house to turn on the Christmas lights. They

always invited Edna—in character as 'Lady Agatha Fin-
try'—a fictitious local lady of independent means who
had pretensions to grandeur. To the delight of all present,
she made a flowery speech, full of deliberate gaffs and
innuendoes, then cut the ribbon and switched on the
Christmas decorations. (I believe they also partook of
some liquid refreshment, which only added to the hilarity).

Me, Edna & Allison, in the courtyard at
Kingspark

Edna and I took early retirement around the same time,
which made room for some of the PT's to step into the
vacancies we left behind. Laura, being younger than the
two of us, continued with a new management team. The
new SMT took their responsibilities very seriously. I got
the impression that Laura missed the banter and fun we
used to have. Even when tackling serious issues, we always found something to laugh about. This was great for
morale and acted as the invisible cement that bound us
together. But we had been performing as a well-oiled machine for years. The newly formed SMT had to work
through the stages of team development which psychol-

ogist Bruce Tuckman classified as 'forming, storming, norming and performing'[1].

Linda Sim was Depute Head in charge of the Secondary department. Originally from Edinburgh, she was a highly capable manager and kept a tight rein on her staff. She worked closely with Inez Robinson, her PT, to improve the curricular resources of the Secondary department. Linda was a remarkable woman. She owned horses, and both she and her daughter were expert riders. In the summer holidays, Linda and her husband used to sail their yacht around the islands off the West Coast of Scotland. She told us of their nerve-wracking experience, navigating the dangerous Corryvreckan whirlpool near the island of Jura. Like many women teachers of her vintage, the one area in which Linda was less proficient, was the use of computer technology. Occasionally, I helped her with that, which earned me several brownie points!

For several years, I taught Art two and a half days a week and attended to management duties on the other two and a half days. It was one thing teaching Primary and Secondary children who could understand and follow instructions—but teaching autistic children, and children with severe physical impairments, was less straightforward. I did my best with both groups but quickly realised I had a lot to learn. Sandra Tosh, a care assistant with one of my ESA classes, was a great help. She was a straight-talking, down-to-earth Dundee girl. She put up with my feeble attempts to engage with the autistic boys in her class for one or two lessons. Then she said, "look Jo, you need to make this a lot simpler. You need to use symbols and you need to show them what you expect them to end up with." She explained the exact procedure I should use and offered to prepare the symbols I needed for my next lesson. With Sandra's expert coaching, I could engage far more effectively with those boys and give them a rewarding experience each time they came to me for art. It involved considerably more preparation beforehand—one could not just 'wing it' with those pupils, the lesson had to be broken down into stages and a visual timetable made up with individual symbol cards, laminated and mounted vertically using Velcro, on a strip of card. I removed the symbol cards one by one as pupils completed each stage of the lesson. When I saw how positively the boys responded to this simple but powerful method of communication, it made all the extra work worthwhile.

Working with severely disabled children in the Unit, re-quired a very different approach. Lynne Martin, Assistant Head in the Unit, had transferred to Kingspark when the children at Strathmartine hospital school joined Kingspark. She explained how important it was to en-gage meaningfully with children who had no way of re-sponding physically apart from a smile, making eye contact, or making sounds. She was critical of teachers who mechanically placed a paintbrush or sponge in a pupil's hand and created a piece of artwork, as if they were working with a chunk of meat and not a human be-ing. Lynne said, "With these children, you need to be-come a larger-than-life personality, make eye-contact and lead them through the activity with empathy and sensitive engagement. Give them time to enjoy the tactile experience of working with the materials."

I did my best to put Lynne's advice into practice, but I was never as good as Louise Laing was when working with those children. She had a tremendous rapport with them and they very obviously enjoyed her art sessions.

Lynne thought the world of Louise and held her up as a great example.

Later on, we re-shuffled our remits, and I had joint responsibility for leading and managing the P&A and the Primary departments. Ann Ross was PT Primary. She was an exuberant character who lived, ate, and breathed the virtues of the Primary Department and her staff.

If there's one thing I miss now that I'm retired, it's the stimulation of daily interaction with staff and pupils. I took this for granted at the time and didn't really appreciate how enriching and valuable such connections are in so many ways. We are social beings and we thrive on the company, friendship and support of others.

～

47   DAD'S LAST DAYS

.

In retirement, Dad enjoyed a daily walk in the countryside around Dunlop. He divided his life between his many Church responsibilities, Bible study, reading, visits to the family and his interest in researching his family history. I helped him format and publish his autobiography 'The Jone Cratur', and arranged for the printing department at Gardyne College of Education in Broughty Ferry to print five hundred copies, which he sold to family and friends for a small profit. He spent a fair bit of spare time typing up the entries in the diaries his Granny and Great Granny had kept, which his mother passed on to him. I saved a copy of these files and hope to publish them one day if I'm spared. Their value as historical documents increases as time goes on.

 In his early eighties, Dad had to go to Ballochmyle hospital for an operation to fix what he called his 'waterworks problem'—an enlarged prostate gland. The procedure entailed a rather unpleasant 're-bore' of the prostate, accessed via a urinary tract catheter. When I visited him in hospital, he said it felt like broken glass in his lower abdomen. Thankfully, this cured the problem for a few years. But, in his mid to late eighties, his health took a turn for the worse. One night he got up to go to the toilet and realised something was wrong with his arm. He couldn't raise it properly. It turned out he'd had a "T.I.A.' — a Transitory Ischaemic Attack — a mini-stroke. Fortunately, he got prompt attention. The doctor pre-scribed Warfarin, Digoxin and a Statin. Warfarin used to be used as a rat poison, which appealed to Dad's sense of humour. As he got older, he became less able to walk his usual two or three-mile round trip and became more and more dependent on a walking stick and more reliant on Mum's help. One day, Mum went into the garden to put some clothes on the line. She slipped and fell on the wet grass and broke her wrist. It was a bad break. This meant she couldn't do so much around the house, so they reluctantly accepted the temporary help of carers from East Ayrshire council.

Dad's 90th birthday celebration, May 2008

IN MAY 2008, we had a family get-together to celebrate Dad's 90th birthday. Little did we know, he only had a few months left. His health took a turn for the worse in October 2008. He didn't want to go into hospital and resisted the carers advice to call an ambulance as long as possible. Eventually things became so serious, he had to give in. The paramedics took him to Crosshouse hospital and admitted him to a Renal Ward, where a dedicated team of nurses and doctors gave him excellent care. His kidneys were failing and medical science could do no more. A very caring and experienced renal nurse said, "your dad's condition is very serious". Over the course of a week and a half, each of the family made the journey to Crosshouse Hospital to visit him. I remember taking Victoria with me after I learned they had taken Dad to hospital. In that moment of crisis, I thought it would be the last time I would see him. To Victoria's alarm, I became emotional as I drove along the motorway. I pulled myself together, and we got there in one piece. Fortunately, I was able to visit him a couple of times after that, and read to him some comforting verses from the scriptures. He said: *"We've all got to die sometime."* On my last visit, he told me he'd seen a figure standing at the bottom of his bed during the night. I listened and said little, but I think it was an angel—the purpose of which may have been to prepare Dad for the fact that his departure wasn't far away.

Dad discovered that the man in the bed opposite was also a Christian, a man from a Brethren assembly in Kilwinning. He had seen Dad reading his Bible and made himself known. Dad was so glad to have his company. For reasons which were not clearly explained, the hospital moved Dad to another, more general ward. We guessed it was because they needed the bed for someone else in the Renal ward. William came over for a few days and took Mum back and forward to the hospital.

I was on holiday from school during that week, so on the Wednesday, Norma and I went to Perth to do some shopping. We had parked the car and were walking up the street that leads to the town centre when my mobile phone rang. It was William. He told me Dad had taken a turn for the worse and I should come to the hospital as soon as I could. We went back to the car and drove across country to Crosshouse. William came out and met us in the hospital car park and told us Dad had collapsed and died that morning. According to the ward nurse, Dad had got out of bed, had taken a few steps, then said 'I feel my power going' and had collapsed and died right there.

They moved Dad's body into a private room. Mum and William sat beside his body for some time. When I arrived, they met me in the car park and we all went in together. Dad was lying on the bed with his mouth open. I said to his body: "I'll meet you in the glory Dad." Elisabeth recently reminded me I also quoted from 1 Cor. 15:43: *'sown in weakness, raised in power.'* It was a traumatic time, but we knew his troubles were over. For him, as the Apostle Paul wrote, it was *'very far better.'*

Dad had specified in his will that we were to choose the plainest, cheapest coffin from the funeral directors, P.B. Wright at Greenock, and that the coffin lid was to be screwed down. Like Uncle Willie, he didn't want anyone gawking at his dead body. John and William went to view the body privately, before the funeral. Dad had bought a grave in Greenock cemetery years before, when Grandad died. There were two more spaces left, one for him and one for Mum.

The funeral director told me the rules had changed, and the cemetery workers now needed to check and see if there was sufficient depth in the grave. I let them know we'd be extremely concerned if there wasn't enough space, since Dad had paid for three 'lairs' (as the spaces in a grave are termed). Fortunately, word came back that there was enough room and we could proceed with arrangements. The funeral director told me there are parts of Greenock Cemetery where there isn't much depth because of the underlying rock. Thankfully, this wasn't the case for us.

Cedar Hall was filled to overflowing. Jim Rankine, Dad's fellow overseer at Kilmarnock, took the service in the hall. I made a few remarks at the end and quoted a stanza (below), from a poem by James Hyslop, the words of which eloquently point beyond the tomb and with poetic licence, give a glimpse of the glories of eternity which belong to all who trust the Saviour. On the back of the Order of Service, we printed Dad's notes on the tremendous 'upper room' prayer of the Lord Jesus, recorded for us in John 17. Dad was preparing to give an address on it at Kilmarnock before he went into hospital. (I've added his notes in the Appendix). James, William, John and I carried Dad's coffin from the hall to the hearse, which was waiting outside. When I shouldered my corner at the front of the coffin, I nearly collapsed under its weight. It felt as if they had loaded it down with bricks. Maybe it was because I'm not as tall as the others and the coffin was angled down toward my end—or maybe I'm just a 9 stone weakling! Jim Cranson took the service at the graveside and we invited everyone back to the Tontine Hotel for something to eat.

> When the righteous had fallen and the combat
>   was ended,
> A chariot of fire through the dark clouds de-
>   scended;
> Its drivers were angels on horses of whiteness,
> And its burning wheels turned upon axles of
>   brightness;
> A seraph unfolded its door bright and shining—
> All dazzling like gold of the seventh refining;
> And the souls that came forth out of great
>   tribulation,
> Have mounted the chariot and steeds of salvation.
> On the arch of the rainbow, the chariot is gliding,
> Through the path of the thunder the horsemen are
>   riding;
> Glide swiftly bright spirits! The prize is before ye—
> A crown never fading! A kingdom of glory!

FROM 'THE CAMERONIAN'S DREAM' BY
JAMES HYSLOP (1798-1827)

48 RETIREMENT

I remember speaking to Ken Weir, a colleague at Kingspark who had recently retired. He was invited to the annual Christmas show and we got chatting afterwards. I had a few years left before I could retire and jokingly said to Ken, "It can't come soon enough!" He replied: "It'll come round a lot sooner than you think, Jo!" He was right. The years flew past. It was a red-letter day when my first monthly pension payment appeared in our bank account!

Dad's advice paid off. He had often emphasised the value of the Scottish teacher's superannuated pension scheme, administered by The Scottish Public Pensions Agency.

I retired from full-time employment in August 2015.

It took me a few months to settle into a routine. I told Allison I'd be available for two or three-day's supply teaching per week—but only after a good couple of months savouring the luxury of not having to rise at seven o'clock every morning! One of the first things Norma and I did was to arrange a two-week holiday in Italy. She had been to Sorrento with her mother many years before, but I had never been further afield than the North of France, when we had a family holiday there one summer when the children were still at school.

Norma and me, St Mark's Square, Venice

We began our two-week Italian adventure in Venice, where we hired a Fiat Panda and drove down the East Coast of Italy to Puglia, via San Marino. We stayed overnight in a farmhouse in the beautiful Abruzzo region where the view across some olive groves to the distant mountains was magnificent. Then on to Locorotondo near Alberobello. On the way there, we took a very inter-esting detour through the forest in the Gargano National Park and down into the fascinating old town of Vieste on the Adriatic coast. In Puglia, we stayed for several nights in a 'Trullo'—the unusual cylindrical, dry-stone houses with conical limestone roofs, a unique feature of that re-gion. After visiting several places of interest, including the elegant ancient city of Lecce, we drove West through the mountains and down through Salerno to the Amalfi coast. We had booked a week's bed-and-breakfast in the hillside village of Atrani, next door to Amalfi. Until then, we had enjoyed driving through the changing scenery on good roads, sampling the excellent motorway restaurants that are unique to Italy. With their reasonably priced, high-quality food, they put to shame the extortionate fast-food outlets on many of the motorway service stations in Britain.

The first inkling that all was not well on the driving front, was when the Sat-Nav, which until then had been reliable, began to take us in circles around the back streets of Salerno. We eventually navigated our way back onto the main road. However, it was when we got onto the twisty, narrow coast road between Salerno and Atrani that the fun started. Every time I slowed down on a hairpin bend, with sheer cliffs on one side of the road and a sheer drop to the waves below on the other, the local Italian drivers behind me became exceedingly irate and tooted their horns aggressively. Even the local bus drivers joined in. At one point I was nearly run off the road when a bus recklessly overtook me on a bend. He was less than an inch from the side of the Panda. I leant on the horn and gave him a long blast in return. It was one of the hairiest driving experiences of my life. The Italians have no patience with inexperienced tourists who have the audacity to attempt the Kamikaze corners on the Amalfi Coast road. With great relief, we reached our destination with life and limb intact. After that, we usually walked or took a ferry to the places we wanted to visit.

During that week, we visited Positano, Amalfi and the island of Capri as well as exploring the hillside town of Ravello. We also drove over the mountains for a day trip to Pompeii, which was one of the most interesting places we've ever been. To walk along streets which had grooves worn into them by chariot wheels, and through houses decorated with ancient Roman paintings and carvings, gave an amazing insight into the lifestyle of citizens in the time of the apostle Paul and the other Jewish preachers, who turned the world upside down, proclaiming the gospel of Christ to both Jew and Gentile. In the amphitheatre, a covered walkway surrounded the exhibition of plaster casts taken from the remains of the poor souls whose lives had been so abruptly cut short by the eruption of Vesuvius. The typical conical shape of the volcano formed a dominant backdrop. The inhabitants of Pompeii lived beside a time-bomb, which suddenly exploded and cut their lives short by pouring out death and destruction.

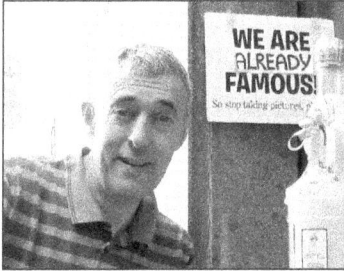

On the Island of Capri—
The sign in the Limoncello shop reads: We are already famous, so stop taking pictures please!

From the Amalfi Coast, we motored up the West side of Italy, by-passing Rome to spend the next couple of nights in Florence, where we returned the hired Fiat Panda to the local Avis depot. We had a nice breakfast and walked along beside the river Arno, stopping briefly to admire some elegant designer shops. We came to the famous Ponte Vecchio bridge and decided to walk across and explore the area on the other side of the river. As we came off the bridge, just outside a little jeweller's shop, Norma tripped on the uneven cobblestones and instinctively put her hand out to break her fall. I lifted her off the ground, and was horrified to see her middle finger bent at right angles to the rest of her fingers. Her face was badly bruised and she was very shaken. The kind shopkeepers from the jeweller's shop brought her inside and gave her a seat while they called the ambulance. We spent the best part of the day in the Accident and Emergency department of the 'Ospedale Santa Maria Nuova'.

Eventually, an X-Ray's showed that nothing was broken. A smiling orthopaedic surgeon took Norma's crooked finger in his hand and expertly snapped it into its normal position. He put a splint in between her fingers and wrapped her hand in a giant white bandage. They discharged her in the late afternoon and we managed a brief walk round some shops just as they were closing for the day. Next day we took the bus to Firenze Airport and vowed to return and 'do' Florence properly another time.

∾

BACK THEN, we took it all for granted. Now—in the name of a prolonged 'case-demic', artificially inflated with false-positive PCR and lateral flow tests, and with the looming spectre of mandatory vaccination passports —it looks as if the freedom to go abroad on holiday without restriction is a thing of the past.

∾

WE RETURNED HOME from Italy and settled into a daily routine of walks around the local countryside and the occasional visit to local cafes and garden centres for a morning coffee and sometimes lunch. I bought a portable Jullian Artist's travel easel and went on several outdoor painting trips. I also set up a backdrop for painting still-life subjects indoors and happily worked away on my art when not preparing for meetings, writing articles for

'Bible Studies' magazine or assisting with the editing of gospel tracts.

Out of the blue one day, Neville Coomer gave me a cutting from a newspaper about the latest craze: Adult Colouring. Had I heard of it? "Yes", I said, but up till then, I'd scornfully dismissed the phenomenon as 'colouring books for baby adults!'

Neville said "With your artistic talents, you could do that." He planted the seed in my mind and over the next month or two, I found out more. It astonished me to discover how many adults, mostly women, who, (it seemed to me) were wasting their time indulging in what I'd always considered a childish activity. But there seemed to be some social and therapeutic benefits, and I saw its potential as a business proposition. So, I invested some money in a second-hand Wacom Cintiq graphics tablet, learned how to use Clip-Studio Paint, and started working on a series of line drawings. Eventually, about a year later, I had enough to justify the production of my very own, self-published adult colouring book, which is still available on Amazon. I asked Jonathan Williams to design the cover, created a 'colouring website' and waited for the cash to roll in. It didn't happen. If I'd done it a year earlier, I might have been in with a chance, but I came too late to the party. Also, I didn't appreciate how much work one needs to do the marketing and advertising front following publication. After some initial sales, the book sank without trace to the bottom of the Amazon ocean. But I learned a valuable lesson—stick to what you know and love and don't allow yourself to be sidetracked by the temptation of a quick buck. It wasn't all wasted effort, though. I also learned a lot about the pros and cons of self-publishing which stood me in good stead later, when I published a colouring book to help children learn their ABC's and co-authored an illustrated primer on Bible Prophecy with Neville Coomer.

In February 2017, Norma and I kept our promise to revisit Italy. We flew out to Florence for a few days' holiday with Joel. We visited many sites of interest, including a fascinating day trip to the ancient city of Siena, where we soaked up the atmosphere and enjoyed delicious Italian cooking in the famous square, the Piazza del Campo.

Back home, I was happily enjoying the retired life, when around Springtime, my lower legs began to swell up during the day. When I pressed my finger into the skin, it left a dent. Very odd. Since it didn't clear up in a week or two, I went to see my GP, Dr David Anderson.

〜

49   DIAGNOSIS, POLAND, HOSPITALS

My sharp-witted GP, Dr Anderson, discovered I was losing massive amounts of protein and referred me to a renal consultant who, after completing a kidney biopsy, suspected a rare blood disorder named Amyloidosis. He referred me to the Haematology consultant, Dr Williamson—a clever but eccentric Englishman who spent most of his meetings with me talking to Norma instead of addressing me directly. He performed an excruciatingly painful bone marrow biopsy, which he extracted from my hip bone with a thick, wicked looking metal needle. (He froze the skin on the hip with Novocain but I got no other pain relief, such as gas and air, which is available in civilised countries like Canada.) The biopsy confirmed a diagnosis of latent myeloma (blood cancer) and Amyloidosis. Dr Williamson told Norma that the best option medical science could offer was a six-month course of chemotherapy, possibly followed by a stem-cell transplant. He sent me for a special type of scan at the NAC (the National Amyloidosis Centre) in the Royal Free Hospital, London. This confirmed that I had "AL Amyloidosis"

—a build-up of mis-folded protein cells which impairs the function of the kidneys.

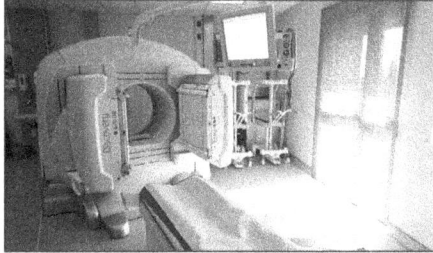

The SAP Scanner at the NAC, Royal Free Hospital, London

This all came as a complete shock. Here I was, a perfectly healthy, fifty-something young man, who took regular exercise and wasn't over indulgent in any way— faced with a diagnosis of a life-threatening condition. It was some time before I got my head around the idea that I might have to say "ta ta" to this world sooner than expected.

Fortunately, in God's goodness, my condition was diagnosed early. If I'd been diagnosed with this fifteen years earlier, doctors could have done little to help. However, due to research by Professor Sir Mark Pepys, a brilliant Jewish doctor from South Africa, the progress of this condition can be arrested by a six-month course of chemotherapy, and in younger fit patients, an Autologous Stem Cell Transplant (SCT for short).

Norma and I had been planning a holiday to Poland. Dr Williamson advised us to do this before treatment began. So, in July 2017, we flew to Krakow and had a memorable holiday there. We visited Auschwitz and Birkenau concentration camps, one of the most sobering experiences of our lives. One image I will never forget was the mountains of shoes and suitcases piled up behind glass in one of the buildings at Auschwitz. It surprised me that so many Poles were also murdered. Hundreds of photographs of Polish victims lined the long corridor, their solemn faces looking out at you from picture frames. All efficiently documented on typewritten papers by the grotesque Nazi war machine.

Auschwitz was a salutary reminder, if we ever needed it, of the capacity for evil that resides in the sinful human heart. Only the redeeming love of God in Christ can save mankind from such awful acts of inhumanity and hatred towards each other. Another day we visited the amazing Wieliczka salt mine, with its carvings of Biblical scenes and inevitably, in ultra-religious Poland, statues of Roman Catholic priests, cardinals and so-called saints.

In August 2017, Andy and Anna McIlree brought Norma's sister Lorraine across to Fife to visit Andy's mother in Glenrothes. They dropped in to see us on their way home. By this time, they'd heard about my diagnosis and impending treatment. Before he left, Andy had a word of prayer. He spoke of how Satan had asked to have Peter that he might sift him as wheat. "But"—the Lord said—"I have prayed for you that your faith fail not". Andy emphasised the intercessory work of the Lord Jesus and thanked God for the necessity that the Lord had to go away and leave His disciples on earth, because then they would have an advocate in heaven, a High Priest who is on the throne. He prayed that the Lord would guide the doctors treating me and that the Lord would heal me and remove the symptoms of the condition. Andy's prayerful concern meant a lot.

Later that day, I switched on the TV and randomly surfed to the TBN channel. A service was being broadcast from Holy Trinity church in Brompton, London. To my astonishment, the preacher alluded to Satan's sifting of Peter, and observed: "Satan had to ask permission"—AND that the LORD said to Peter: "BUT I have prayed for you." The thought struck me with fresh force: HE—THE LORD OF ALL GLORY—prays for us. For ME! What more do we need!

On 23rd September 2017, we joined the extended Johnson family in a restaurant near Dunlop in Ayrshire for Mum's 90th birthday celebration. I let Norma off and parked the car. As I walked towards the restaurant, I tripped on a kerbstone and fell full length onto the grass. I jumped up, feeling rather foolish. Norma, waiting a few yards in front of me, burst into tears. I think she thought I was a goner! It suddenly struck me—I wasn't the only one struggling to come to terms with my diagnosis. She, too, wasn't finding it easy to confront my fragile mortality.

I had strong reservations about chemotherapy and explored alternative, naturopathy options. Norma's niece Helen recommended a well-researched book on the subject by Dr Xandria Williams, which I read. One of the few areas where she recommended using the Allopathic method was in the treatment of blood disorders. After much heart-searching, I reluctantly went through with the chemotherapy treatment. This involved a weekly visit to the Victoria Hospital in Kirkcaldy. We would arrive about ten o'clock in the morning and sit in the waiting area for fifteen to twenty minutes before being called. I had to learn to be a 'patient' patient, since our chronically overwhelmed NHS appointment system invariably kept us waiting beyond the appointed time. Often, we had to wait for half an hour or more before being called. Once admitted to the day ward, however, things usually progressed at a reasonable pace. One thing constantly surprised and annoyed me—the inconsistency between the chemotherapy schedule prescribed by the NAC consultant in London and the default chemo schedule on the computer system at Kirkcaldy. The nurses always insisted the Fife system was correct (Computer says it, so it must be right—a dangerous mindset). My chemotherapy involved a schedule of ten different drugs administered over a six-week cycle, but the default schedule at Kirkcaldy was a four or five-week cycle. I lost count of the number of times I told them, 'No, I'm not supposed to get my Velcade injection till next week!' This triggered a back-and-forth discussion between the nurse and me until I either produced the letter from the Royal Free, listing the frequencies of the various drugs and dosages, or if this didn't satisfy them, I had to ask them to check with Jill Livingstone, the Pharmacist who was overseeing my chemotherapy regime. At my initial meeting with Jill, she carefully made notes of the programme of drugs I was to be given, exactly as prescribed by the consultant at the National Amyloidosis Centre. She then went away and created her own spreadsheet based on this—different from the default chemo regime on the Kirkcaldy computer. The major flaw in the Fife IT system was that the programme did not allow Jill to edit and save an individualised chemo programme, which could be accessed by the nurses when they brought up my records—she had to create her own customised spreadsheet. I had typed the spreadsheet data into the electronic diary on my mobile phone—so I knew exactly where I was on the chemo schedule in any given week. I was so thankful Jill had been so careful, because it meant I could insist with absolute confidence that the nurses should double check before proceeding. This underlines the fact that the NHS is only as good as the people who work for it. People like Jill Livingstone, who maintain that level of professionalism, are worth their weight in gold.

50 POISON THERAPY, DOUBTS AND FEARS

The consultant at the NAC put me on a six-month course of 'VCD' chemotherapy—which stands for Velcade, Cyclophosphamide and Dexamethasone.

Velcade (also called 'Bortezomib'), is an anti-cancer drug, which targets and kills protein cells, administered by injection.

Cyclophosphamide is a 'cytotoxic' chemical derived from nitrogen mustard; the compound used to produce mustard gas. It suppresses the immune system and triggers the self-destruct mechanism in the body's cells.

Dexamethasone is a steroid which enhances the effects of the other two drugs—interestingly, recently found effective against the acute respiratory syndrome caused by Coronavirus. Dexamethasone wound me up like a spring. For 24 hours, my mind worked overtime, and I had a surge of manic energy. It was impossible to switch off and go to sleep. When it wore off, I was exhausted.

They also gave me a cocktail of anti-sickness drugs and laxative concoctions to counteract the severe constipation — another side-effect of this so-called 'therapy'. Did I mention the side effects? Severe nausea, tiredness, flu-like symptoms, horrible constipation that clogged me up for days on end, food and drink tasting like nothing and loss of appetite. My hair became really thin and hardly grew. But, every cloud has a silver lining—it saved me spending money at the barber's shop.

In December 2017 after three six-week cycles of chemo/poison therapy, I had what they called a 'Complete Response': The excess levels of 'monoclonal kappa and lambda serum free light chains (FLCs)' (the cause of amyloid deposition in my kidneys), was now within the normal range. However, Dr Williamson insisted I continue for one more six-week cycle of chemotherapy, just to be sure.

On Thursday 1st Feb 2018, Norma and I met with Dr Huw Roddie, Haematology Consultant at the Western General Hospital, Edinburgh where I signed the consent forms for the Stem-Cell Harvesting and Transplant procedures.

Dr Roddie explained the process in detail, including the high dose of Melphalan with its major side-effects. It would effectively wipe out my immune system. The side effects included severe ulceration of the gastro-intestinal tract, diarrhoea, hair loss, vomiting, nausea, exhaustion and fatigue. They would give me powerful anti-sickness drugs, but these also come with unwanted side-effects. The main concern during the transplant period would be my susceptibility to infection—which, he said, was virtually guaranteed, and would require intravenous antibiotics and blood transfusions to counteract the effects of low blood-cell counts during the isolation period (at least three weeks). Thereafter, if all went well, I would go home but would continue to be monitored by the Victoria Hospital and receive further blood transfusions as needed. There would be a gradual recovery over the following three months, but I would still be susceptible to infections and would require to be re-vaccinated a year later. Nothing to worry about.

Specialist nurse Liz Brown met with us and reiterated all the above in graphic detail. She took Norma and me to see the Ward where I would spend the three-week isolation period during the transplant process.

Although I'd previously read about the stem-cell transplant procedure, I had put it all to the back of my mind. Now, as I considered all this information afresh, the reality hit me — it was about to happen. To me. As Lance Corporal Jones of 'Dad's Army' fame often said: "DON'T PANIC!"

I had a sleepless night, wrestling with all the details in my mind. I remember praying over the following scriptures: "In nothing be anxious but in everything make supplications with thanksgiving" — "sufficient unto the day is the evil thereof" — "let the morrow be anxious for itself". In my prayer to the Lord, I acknowledged how easy it is to say these words but how difficult to do them. Eventually, I came to an end of myself. I could do only say: "Lord this is too much for me to carry on my own, you'll have to carry it for me."

Next morning, 2nd February 2018, I got up and, as usual, tore off yesterday's calendar reading on the Golden Bells calendar to read that day's text. Amazingly, it was one I had chosen and written the comment for, more than a year beforehand:

"Behold, I am the LORD, the God of all flesh. Is anything too hard for me?" (Jeremiah 32:27)

When the storms of life threaten to overwhelm, we "take it to the Lord in prayer". Like Hezekiah did with the hostile letter he received, we should "spread it before the LORD"! (2 Kings 19:14-20...) But it's also great to know, "Our God is so big, so strong and so Mighty, There's NOTHING that He cannot do!"

Unmistakably, the voice of God spoke to me through those words, answering my fears of the previous night and reassuring me of His help. Nothing is too hard for Him. Not even a stem-cell transplant.

Victoria phoned me that morning. I told her about the calendar reading and said, "it reminds me of the scripture in Ecclesiastes:

"Cast your bread upon the waters and it will return to you after many days" (Ecc. 11:1).

As if to underline the message on the calendar, my daily reading portion for that day included this passage:

> Ask, and it shall be given you; seek, and ye shall find; knock, and it shall be opened unto you: for every one that asks receives; and he that seeks finds; and to him that knocks it shall be opened. Or what man is there of you, who, if his son shall ask him for a loaf, will give him a stone; or if he shall ask for a fish, will give him

a serpent? If ye then, being evil, know how to give good gifts unto your children, how much more shall your Father which is in heaven give good things to them that ask him?

MATTHEW 7:7-11

In prayer, I asked the Lord to grant me a long and complete remission so that I could serve Him faithfully until the Lord returns or until He calls me home. Also, that He would bring me through these procedures UNSCATHED and that the doctors and nurses would be amazed at the transformation in me and be caused to acknowledge that a higher hand than theirs had been at work in my recovery.

"He asked life of you, you gave it him; even length of days for ever and ever." (Ps 21:4)

At the end of February 2018, I went down to London for my six monthly, two-day assessment (a battery of scans and tests) at the Royal Free Hospital. Dr Helen Lachmann told me my results were excellent—I'd had a complete response to the chemo, my kidney function was good and there was slightly less amyloid in the kidneys. I was therefore an ideal candidate for a stem-cell transplant. I had three options:

1. Do nothing.
2. Have the Stem Cell harvesting, then wait and see, or
3. Go ahead with the stem cell harvesting and transplant.

After discussing of the pros and cons and risks involved, I agreed to proceed with the stem-cell transplant. Dr Lachmann said I had a lower risk of death during the transplant because the condition was at an early stage. Coupled with my age and a good level of health and fitness, this meant I was physically more able to withstand the severity of the treatment.

Despite those reassurances, though, the nagging doubts kept coming back. Should I go ahead with both stem-cell harvesting and transplant, given the risk of kidney damage and the five per cent risk I might not survive? There were unknown factors. Statistically, I could expect five to eight years remission.

Martin and Evelyn Notman

If I survived, it would be impossible to say whether remission was solely the result of successful chemo treatment, or of chemotherapy plus the stem-cell transplant.

My good friend Martin Notman, whom God has preserved since he had his kidney transplant fifty years ago — phoned me on the evening after I returned from the final check-up in London. He said "Jo, I believe the Lord is going to bring you through this. I think you should go ahead with stem cell therapy." Amazingly, the very next morning, 23 February, the reading on the calendar was another of the ones I had compiled. This had to be more than coincidence:

"… The Lord said to Moses, "Why do you cry to me? Tell the people of Israel to go forward..." (Ex 14:15).

Sometimes it is necessary to "halt (no track discovering), Fearful lest we go astray…" At such times it is wise to wait on the Lord in prayer. But when the clear direction of God comes, we must step out in faith, "being fully per-suaded that what he has promised he is able also to do…" (Rom 4:21 Derby) Today the clear word of the Lord is: "GO FORWARD!"

 Once again, God strengthened my confidence in Him. I put my hand in His, and, tentatively I have to admit, went forward in faith.

A few days later, on 8th March, our good friends Martin and Margaret Dyer in Edinburgh sent me this verse:

"the LORD is on my side among them that help me" (Psalm 118:6,7).

Martin Notman had quoted that same verse to me some time ago as a word of encouragement. I found much comfort in all this, realising that the medical professions and specialisms, with their amazing skills coupled with all the modern technology at their disposal, were being guided by the LORD, who was on my side. He was fighting my battles! My future was safe in His hands. I don't deny the importance of having a 'positive attitude'. I believe one's state of mind will significantly influence physiological changes in the body for good or ill; how-ever, sometimes constant exhortations to 'think positive' can make one feel that, no matter how physically or men-tally depressed one may be, 'we must keep trying to BE POSITIVE!' For me, Psalm 118 took away that unfair pressure. It brought to my mind an old hymn on the LP Dad had given Mum, beautifully sung by Kathleen Ferrier: "Rest in the LORD and wait patiently for Him", a direct quote from Psalm 37 Each verse in that Psalm begins with a letter from the Hebrew alphabet. Verse seven begins with the letter Dalet—in Hebrew the word rest is 'damam' [daw-mam] which means 'Cease'—cease from struggle. If the LORD is on your side, He'll do the fighting for you—you can relax. Trusting God is so much easier than the strain of always having to 'think positive'.

On Monday 12th March, to prepare for stem-cell harvesting, I went to the Victoria Hospital for an infusion of High-Dose Cyclophosphamide, administered overnight via a drip in my arm. With a cheery smile, Dr Williamson said: "Your hair will fall out within three weeks." As I understand it, the High-Dose Cyclophosphamide suppresses the production of abnormal proteins, so that they can then administer another drug to boost the production of normal stem-cells which are then harvested on the 'Apheresis' machine. It seemed counter-intuitive. Can stem-cells really be healthy after such a massive dose of a mustard gas derivative?

By Wednesday 14th March I felt awful—extremely tired and unwell. I spent most of the day in bed. The very thought of food made me sick. I was shivery all the time. On Thursday 15th, two cards arrived in the post: one from Lorraine and one from Joan and Brian Fullarton. I especially appreciated their thoughtful and kind messages of support.

On Monday 19th March, Norma and I got up early and drove to the "Apheresis Unit" at Edinburgh Royal Infirmary (ERI), where I expected to be hooked up to the machine, which would circulate the blood from my left arm, through a centrifuge to separate the stem cells, returning the 'skimmed' blood to my body via a canula in my right arm. First, I had a blood test and had to wait for an hour before the lab processed it. My blood count was too low, so they sent us home and told us to come back next day. The same happened on Tuesday. By Wednesday, my blood count was high enough to start the procedure. The friendly and competent nurses hooked me up to the machine. It whirred away for several hours, after which a transparent plastic bag of yellowish liquid—my stem-cells—had been 'harvested' from my blood. I went back again on the Thursday for a second round. The nurse labelled the plastic bags with my details and sent them off to be kept in a deep freeze somewhere until needed for the stem-cell transplant. Two bags of stem-cells were collected so that, God forbid, if I ever needed a second transplant, I wouldn't have to go through the harvesting procedure again.

On 12th April, Norma and I did some shopping in St. Andrews in the morning. When we got home, a letter had arrived from the Western General hospital in Edinburgh, informing me that a PICC line was to be inserted on 19th April, prior to transplant (A PICC line is a thin plastic tube, threaded through a vein in your arm until it reaches the heart, so that they can administer medication without constantly stabbing you with a needle). The letter also confirmed my transplant admission date: Monday 23rd April.

After lunch, I opened my email and found a message from Ruth McCarty in Belfast, in which she encouraged

Norma and I to rest on the promises of God. She passed on the following verse:

"I know that thou canst do all things, and that no purpose of thine can be restrained". (Job 42:2)

This thought was very precious. I felt the steadying hand of God, reminding me that He was with me.

～

51 STEM-CELL TRANSPLANT AND BEYOND

I was admitted to the Western General in Edinburgh on the afternoon of 23 April 2018. I sat in a little conservatory area for a wee while and read a book. One of the other patients came and sat down opposite me. A friendly chap named Bill. Next morning, about eleven o'clock, they gave me the High Dose of 'Melphalan' via the PICC line in my arm. It took just over an hour to drip feed into me. They advised me to suck ice pops to prevent ulcers forming in my mouth. Unfortunately, the ice pops numbed my mouth and the inside of my cheeks and I bit the insides of my cheeks without realising. I began to spit great gobs of blood. The inside of my cheeks were in quite a mess and took several days to heal. That was nothing compared to the effects of the Melphalan, which immediately caused substantial damage. My white blood count plummeted. I felt weak and extremely ill. I lost my appetite. Hospital food tasted even more cardboard-like than usual, and the very thought of eating was nauseating. I forced myself to eat in order to stay alive, but my intake was much reduced. This is known as an 'iatrogenic illness'—illness caused by medical intervention. (So much for the Hippocratic promise, 'do no harm'). Within a few hours, I went from being healthy and full of energy to feeling like a wet rag with holes in it. I lost my appetite, my joints ached, and I was shivery, as if I had a bad dose of 'flu. A medically induced illness to make me better? It didn't seem right.

On Thursday (26th April), a technician arrived with what looked like a picnic cool-box. Inside was one of the plastic bags of stem-cells, harvested from me at Edinburgh Royal in March. The bag had to be defrosted gently for an hour or two before a nurse hooked it up to drip-feed it via my PICC line. This took a couple of hours in the afternoon. So far so good. Around tea-time, my heart started beating irregularly. I called a nurse, who called Dr Roddy. I was suffering a severe arrhythmia—a dangerously irregular heart rhythm which, if not corrected, might lead to sudden death. Twice, to no avail, Dr Roddy injected me with something which was supposed to slow the heart rate—my heart seemed to stop dead for two or three moments; I've never felt such an alarming, awful feeling in all my life; I thought I was going to die. Dr Roddy then tried a Beta Blocker injection. To his, and my even greater relief, this settled things down and averted catastrophe.

That evening, for reasons that seem to have more to do with making life easier for nurses than patients, a business-like nurse arrived and inserted a catheter to empty my bladder into a bag, so that they could measure the output. I couldn't stand the feeling of that horrible plastic tube dangling from that most sensitive part of my anatomy, so later that night, I tried to pull it out. No-one had told me there's a balloon thing at the bladder end which must be deflated before they can extract it. I can tell you from experience, both the insertion and removal procedures were extremely uncomfortable.

On the Sunday, my brother James texted the words of Psalm 41:3

"The LORD sustains him on his sickbed; in his illness you restore him to full health."

That morning I recorded in my diary,

"I had three severe bouts of diarrhoea. Norma and Evelyn Notman came on the bus to visit me. I'm afraid I wasn't good company."

Next day, Monday 30th April, I was extremely tired and weak. Norma and Joel came to visit me that evening. Norma was visibly upset by the deterioration in my condition. When they left, I prayed and asked the Lord to heal me quickly and turn around my situation. I reminded Him of the words of the Lord Jesus: "What father, if his son asks for a loaf, will give him a stone?" I prayed, knowing that my Father in heaven wants to give good gifts to His children (Matt 7:9). At ten o'clock that evening, I felt a definite change. I felt much stronger. It was as if someone flipped a switch. God answered my prayer. That night, I heard Bill, who was in the room next to mine, crying out several times. I don't remember seeing him afterwards and have always wondered if he made it out of there alive.

Until this point, I kept a daily diary of my treatment and the events that occurred. The diary entries became more irregular between May and October. I guess I needed to focus my energy on getting better.

On Tuesday 1st May I wrote:

"Last night about 10.00pm I suddenly felt much stronger. An answer to prayer. Before, I was so weak and had no appetite and felt cold all the time. This morning I was able to eat more than just picking at food, my appetite is returning! I had a biscuit and a coffee at 11.00am, something I couldn't have faced yesterday. Nurse Julia Yen reported she had dipped my urine and sent off a sample - possible infection. I hope and trust the Lord will continue to overrule and grant me a steady recovery. "The Lord is on my side among them that help me." I have no doubts about that. Julia came in again to tell me my neutrophils have dipped again—to 0.6 from 0.9 yesterday and 7.5 the day before. So still a road to travel before I get out of here. God is over all."

The following week, on Tuesday 8th May, a tall, well-spoken, sun-tanned consultant—called Peter Johnson remarkably enough (hey, same name!)—brought six medical students into my room. For the benefit of his students, he asked me to relate the steps I'd undergone in my diagnosis and treatment. I summarised my medical journey in layman's terms. He seemed impressed by my knowledge of the process and asked the students to especially note the steps that resulted in the confirmation of my diagnosis. Later that afternoon, I got the first of several blood transfusions to help raise my blood cell levels. It was about this time that an officious nurse put her angry little head around my door and said, "Stop pressing the buzzer. There are other patients in this ward as well, you know." I didn't say it, but thought to myself: "Well if you hadn't taken so long to respond, I wouldn't have kept pressing the buzzer."

Martin, Evelyn, and Norma came and visited me that evening. It was good to see them, even for a short time.

The massive dose of Melphalan wiped out my immune system. I was very weak and unwell for several months while my stem cells slowly regenerated. Those grim days and weeks in the isolation ward at the Western General seemed to drag on forever. All I could do was hold on to the precious promises God had given me.

My hospital stay in Edinburgh was made worse because of the Acute Kidney Injury (AKI) I suffered, caused by the infection which happened while I was there. I clearly remember an older nurse who took blood from me one day. She didn't bother washing her hands and didn't put on a pair of latex gloves the way the others did. On top of this, she went through her pockets looking for something, taking out a used paper hanky and other detritus—all potential sources of infection for someone with low immunity. She may not have been the culprit—I'll never know for sure—but it was just after this that Julia Yen dipped my urine and the AKI was diagnosed. They treated the infection with successive infusions of high strength, intravenous antibiotics, which weakened me even more.

They released me from the Western General 'Penitentiary' on Thursday, 10th May. Norma picked me up. I was too weak to drive, but so thankful to be getting home at last. Unfortunately, my freedom didn't even last twenty-four hours. The Western General had arranged an appointment for me at the Victoria Hospital, Kirkcaldy, next morning. 'The Vic' is only ten minutes from our house, so Norma dropped me off and went home, expecting me to call her when my checks and tests were all done. To her immense disappointment, I phoned—not to tell her to

come and pick me up—but to bring my toothbrush, py-
jamas etc., as the doctors had decided I wasn't well
enough to go home and needed to spend more time in
hospital until they got on top of the kidney infection. Consultant Kerri Davidson said, "The Western General let you
go too soon!"

Another Consultant, Victoria Campbell, a very competent
young doctor, knelt beside my bed and said: 'Don't
worry, we're going to get you to the other side of the
bridge.' Those words filled me with confidence that the
medical expertise of the doctors at Kirkcaldy would be
effective. I spent the next two weeks in 'The Vic', where I
got the very best care and attention, in a bright new hospital wing which was so different from the tired old
building I'd been in at the Western General. The nurses
also seemed friendlier. One, named Holly, was so empa-
thetic and caring in the way she did her job. It was like a
tonic and reminded me how much physical environment
and social interactions affect our mood and our health
and wellbeing. Vitally important for both patients and
staff.

Unfortunately, because of the copious amounts of intravenous fluids pumped into me, my legs and feet became
very swollen. I got two huge blisters—one on top of my
right foot and the other on the inside of my right ankle,
which took weeks to heal and curtailed my ability to walk;
they were so tender I had to wear soft slippers—eventually, a cheery specialist nurse came in and burst them
with a scalpel. You'd need to be cheery in a job like that! I
had to have the raw sores dressed for a week or two until
they healed.

One of my abiding memories of my stay at 'The Vic', in contrast to the rather static view from my window in the Western, was the excellent view I had of the hospital plant room, where on certain days, a lorry arrived and the plant room operators opened up remote controlled metal doors over two gigantic pits. The lorry then backed up and shed its load of biomass fuel into the pit. The giant metal doors slowly returned to their place, the lorry drove off, the plant room operators disappeared inside, and the scene returned to its usual state of not-much-happening-at-all. At certain times of day, I watched the same dog walkers emerge like clockwork from the housing estate near the back of the plant room and hang about on the grassy area until their pet 'performed' its business. This, and the regular flow of local buses picking folks up and dropping them off at the bus stop below my window, were the only distractions from daytime T.V., which bored me stupid. Unfortunately, I missed the excitement in the car park one day—a nurse told me there had been a fight between a pensioner and a pregnant woman over a space in the disabled parking area. Security had to be called to restore order!

I finally got home for good on 23rd May 2018. Over the summer, I made a slow but steady recovery. In July, Norma and I went for a few days' holiday to a bed-and-breakfast on the beautiful Ardnamurchan peninsula. It was great to be out and about again after being cooped up for so long. By that time, I could do most activities without getting out of breath. One day Joel and I climbed Falkland Hill. Joel ran up the hill while I plodded on after him, eventually reaching the top. At last, I felt more like my normal self.

Every four weeks between August and October that year, I attended the Queen Margaret Hospital in Dunfermline to have a Pentamidine infusion (inhaled via a plastic tube), to protect against pneumonia infections. First, I had to blow into a plastic gadget which measured how strong my lungs were. If it had registered below a certain threshold, it would not have been safe to proceed. Fortunately, my lung capacity was always good.

The first Sunday in August was a red-letter day. The consultant had advised me to avoid crowded places where someone could infect me with a cough or sneeze—so I wasn't able to attend the meetings of the church until then. It was wonderful to get back among the saints and be able to worship the Lord with His people in the House of God.

In September 2018, we took our regular trip to London for my six monthly check up at the Royal Free hospital, Hampstead. This time I didn't need the SAP scan, and all the blood results were good. I didn't have to go back until October 2019.

God restored my health. He answered my prayer and brought me through 'unscathed'. Other Amyloidosis patients have suffered ongoing 'peripheral neuropathy' (painful nerve damage plus constant tingling and loss of feeling, in hands or feet) because of the damaging chemotherapy. I was spared that. Apart from dizziness if I bend down for too long because of my low blood pressure, I feel fine. I don't know whether the doctors were amazed at my recovery. The only thing Dr Clark, the Haematology consultant told me, was that my eGFR count (a measure of how well kidneys are functioning)—had at one point reached a low of 12ml/min when I had the Acute Kidney Infection but had since risen to within the normal range at 60ml/min. If they were amazed, they didn't show it. But I have everything to be thankful to God for.

Why did the Lord give me another chance, yet take away better men than me? My younger cousin Joel in Vancouver was called home a few years ago in his fifties. He always kept himself extremely fit and loved to hike in the mountains around Vancouver with his wife Carol and their family of three teenage boys. Why was he taken and not me? I don't know. As George Whitefield said, "Man is immortal until his work is done." I can only conclude that God has more work for me to do for Him—and, I don't doubt He has further work to do in me: that I might be "conformed to the image of his Son" (Rom 8:29)

> I know not why God's wondrous grace
> To me hath been made known,
> Nor why, unworthy as I am,
> He claimed me for His own!
> But I know whom I have believed,
> And am persuaded that He is able
> To keep that which I've committed
> unto Him, against that day.

PHSS 326

52 MUM'S LAST DAYS

Eventually, to my great relief, I didn't have to swallow a daily cocktail of pills. My strength returned and life got back to normal. I started painting again; I started work on this book; I co-authored and self-published an illustrated primer on Bible prophecy with Neville Coomer, and I joined the editorial team of Bible Studies magazine. Karl Smith stepped down from the Tract committee and I took over from him as senior editor. It's good to be productive.

Best of all, Norma and I were able to visit Mum again, and along with the rest of the family, give her the extra support she needed.

As she got older, her hearing deteriorated and phone calls became increasingly difficult. Amusingly, there was a phase of her deafness when she would say: "Wait a minute, I'll take my hearing aid out so that I can hear you better!" Sometimes that worked, but eventually, the only way we could communicate effectively was when we were physically present with her. If she didn't catch what we said by watching our lips, we could write it down for her to read. I also used an app on my phone which translated spoken words to written text.

At one stage, we talked about the possibility of Mum going into sheltered housing. Elisabeth and I explored the options in Ayrshire and Fife. We went as far as arranging appointments to view several vacancies. I remember taking Mum to visit a self-contained flat in a sheltered housing complex in Glenrothes, ten minutes from our house, where we could have kept an eye on her and given support when needed. She liked the accommodation well enough, and I thought we might just persuade her just to make the move. We then went and sat down for a chat with some of the other residents in the communal area where residents could meet, as well as participating in regular social events organised by the manager of the complex. All went well until one resident, a man in a wheelchair, made a lewd remark about one of the other residents: "They call her Jenny drap your pants" he said. He thought he was being funny. The expression on Mum's face told me she thought it was anything but. From that moment on, she firmly decided, that since Dad had bought the house in Dunlop, she should stay there as long as she was able. Who could blame her? In the end, it probably worked out for the best.

With the rest of the family, we visited regularly. John visited every Tuesday night and played a game of dominoes with Mum, which she very much enjoyed, and Elisabeth and Jolie took turns at doing Mum's hair on a Saturday. Every month or two, James and William faithfully made the journey from Aberdeen and Armagh, respectively. Between daily visits from carers and weekly visits from at least one of the family, she continued living on her own.

In her youth, Mum crushed her toes into stiletto-heeled pointy shoes, which resulted in chronic bunions and severely deformed toes on both feet. In her last four or five years, the circulation to her feet became progressively worse, and she developed weeping sores between some of her toes, which then became 'necrotic' and died from lack of sufficient oxygen and blood flow. Eventually, two of her toes fell off. Mark, the podiatrist who dressed her wounds twice a week said there was nothing he could do, except keep the wounds clean to avoid infection. An operation to widen the veins in her legs, was too risky. As Mark explained, and Mum knew from experience, those kind of sores are as painful as severe frostbite. Mum always had a high pain threshold—she always refused a local anaesthetic when having her teeth drilled at the dentist! But the pain in her feet kept her awake most nights, despite using painkillers. She bore it with amazing fortitude.

Mum and Norma, Dunlop 2020

In the last couple of years before she died, Mum had several falls. We installed grab bars and signed up for the personal alarm system run by the local council via an intercom linked to the telephone. We also installed cameras in the living room, kitchen and study so that we could monitor her via an online app on our mobile phones. Sometimes I checked the cameras before I went to bed or when I got up in the middle of the night. Often, I saw Mum still hobbling around the house, going back and forth between the cupboard under the stairs where she kept biscuits and breakfast cereal, or between kitchen and living room. Day merged into night. She often made up for lost sleep by dosing off in the chair in the living room during the day.

Life for Mum went on in this way, largely without incident. She thrived on the regular visits of care staff, family and friends. With John's faithful taxi service—he came all the way from Clarkston in Glasgow every week—she was able to get out to remember the Lord each Sunday morning. Then, in early 2020, the political 'panic-demic' known as COVID-19 changed everything.

Scottish government travel restrictions during 'lockdown' forbade me to travel across country to Ayrshire. Norma and I continued to visit her, regardless. Mum's quality of life was far more important than the tiny risk of transmitting, or indeed, catching the virus, when not one of us had any symptoms.

Mum had three visits a day from carers, who assisted with meals and personal care, plus two visits a week from a podiatrist to dress her foot. Each of these professionals continued to visit multiple households every day, while Norma and I, being retired, hardly saw anyone from day to day.

At the end of October 2020, Mum's condition worsened. I took her to see her GP in Beith, Dr Dimitar Nechev, a sympathetic doctor, originally from Bulgaria. He arranged an immediate scan at A&E in Kilmarnock. I drove her from the surgery to Crosshouse Hospital, in East Ayrshire. As I wheeled her into the emergency department, large unfriendly notices on the door confronted us, one of which read: **NO RELATIVES.**

Unfriendly notices on the doors of the A&E department, Crosshouse Hospital, October 2020

I parked Mum in her wheelchair beside a row of seats in the waiting area and sat beside her. When her name was called, I handed her over to the triage nurse, who took her into the inner sanctum of the department. Some time later, a doctor emerged and informed me they were going to admit Mum to the 'Combined Assessment Unit'. I asked to see her, to reassure her and make sure she knew what was happening before I left. He said 'No, that's not allowed'. I asked if he could bring her to the door of A&E so that I could at least wave goodbye through the windows on the door. That wasn't possible either. I barely controlled my anger and frustration. I went to the Combined Assessment Unit and asked the receptionist how long they would keep my mother in A&E before being transferred to the unit. A nurse, who was standing beside the receptionist, told me that another patient had recently waited seventeen hours in A&E before a bed became available. I went home feeling that I had abandoned Mum to lie on a plastic plinth for hours, her contact with me abruptly cut off. Of course, they were only doing their job, keeping everyone safe. Too bad if one or two patients forfeited reassurance from a familiar family member.

In the days that followed, they denied Elisabeth and the rest of us any contact with Mum. We had to rely on daily phone calls to the assessment unit to find out how she was. Then, when they transferred her to another ward, still no access, only phone calls. Calls which sometimes were not answered, or when they were, they left us in no doubt that staff were being run off their feet. One wonders where all the money has gone, supposedly poured into the NHS over the last few years.

We wrote to local MSPs and also to Ayrshire and Arran Health Board officials, asking for a relaxation of the 'no relatives' rule so that at least one of us could visit. We were refused permission. Mum was then transferred to a rehabilitation ward in another hospital, (Ayrshire Central, in Irvine), where they granted us the concession of daily, pre-arranged, fifteen-minute Zoom calls. We were also—grudgingly—granted the 'privilege' of visiting Mum's window since her room was on the ground floor, facing the access route to the hospital entrance.

Enter, a wonderful pink-haired, down-to-earth nursing assistant named Marisha, with a straightforward Ayrshire accent, whose job it was to facilitate Zoom calls for patients and their families during the COVID-19 crisis. What a difference she made! For two and a half months, James, William, John, Elisabeth and I had a fifteen-minute Zoom call with Mum on weekdays. (Marisha didn't work weekends and none of the other staff volunteered to do it on Saturdays and Sundays.) Marisha was so kind and good to Mum. She was good with us too! A caring, friendly, practical girl whom we got to know well over those weeks. To my surprise, one day, I discovered Marisha had also gone to Duncan of Jordanstone College of Art, where she'd studied Ceramics and had become an art teacher after graduation. However, like me years before, she only got supply work, since there were too few Art Teacher vacancies. She got fed up doing supply work and retrained as a nursing assistant. How thankful we were for Marisha! She made the intolerable 'no relatives' rule almost bearable for Mum and we will be forever grateful for the light she brought us in those dark days. She was on holiday over Christmas and New Year, so Zoom calls were spasmodic and only happened if a member of staff was available to do it. Mum grew steadily weaker over this period. More than ever, she needed the comfort of our physical presence. Whenever she saw us at the window, she beckoned us to come in and couldn't understand why we had to stay outside.

Elisabeth and John faithfully visited, waving at Mum's window and holding up written whiteboard messages for her to read. James, William and I were more limited in our visits because of our greater distance from the hospital. Just after Christmas, following renewed fears about a new Coronavirus strain, hospital policy appeared to change; they actively discouraged us from coming to the window—an A4 notice appeared on the inside of the window commanding us to stay two metres away if we came at all. When a nurse saw Elisabeth outside one day, she opened the window and told her to stay away. On Monday 4th January 2021, Elisabeth visited Mum's window several times. On each occasion, the curtains were closed. When she phoned to ask why, she was told that Mum may have been getting personal care. The next day, she arrived at Mum's window and discovered the room was empty. No bed, nothing. Her mind racing, she phoned the ward and was told they had moved Mum to another room. When she located the room, Mum was asleep. Eventually, she woke up and saw Elisabeth, but stared blankly at her, not recognising her.

It seemed as if the hospital held all the cards. As a family, we felt an increasing sense of dismay. The odds were firmly stacked against us. "How many other families were enduring that same nightmare?"

We understood the need to protect patients. Ward staff told us there were Covid-positive patients in Mum's ward, so we had to accept the situation in order to provide what limited support we could. But Zoom calls and window visits at a two-metre distance were far from ideal for a ninety-three-year-old lady with acute hearing loss and fragile mental acuity who was too weak to get out of bed. At the very moment she needed her children with her, the hospital tightened the already restrictive concessions. It was distressing and frustrating—even more so when nurses, auxiliaries, cleaners, doctors and other health workers had free access in and out of Mum's room in the course of their work. Would the risk to anyone else really have been exponentially increased if a designated, masked, and gowned family member had been allowed into Mum's room to hold her hand for a brief visit every other day?

On 4th January 2021, we learned about Nicola Sturgeon's latest measures: another extended, Scotland-wide, total lockdown for at least the next month, perhaps longer. In the diary notes which I kept of Mum's incarceration in Ayrshire Central, I wrote: "Make no mistake; if our mother dies without the comfort of her family beside her, we will place the blame firmly at the door of Ms Sturgeon and Jason Leitch, her blowhard 'National Clinical director', and their equally guilty confederates in London. Our hearts cry out to God, for 'vain is the help of man'."

On Monday, 11th January, Mum was unresponsive during our midday Zoom call. Marisha couldn't hide the concern in her voice. "She's no' good th'day," she said. There was no point in continuing with the video call. About an hour later, my phone rang. It was the consultant in charge of Mum's case. She said: "I think your Mum is going to die soon." Suddenly, they relaxed the rules and granted us access to Mum's room to sit beside her. John and Elisabeth got to the hospital before me. The three of us took turns to sit with Mum and hold her hand. Over the next two days, John and I took turns to travel back and forth between the hospital and Dunlop to snatch a few hours' sleep. Elisabeth lived in Beith, so she could go home. Sometimes Mum tried to speak to us but could only move her lips. At least she knew we were there. On Wednesday 13th January, James drove down from Aberdeen. Mum rallied a bit while he was there. She smiled and responded with an appreciative nod as he held her hand and wrote some Bible verses and messages of love and support on the whiteboard. About an hour after he left, she took a turn for the worse. Motionless from then on, she never opened her eyes or lifted her head from the pillow. Elisabeth was sitting with her and John and I had started talking about something, when Elisabeth said "Boys." Mum made a couple of slight coughing noises and her shallow breathing stopped. It was 9.30 pm.

I went into the corridor and called the nurses. I think one of them was Holly, a nursing assistant who had filled in for Marisha a few days previously. It was hard to identify her with her face half covered with a mask. She said, "We'll take good care of her." There was some comfort in those words, knowing that even though Mum had passed into the presence of the Lord Jesus, those who had to deal with the body she had just vacated, would do so with care and dignity. We packed Mum's belongings into plastic bags and a couple of boxes and took them back to Dunlop before going home.

While we know a glorious day is coming when we'll see Mum again, that doesn't mitigate the seriousness of the injustice done to her by the authorities. For two and a half months, they denied her the physical contact with family that she so desperately needed. Whether out of sincere concern or political motivation, we felt that Sturgeon, Leitch and the Ayrshire and Arran hospital authorities—stole that time from Mum and from us because of the excessively restrictive measures they imposed. They made all the right noises, but in my opinion, their refusal to listen when we pleaded for limited family access revealed a monumental failure to show practical compassion to patients like Mum and their families.

As we adjust to life without our loving mother, we know that each of us did all we could to support her during her stay in hospital. We are glad that her suffering is over. Now, she has the wonderful joy and comfort of being with the Lord Jesus. As the apostle Paul wrote: 'To depart and be with Christ, is very far better'. We look forward to meeting again when all the perplexing challenges and injustices of this imperfect world will seem like a dream of the night. Isaiah sums it up well: 'For behold, I create new heavens and a new earth, and the former things shall not be remembered or come into mind.' (Is. 65:17) Thank God for that.

53 THE FUTURE FORETOLD

I've read the last chapter
JESUS CHRIST
Wins!
Do not take the
'Mark of the Beast'

The above message was written on a placard held aloft by one of hundreds of thousands of people who turned out to join the 'Freedom March' of British citizens on Saturday 29th May 2021. Some estimated the number of marchers was around one million. Photographs taken on the day[1], recorded a twelve-mile sea of people who marched from Parliament Square to Shepherd's Bush in London, protesting the Draconian measures imposed by politicians. True to form over the last year, the BBC and Sky News were curiously absent and hardly mentioned the march in their news bulletins.

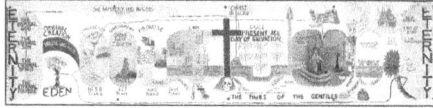

The Bible prophecy chart which I painted on canvas for Neville and Helen Coomer, was based on Harry King's original chart which Jackie Forbes had painted for Harry on a sheet of cotton.

From From October 2019, through 2020 and 2021, contributors to our 'Bible Studies' magazine studied the book of Revelation. Editing and reviewing their articles revitalised my interest in prophetic events. The sudden and far-reaching changes currently taking place under the pretext of bio-security are yet another sign that our world is approaching the end times illustrated in the prophetic chart. After the Church the Body of Christ is taken to heaven, the world will fall under the diabolical dictatorship of the man called in scripture, 'the Beast' and 'the Antichrist'. During that time, God will unleash fearful judgements on all who reject the gospel of the coming kingdom of Christ, which will be proclaimed by 144,000 fearless Israeli preachers. After an apparent solution to the Middle East problem, a seven-year covenant agreed between Antichrist and Israel, 'the Beast' will break his covenant in the middle of the seven years. The nation of Israel and all who support her will undergo the three-and-a-half-year period of intense suffering, known as the Great Tribulation, "the time of Jacob's trouble" (Jer. 30:7).

Who would have imagined at the beginning of 2019 that the liberty we and our parents and grandparents enjoyed all our lives would be so easily taken from us? In the space of twelve months, we' went from a nation of autonomous individuals, free to travel, free to socialise, free to start a business, free to worship God without restriction—to a nation of fearful, subservient sheep, forbidden by the state from living normal lives and even prevented from working—cowed into submission by a relentless propaganda machine which convinced the vast majority that COVID 19 and it's 'scariants' poses such an ongoing danger that only an experimental, gene-based injection, can save us. Seasonal coronaviruses have been with us for years. The NHS has been convulsed by an annual winter crisis for years. Our marvellous, God-given immune system has protected us from airborne viruses for thousands of years. But now, in these scientifically 'enlightened' times, we must compromise both our physical and mental health by obstructing our airways with useless, unhygienic masks and denying ourselves the comfort of human contact, whether we have symptoms or not.

Besides the unacceptably high rate of adverse reactions to messenger RNA injections, one major concern, completely ignored by mainstream media, is the likelihood that they'll cause permanent damage to our immune system's ability to fight off infection. Yet politicians, GP's, medical professionals and so-called experts have promoted 'the jab'—or 'the jag' as our Radio Scotland reporters insist on calling it (we've always got to be different)—as the answer to all our fears. Regardless of any supposed protection these 'vaccines' may offer, we were subjected to a never-ending cycle of house arrests, even though 'lockdowns' did little to control the spread of the virus. Reason, caution and common-sense were thrown to the wind. Now they're injecting healthy children, who are at zero risk from the virus. This, despite many reports of serious damage to the heart. The world appears to have gone mad.

I salute the few brave souls who've had the courage and integrity to take a stand against the tsunami of propaganda and coercion that has engulfed our world: notably, Mail on Sunday journalist Peter Hitchens, Neil Oliver on GB News, Professor Sucharit Bhakdi, Dr Mike Yeadon (former head of Pfizer's research department), the internationally respected epidemiologist John Ioannidis, Pathology professor Dr Roger Hodkinson in Canada, Lytton GP Dr Charles Hoffe in British Columbia, Dr Sunetra Gupta at Oxford University, Dr Peter McCulloch in America, and many others. But their voices are deliberately suppressed and disgracefully vilified. People are being conditioned to accept at face-value everything the government and the media tell them. Dissenting opinions are not welcome, even from highly qualified experts; a disturbing state of affairs. Whether we attribute the actions of those in authority to panic and sheer ignorance, or to more sinister motives, I believe that behind the scenes, Satan, God's implacable enemy, knows that the purposes of God are ripening fast. He knows his time is short. The Devil is preparing the ground for the cataclysmic conflict between himself and God in the time of the end, predicted thousands of years ago in the Bible by men of God..

If you want to find out more about what the Bible says about the time of the end, I recommend 'The Finger of Prophecy'[2], jointly written by Jack L. Ferguson and Bob Armstrong—a Scotsman and a Canadian—both of whom I had the privilege of listening to and talking with in my younger days. They were outstanding Bible students and preachers.

I believe the return of the Lord Jesus to the air is just around the corner. How wonderful it would be if I were visiting Dad and Mum's grave at the very moment when the Lord descends to the upper atmosphere and calls us home! To see my parents rise from the dead, in new, incorruptible bodies would be marvellous. Even better, to be caught up together with them to meet our Saviour in the air, with myriads of the redeemed; that moment will surpass our wildest dreams.

When I was a teenager, I had a dream which happened regularly. In the dream, I could defy gravity. I could step up into the air and in a few moments, be high above the landscape, able to soar through the air like a bird. One day soon that dream may well become a reality; not that I'll be able to step up into the air and fly about wherever I want, that's fantasy. But when the Lord Jesus returns, at His command, I will be "caught up to meet the Lord in the air!" as 1 Thessalonians 4 tells us. That's the golden prospect which lightens the demoralising events of recent times, The Lord Jesus promised His disciples: "If I go, I will come again and receive you unto myself." (John 14)

After 'the rapture', events on earth will move faster than ever. There will be no freedom for people to act independently or according to their conscience. Everyone will be obliged to comply with the authoritarian rule of the world system and the man who will emerge from obscurity to dominate the world; both of which—the system and the man—the Bible calls 'The Beast'. Compliance with his diabolical agenda will be mandatory. He will ensure that those who refuse will suffer for it.

Around 1988/89, I attended a series of seminars about Bible Prophecy by evangelist Harry King (see my note, below). He used the chart painted by Jackie Forbes in Kirkintilloch to illustrate those talks. In one of the plenary sessions, someone asked Harry whether everyone who takes the mark will be in the Lake of Fire. He pointed out that in every case where those with the mark are consigned to the Lake of Fire, they are also described as worshippers of the Beast. Without being dogmatic, this opens the possibility that some may be spared who take the mark of the Beast on their hand, just to feed themselves and their family, even if they believe on Jesus and refuse to worship the Beast. When the Lord Jesus gathers the nations before him and 'separates the sheep from the goats' (Mat. 25:31-46), He will adjudicate between those who are admitted to His Millennial kingdom and those who will join the Beast and the false prophet in the place of torment. But thousands, (probably millions), who deify the Beast and unashamedly accept his mark on hand or forehead, will sign their eternal death warrant by so doing.

This warning will sound far-fetched to the modern mind, conditioned as it is, to believe that the material, physical world is all we have. Many say, "when you're dead, you're dead." But just because the majority believe a lie doesn't mean the truth is any less valid.

I challenge you to read the Bible with an open mind. Ask God to reveal Himself to you in His Living Word. If you do that, the Bible will come alive and the Holy Spirit will speak to your heart.

. . .

[NOTE: Some years ago, I transferred the cassette tapes of Harry's seminars to audio files and uploaded them to the Internet Archive — https://archive.org/details/HarryKingTrack2 — They were recorded at Wishaw around 1988 and are well worth listening to. If you listen carefully, you'll hear my younger self in the recordings of the plenary sessions, asking questions on behalf of my discussion group!]

～

THE MYSTERY HID IN GOD
EPH 3:9

ETERNITY

THE ETERNAL GOD

THE ETERNAL SON

THE ETERNAL SPIRIT

THE ETERNAL PURPOSE

ORIGINAL CREATION

CHAOTIC

EDEN

CONSCIENCE

SETHITES
ENOCH

CAIN
ABEL

CAINITES
LAMECH

1656 YEARS

GOVERNMENT

SHEM
HAM
JAPHETH

BABEL

427 YEARS

PROMISE

ABRAHAM
ISAAC
JACOB
JOSEPH

MELCHIZ
JOB

ISRAEL

430 YEARS

LAW

MOSES
JOSHUA
SAUL
DAVID
SOLOMON

ISAIAH
JEREMIAH
EZEKIEL

DANIEL

ZEPHANIAH
MALACHI

ZERUB
EZRA
NEHEMIAH

TABERNACLE

TEMPLE OF SOLOMON

EXILE 70

TEMPLE OF ZERU

10 TRIBES

1491 YEARS

EPILOGUE

Looking back, I'm thankful I was born and brought up in the family, in the church and during the times in which I've lived and worked. Even if there had been no 'case-demic', I have thought for many years that my generation had the best of it. I fear for my children and grandchildren's future as I see the continuing downward spiral of moral, spiritual, economic and social conditions. Of course, each generation makes the best of the world in which they find themselves and I'm sure my descendants will rise to the challenges in their own way. I can't change things for them. All I can do is pray for their welfare and trust that God will look after them.

David, Victoria and Joel

Until the Lord returns, or until I'm called home, whichever is sooner, I'll do my best to serve Him and care for my nearest and dearest, within the limits imposed by circumstance, time and place. One thing life's experiences give us, is a more reflective spirit. What lessons have I learned? One thing is the importance of personal integrity. Another, the value of faithfulness to the word of God, even though that means being increasingly out of step with a Godless world.

My recent health scare moved me to write this book while I still had time. By the grace of God, the story's not over yet.

> 'How dull it is to pause, to make an end,
> To rust unburnish'd, not to shine in use!'
> As tho' to breathe were life!

Those words from the poem I learned at school all those years ago, encapsulates my desire to end the race well. Here it is in full:

ULYSSES

It little profits that an idle king,

By this still hearth, among these barren crags,

Match'd with an aged wife, I mete and dole

Unequal laws unto a savage race,

That hoard, and sleep, and feed, and know not me.

I cannot rest from travel: I will drink

Life to the lees: All times I have enjoy'd

Greatly, have suffer'd greatly, both with those

That loved me, and alone, on shore, and when

Thro' scudding drifts the rainy Hyades

Vext the dim sea: I am become a name;

For always roaming with a hungry heart

Much have I seen and known; cities of men

And manners, climates, councils, governments,

Myself not least, but honour'd of them all;

And drunk delight of battle with my peers,

Far on the ringing plains of windy Troy.

I am a part of all that I have met;

Yet all experience is an arch wherethro'

Gleams that untravell'd world whose margin fades

For ever and forever when I move.

· · ·

HOW DULL IT is to pause, to make an end,

To rust unburnish'd, not to shine in use!

As tho' to breathe were life! Life piled on life

Were all too little, and of one to me

Little remains: but every hour is saved

From that eternal silence, something more,

A bringer of new things; and vile it were

For some three suns to store and hoard myself,

And this gray spirit yearning in desire

To follow knowledge like a sinking star,

Beyond the utmost bound of human thought.

THIS IS MY SON, mine own Telemachus,

To whom I leave the sceptre and the isle, —

Well-loved of me, discerning to fulfil

This labour, by slow prudence to make mild

A rugged people, and thro' soft degrees

Subdue them to the useful and the good.

Most blameless is he, centred in the sphere

Of common duties, decent not to fail

In offices of tenderness, and pay

Meet adoration to my household gods,

When I am gone. He works his work, I mine.

. . .

THERE LIES THE PORT; the vessel puffs her sail:

There gloom the dark, broad seas. My mariners,

Souls that have toil'd, and wrought, and thought
with me—

That ever with a frolic welcome took

The thunder and the sunshine, and opposed

Free hearts, free foreheads—you and I are old;

Old age hath yet his honour and his toil;

Death closes all: but something ere the end,

Some work of noble note, may yet be done,

Not unbecoming men that strove with Gods.

THE LIGHTS BEGIN to twinkle from the rocks:

The long day wanes: the slow moon climbs: the deep

Moans round with many voices. Come, my friends,

'Tis not too late to seek a newer world.

Push off, and sitting well in order smite

The sounding furrows; for my purpose holds

To sail beyond the sunset, and the baths

Of all the western stars, until I die.

It may be that the gulfs will wash us down:

It may be we shall touch the Happy Isles,

And see the great Achilles, whom we knew.

THO' much is taken, much abides; and tho'

We are not now that strength which in old days

Moved earth and heaven, that which we are, we are;

One equal temper of heroic hearts,

Made weak by time and fate, but strong in will

To strive, to seek, to find, and not to yield.

APPENDICES

I have copied two of my own sermons here. The first, a gospel message, bringing before you the claims of the eternal Son of of God.

The second is an appeal to my fellow believers, to consider one of the most neglected, yet most important of truths which runs like a golden thread throughout both Old and New Testament writings. The glorious subject of 'The House of God'.

The third appendix reproduces the notes Dad made for an address he was due to give on John chapter 17 at Kilmarnock in October 2008. He died before he could fulfil that fixture. We printed his notes on the back of the order of service at his funeral.

Appendices IV and V show the music and words of the hymns sung before and after meals at Camp.

Appendix VI gives a sample of the Shetland poet referred to earlier.

APPENDIX I: THE DEITY OF CHRIST

I want to show you from scripture the sublime truth of the Deity of Christ.

It's beyond the grasp of human logic—but not beyond the grasp of faith in the life-giving word of God.

When I was a boy, my father taught me how to say the opening words of the Bible in Hebrew: the first line of Genesis chapter 1, the first book of the Old Testament:

בְּרֵאשִׁית בָּרָא אֱלֹהִים אֵת הַשָּׁמַיִם וְאֵת הָאָרֶץ

'birishith bara Elohim ayth hashamayim v'ayth ha-aretz'

That's the English transliteration. In English it means:

"In the beginning God created the heaven and the earth." (Gen 1:1)

Link this with the opening words of John's Gospel in the New Testament:

"In the beginning was the Word, and the Word was with God, and the Word was God..." (John 1:1)

John writes: "All things were made by him"—All things! A grain of sand, the far-flung star, a tiny flower, the blazing sun.

William Blake, one of our finest English poets wrote a poem about the essence of a tiger—in which he posed a terrifying question, which is really about the majesty of the Creator, who is so much greater than ourselves, the very essence of whose being deserves our utmost reverence:

> "Tyger! Tyger! burning bright,
> In the forests of the night,
> What immortal hand or eye
> Could frame thy fearful symmetry?
> Did he smile his work to see?
> Did he who made the Lamb make thee?"

WILLIAM BLAKE

John goes on in chapter 1: "and the Word became flesh…"

"No man has seen God at any time; the only begotten Son, which is in the bosom of the Father, he has declared him." (John 1:1,14,18)

John is not talking about an ordinary mortal man like you or me. He's talking about a man who is both God and man; a man who, though subject to the limitations of a human body, is at the same time OMNIPOTENT, OMNI-SCIENT, OMNIPRESENT: All powerful, all seeing/all knowing, present everywhere at the same time.

God is omnipresent: everywhere at the same time

Jeremiah 23:24: "Can any hide himself in secret places so that I shall not see him? saith Jehovah. Do not I fill heaven and earth? saith Jehovah." John Wesley said: "the universal God dwells in universal space."

In His prayer to God the Father, before He went to the cross, the Lord Jesus said in John 17:5:

"..Father, glorify thou me with thine own self with the glory which I had with thee before the world was…"

He had a prior existence.

When Moses heard the voice of God speaking to him from the burning bush, the LORD said to him: "I AM has sent you" (The Hebrew word for LORD is Yahweh or Jehovah] (Ex 3:14)

Jesus said to the Jewish religious leaders who questioned His identity: "Before Abraham was, I AM" (John 8:58) He attributed the Divine Name of the Supreme Being, who exists outside of time and place in the eternal here and now, to Himself.

God is Omniscient: All knowing, all seeing

Proverbs 15:3 says: "The eyes of Jehovah are in every place, keeping watch upon the evil and the good."

 To Nathanael Jesus said:

 Before Philip called you, when you were under the fig tree, I saw you.

JOHN 1:48

Jesus told His disciples, not a sparrow falls to the ground, but God knows about it, and He added:

the very hairs of your head are all numbered

MATTHEW 10:29

He knew all about Moses—knew his exact position. God has no need for a GPS tracking system, no need for an out-of-date satellite picture. He saw him in real time.

He knows all about you. He knew all about you before you were born; He knows "your downsitting and your up-rising" (Ps 139:2) He cares about your welfare; He has a purpose for your life; He wants you to enjoy fellowship with Him.

God is Omnipotent: all powerful.

The Bible presents us with evidence of His Power.

In Romans 1:20, Paul writes: "For the invisible things of him since the creation of the world are clearly seen, being perceived through the things that are made, even his everlasting power and divinity; that they may be without excuse."

The Lord Jesus Christ is Immanuel—a Hebrew name meaning 'God with us'. In Matthew 1:23, we read: "Behold, the virgin shall be with child, and shall bring forth a son, And they shall call his name Immanuel; which is, being interpreted, God with us." This is a direct quote from the book of Isaiah in the Old Testament (Isaiah 7:14)

The Greek name 'Jesus' means "Jehovah the Saviour".

Jesus raised the dead: "Young man, I say to you, arise." (Luke 7:14)

He calmed the raging storm with a word: "Peace, be still" (Mark 4:39)

He said to His disciples: "Peace I leave with you; my peace I give unto you: not as the world gives, give I unto you. Let not your heart be troubled, neither let it be fearful." (John 14:27) That's why I can sing with confidence the words of the hymn writer: "There's a peace in my heart that the world never gave, a peace it cannot take away…"

Jesus healed the blind: "two blind men … according to your faith, be it done to you" (Matt 9:29)

He healed the leper "Be made clean …" "… immediately his hand was restored, whole as the other." (Matt 8:3)

He opened the mouth of the dumb: "Be opened"—immediately his tongue was loosed and he spoke clearly" (Mark 7:34)

This is none other than our great Creator, of whom it is written:

"He commanded and it stood fast; He spake and it was done". (Ps 33:9)

"In the beginning God created the heaven and the earth." (Gen 1:1)

Therefore, the heaven and the earth including you and me—belong to Him.

"He has made us and we are His." (Ps 100:3)

This is the one who was born in Bethlehem, who grew up in Nazareth, who for three and a half years walked the length and breadth of the land of Israel preaching and teaching and healing people, and then, at the time appointed by His God and Father, laid down his life on a

Roman cross outside Jerusalem. This is "Immanuel" — "God with us."

This is the one, who called Abraham out of Ur of the Chaldees; who took Moses from watching over a flock of sheep in the wilderness and made him leader of his people, Israel.

This is the one who brought Israel out of Egypt with a powerful hand; who tabernacled among them through all their wilderness journey despite their unfaithfulness, because he had purposes of grace in them; this is the one who answered their prayers and gave them victory and brought them into the promised land.

This is the one who sent his prophets to Israel when they went astray, the one who came seeking fruit from his vineyard. He had invested so much in them through the centuries. Yet John sadly had to record their rejection of Him:

"He came unto his own, and they that were his own received him not." (John 1:11)

This is the one who saw YOU from eternity past and who came to die for you.

"No man has seen God at any time; the only begotten Son, which is in the bosom of the Father, he has declared him." (John 1:18)

The writer to the Hebrews says in chapter 1 verse 3: "He is the effulgence of God's glory, the very image of his substance".

This mighty one told Peter on the very night of His betrayal that He could have called ten thousand times ten thousand angels to destroy the world. But He hadn't come to judge the world; He came to save it. In Christ we see the wonderful love of God, revealed in his submission to the will of God, despite men's hatred and rejection.

A mortal man would have given up. You or I, faced with such hatred and rejection, would have said "they're not worth it". That's what the Devil tried to make Him do when he spoke to Jesus through the scribes and Pharisees at the cross. They said: "Save yourself; if you're the King of Israel, come down from the cross and we'll believe on you". What provocation! Just as well it was no mere mortal hanging there; we can be thankful it was the gracious Son of God from heaven, the effulgence of God's glory, the one whose very nature is Divine, whose love for sinners like you and me took Him all the way to Calvary's cross.

The Son of God came down from heaven to fulfil the purpose of the ages—to show to all creation the glorious character of God—"God is Love" and "God is Light". It was out of of love beyond human comprehension that He, the Holy One of God, entered the darkness of Golgotha. That dark, dark place where my sins and your sins and the sins of His ancient people, the Jews and the sins of this guilty world of Adam's children—were laid upon him. Why?

Why? So that God in righteousness could justify the sinner who comes to God through Jesus Christ. Sin has to be dealt with; God cannot ignore your sin. Unless you come to God on the basis of Christ's shed blood, there can be no remission of sin.

This Mighty One, this loving God, commands each one of us to repent. As children of Adam, we are inherently rebellious, proud, and selfish by nature. Our sins are an un-bearable burden. If we don't get rid of them, they will take us to a lost eternity, away from the presence of God forever. Yet God does not and will not force you to turn from your sin and come to Him. The all-powerful, divine Creator invites us in the person of His Son, in the most gracious and winsome way, to lay our burden of sin at Jesus' feet. He paid the price for your sinful condition as well as all the sins of commission and sins of omission we have committed, when He bore our sins 'in His own body on the tree', where 'God laid on Him the iniquity of us all' (Isaiah 53).

Let Him take away that burden of sin. Put your trust in the Saviour who came to bring you back to God. Have faith in Him and you'll enter the peace and calm of knowing God's forgiveness. He'll come into your heart and give you new life - 'eternal life'. With increasing joy, you'll have fellowship with God. You'll know His guidance and support throughout life's journey. He sees the end from the beginning. He created you for a purpose. Unlike you and me, He never makes mistakes.

This Mighty One speaks to you today, in the still, small voice, the sound of gentle stillness that Elijah heard when he had come to an end of himself.

Listen to the voice of Jesus: He simply says: "Come."

"Come unto me all ye that labour and are heavy laden and I will give you rest." (Matt 11:28-30)

Turn away from the confusing babble of this world and place your life in His hands. Only the One who raised the dead, who died a sin-atoning death on the cross for us, can give hope to the hopeless, strength to the weak, power to the helpless. As the old Sunday School chorus says: "Only Jesus, only Jesus, only He can do all this."

Jesus said: "I am the way, and the truth, and the life: no one comes to the Father but by me." John 14:6)

Why not bow your heart in prayer and say:

'Lord Jesus, thank you for going to the cross for me. I believe you died to be my Saviour. Please come into my heart and guide my life from this day forward. Amen.

APPENDIX II: THE HOUSE OF GOD

The garden of Eden was a place of communion, a place where God and man enjoyed unbroken friendship. Man, the creature of God's hand, had fellowship with God before sin came in and destroyed their relationship. When He cast out Adam and Eve, God placed the Cherubim East of Eden and "the flame of a sword ..." prevented access to the tree of life. Cherubim are associated with the throne of God—with the heavenly sanctuary: In Ezekiel 10:19, The Cherubim stood at the East Gate of the Lord's House.

God still longed to restore fellowship and communion with mankind. But this could only happen on God's terms because God is Holy.

Fast forward to Genesis chapter 28. Jacob left home because of Esau's anger at his 'stealing' the birthright from him. With Isaac's blessing, Jacob went to Padanaram, and lighted upon a certain place: He afterwards named it Bethel - the House of God. In the visionary dream which God gave him that night, he saw a ladder between heaven and earth on which angels were ascending and descending.

"I am the Lord…. in you and in your seed, shall all the families of the earth be blessed." (Genesis 28:14)

God revealed himself and his purposes to Jacob, who responded to the awesomeness of what he had witnessed by exclaiming: "How dreadful is this place! This is none other than the House of God and this is the gate of heaven."

Jacob needed that personal Revelation from God to enable him to continue steadfastly in the footsteps of his father Isaac and his grandfather Abraham, men of great faith. Through their descendants, God would ultimately work out His purposes of grace for all mankind. Jacob called God "The fear of Isaac" (Gen. 31:42), meaning the God whom his father worshipped and revered. The vision of the house of God, given to him by the God of his fathers, kept Jacob from straying from God's purpose for him, in contrast to Esau his brother (who was a grief of mind to his parents, Isaac and Rebecca).

My spiritual forefathers also had a vision. Ultimately, after years of trying to share it with their fellow believers, that vision caused them to separate themselves from their dear friends who remained in what we sometimes term

'Open Brethren.' The vision of the house of God, as revealed in the New Testament, was so important to them.

Under the Old Covenant, when God called Israel out of Egypt, He said:

"Let my people go that they may serve me"—God's purpose in calling them out was so that Israel could enjoy communion with God as a people. But it required close attention to God's instructions.

God said, "I bare you on Eagles Wings and brought you unto myself" (Ex.19:4)

In Exodus 28, God revealed His central purpose in this extraordinary intervention in the course of Israel's history: "Let them make me a sanctuary, that I may dwell among them." (Ex. 25:8)

God's purpose in separating them from other nations was so that He could dwell among them! So that He could have fellowship with them as a collective people, a holy nation, willing to do things HIS way.

Many years later, when Solomon dedicated the "exceeding magnifical" temple he'd built, he asked a question which has resonated down the centuries ever since, the answer to which is utterly astonishing:

"Will God in very deed dwell with men? Behold, heaven and the heaven of heavens cannot contain thee, how much less this house which I have builded!" (2 Chron. 6:18)

Solomon recognised the inadequacy of the best this earth could provide compared with the glory of the great Almighty God, maker of heaven and earth.

Yet, the astounding answer to the question—"Will God in very deed dwell with men?"—is "Yes!" Ever since Adam was banished from Eden, it has been God's desire to dwell with men on earth. His delight was with the sons of men (Proverbs 8:31) Sadly, very few reflected this desire back to God. It has been well said, 'God isn't looking for numbers, He's looking for hearts.'

Ezra and Nehemiah returned from exile in Babylon to re-build the house of God. The house of God was in ruins. God recognised their valiant endeavours, even though the rebuilt house was only a shadow of its former glory.

My spiritual forefathers came out from Open Brethren to give effect to the vision that God revealed to them about the house of God as taught by the apostles of the Lord Jesus in the New Testament. They separated themselves from those who didn't share their vision in order to re-build the spiritual house of God, according to the pattern given by God in the New Testament.

That doesn't mean God got nothing from believers in Open Brethren after the separation that took place in the 1880s, or from other believers today:

"For from the rising of the sun even unto the going down of the same my name is great among the Gentiles; and in every place incense is offered unto my name, and a pure offering: for my name is great among the Gentiles, saith The Lord of hosts." (Malachi 1:11)

But God is looking for something more from those who have caught the vision of the House of God as taught by the Lord to the Apostles after His resurrection, during the forty days He spent teaching them before His ascension from the Mount of Olives.

"ye also, as living stones, are built up a spiritual house, to be a holy priesthood, to offer up spiritual sacrifices, ac-ceptable to God through Jesus Christ." (1 Peter 2:5)

"in whom each several building, fitly framed together, groweth into a holy temple in the Lord" (Ephesians 2:21)

"God isn't looking for numbers, he's looking for hearts." He wants us to have obedient hearts, willing hearts, consecrated hearts; hearts that have seen the vision, that have heard the call of the Saviour who laid down his life for them, calling them as he called twelve ordinary men by the shores of Galilee when He was here on earth. Acting on His authority, they called both Jew and Gentile believers to join them in this unique, spiritual house:

"God is faithful, through whom ye were called into the fellowship of his Son Jesus Christ our Lord." (1 Corinthians 1:9)

God began with just two souls in the garden of Eden. Then, He revealed the truth of the house of God to one man (Jacob). Israel was a people so insignificant that they were "not reckoned among the nations", yet God put his name there and dwelt among them when they became obedient to his revealed will. Their service in the House of God, the tabernacle and later the Temple, under the Old Covenant, was conditional on their obedience. The service of God's New Covenant people in God's spiritual house is also conditional upon our obedience to the pattern revealed through the apostles.

God's Old Covenant people brought their sacrifices to the priest, who offered them to God. Those sacrifices pointed forward to the atoning sacrifice of the Lord Jesus Christ on the cross. So disciples of Christ today, who answer God's call and become obedient to the divine pattern, may also offer spiritual sacrifices to God, in thanksgiving for that great atoning work, through our Great High Priest, the Lord Jesus Christ. That's a central part of God's purpose in saving men and women from their sins.

"God is a spirit and they that worship him must worship in spirit and in truth." (John 4:24)

"For every high priest is appointed to offer both gifts and sacrifices: wherefore it is necessary that this high priest also have somewhat to offer." (Hebrews 8:3)

God is looking for nothing less than communion with a sanctified, people, who out of love for their Saviour willingly align their lives with "the faith once for all delivered to the saints"—the body of teaching which brings disciples of Christ together into a visible unity, a worshipping people gathered according to the Word of God, among whom God can dwell and with whom He and they can enjoy sweet communion week by week. The greatest privilege any believer can have this side of eternity is to prepare some precious thoughts each week and bring to God their appreciation of His beloved Son; to fill the hands of their Great High Priest as they gather in Churches of God, remembering Him each week in broken bread and poured out wine.

In aggregate, individual churches of God are "fitly framed together"—just as the curtains of the tabernacle were joined with golden clasps (Exodus 26) and the tabernacle became one.

"in whom each several building, fitly framed together, groweth into a holy temple in the Lord." (Ephesians 2:21)

"But ye are a elect race, a royal priesthood, a holy nation, a people for God's own possession, that ye may show forth the excellencies of him who called you out of darkness into his marvellous light, who in time past were no people, but now are the people of God: who had not obtained mercy, but now have obtained mercy." (1 Peter 2:9,10)

God's priority is not numbers. He's not looking for academic or intellectual brilliance, although He may use that too.

God is looking for hearts that love the things that He loves and are central to His purposes. One of those purposes is to dwell with us in His spiritual House, where we may collectively enjoy sweet communion with Him through our Lord Jesus Christ.

God plans an eternal relationship with mankind in the New Jerusalem where, "its temple is the Lord God the Almighty and the Lamb" (Rev. 21:22)

Unquestionably, God's heart is in the House of God—is yours?

∼

Want to find out more about the present day expression of God's house on earth? Visit: https://churchesofgod.info/

APPENDIX III: DAD'S NOTES ON JOHN CHAPTER SEVENTEEN

JOHN CHAPTER 17: THE GLORY OF GOD

This chapter might be described as the Lord's prayer rather than the prayer which begins "Our Father who is in Heaven...", which is better described as "the disciples' prayer". The chapter has many important truths. Prominent is the glory of God. The glory of the Lord Jesus is also the glory of God, and the glory of God is also the glory of the Lord Jesus.

Verse one opens with the awesome "Father, the hour is come". This was a time decided by the triune God in the ages of a bygone eternity, before the foundation of the world, long before the creation of Adam and Eve. It was to be a crisis event in the annals of God, an event which would result in an eternally greater glory of God than His glory as Creator of heaven and earth. The glory of God's grace would exceed His glory as Creator, a glory that would call for the spontaneous worship of the Creator by the creature not only because of His holiness, His omnipotence and not only because He is the everlasting God who was, who is and who ever shall be; but because of His amazing grace and His incomparable love, which was about to be displayed on the cross of Calvary.

"And now O Father" (v5) ... "glorify Thy Son that the Son may glorify Thee." (v1). NOW means not immediately, but as a result of His sacrifice on the cross. For millions would believe: "Jesus died for me" and the Lord Jesus would be glorified. He would be highly exalted and given the name which is above every Name, that at the Name of Jesus every knee will bow and every tongue will confess that Jesus Christ is Lord to the glory of God the Father. (Phil 2) "Glorify thy Son that the Son may glorify Thee". The following verse is epexegetic of this statement, i.e., is added as explanatory of it:

"Even as Thou authorised, or gave Him power over all flesh, that whatsoever Thou gavest Him, to them He should give eternal life."

This embraces the subject of election and reminds us of the Lord's words to the apostles (and to you and me), "You did not choose Me but I chose you"—See Romans chapter 9:10 - 23 which deals with the subject of election. There Rebecca exclaims, "Wherefore am I thus?" as the twins struggled in her womb. God answered "The elder shall serve the younger."

"Jacob I loved but Esau I hated" (Rom 9:13). Was Esau excluded from God's love? Not at all; but God chose Jacob "that the purpose of God according to election might stand" In Rebecca's question, we see the truth of the believer's two natures—the old Adam nature or the flesh which is ever ready to assert itself in unholy thoughts and deeds and the new nature which cannot sin. This struggle goes on until the Lord comes. The truth of the church the body of Christ, is also in the Lord's words and Ephesians chapter 1 shows that Christ is glorified, in that He is "Head over all things". The church the body is also the Bride, the wife of the Lamb.

"I glorified Thee on the earth having accomplished (or finished) the work which Thou gavest Me to do." (John 17:4) The finished work includes all the works of healing, all those whose sins were forgiven, all the sermons He spoke and His Sacrifice which He would make on the cross in 18 hours' time. He saw the sacrifice finished, accomplished. This is characteristic of God, who knows the end from the beginning. Other instances of God's foreknowledge are, Isaiah 53, written about 600 years before it happened, "He was wounded for our transgressions, He was bruised for our iniquities."

"Whom He (God) foreordained, them He also called, and whom He called, them He also justified and whom He justified, them He also glorified." (Rom 8:30) When we believed we were called, and justified (accounted righteous). The calling and justifying take place when we believe, but we will not be glorified until we get to heaven. But God sees it as already done! And in Revelation 21, where the new heaven and new earth are foretold, God says, "It is done" or "It is come to pass." (Rev 21:6)

"And now O Father, glorify Thou Me with Thine own self, with the glory which I had with Thee before the world was." (John 17:5) This is the glory of light unapproachable.

John Holmes Johnson, October 2008

~

APPENDIX IV: O GOD TO THEE WE RAISE OUR VOICE

O God to Thee we Raise our Voice
(Number 490 in the PHSS Hymnbook)

FOR MEALS

490 C.M.D. BETHLEHEM

Moderately fast

A - men.

O GOD, to Thee we raise our voice
    In thanks for these good things;
Thy kindness makes our heart rejoice,
    Each hour fresh token brings;
Yes, for Thy mercies every one,
    A grateful song we lift,
But chiefly for Thy blessèd Son,
    Thy richest, greatest gift.   Amen.

Doh is C

{ :s |d':d'|t :l |s :—.l |s ||s |l :r'|d':t |d':—|—||s |d':d'|t :l |s :—.l |s ||
{ :s |m :l |s :f |m :—.f |m ||s |f :l |s :s |s :—|—||s |m :s |s :f |m :—.f |m ||
{ :s |d':d'|d':d'|d':—.d'|d' ||d' |d':f'|m':r' |m':—|—||s |d':d'|d':d' |d':—.d'|d' ||
{ :s |d :d |d :d |d :—.d |d ||m |f :r |s :s |d :—|—||s |d :m |f :l |d':—.d |d ||

{ :m' |r':d'|t :l |s :—|—||s |t :s |d':s |r':s |m'||d' |f':m'|r':d'|d':—|t ||
{ :m.fe |s :l |s :fe |s :—|—||t, |r :t,|d :s |f :f |m ||m |f :s |l :l |s :—|—||
{ :s .l |t :m'|r':d'|t :—|—||s |s :s |s :d'|t :t |d'||d' |d':t |l :r' |r':—|—||
{ :d |t,:d |r :r |s :—|—||s |f :f |m :m |r :r |d ||ta,|l :s |f :fe |s :—|—||

{ :s |d':d'|t :l |s :—.l |s ||s |l :r' |d':t |d':—|—||D' |D'
{ :f |m :l |s :f |m :f |m ||m |f :l |s :f |m :—|—||F |M
{ :t |d':d'|d':d'|d':t |d' ||d' |d':f'|m':r' |d':—|—||L |S
{ :s |d :d |d :d |d :r |m ||d |f :r |s :s |d :—|—||F |D
                                                        A - men.

APPENDIX V: LET US WITH A GLADSOME MIND

Let us with a Gladsome Mind
(number 158 in the PHSS hymnbook)

158 7.7.7.7. MONKLAND

Moderate

1.

LET us with a gladsome mind
Praise the Lord, for He is kind;
For His mercies aye endure,
Ever faithful, ever sure.

2.

He, with all commanding might,
Filled the formless earth with light;
For His mercies aye endure,
Ever faithful, ever sure.

3.

All things living He doth feed,
His full hand supplies their need;
For His mercies aye endure,
Ever faithful, ever sure.

4.

He hath with a piteous eye
Looked upon our misèry;
For His mercies aye endure,
Ever faithful, ever sure.

Doh is C

d :m	s :m	f.s :l .t	d' :—	m' :m'	r :d'	t :l	s :—
d :d	r :d	d :f	m :—	s :s	s :s	s :fe	s :—
m :l	t :s	l :f	s :—	d' :d'	t :d'	r' :—.d'	t :—
d :l,	s, :d	f :r	d :—	d.r:m .f	s :m	r :r	s, :—

r' :r'.d'	t :s	d' :m'	r' :—	m' :r'.d'	t :d'	d' :t	d' :—
s :r	r :s	s :s	s :—	s :s	s :s	s :r	m :—
t :l	s :t	d' :d'	l :—	d' :t .d'	r' :d'	r' :s	s :—
s :fe	s :s .f	m :d	s :—	d :r .m	f :m	s :s,	d :—

APPENDIX VI: ELLEN JEAN BAIRNSON'S POETRY

CANA
They were feasting with their comrades,
Tasting pleasures one by one,
But they knew not One among them,
Was their Saviour, God's own Son.

And like all of earth that charms us,
As the rose by garden wall,
When the flower is full and fragrant,
Soon the petals shrink and fall.

So like all of earthly pleasure,
Soon their vessels empty stand,
But there's One alone can help them,
If they will do His command.

See them bring their vessels to Him,
Fill with water clear and fine,
Look to Christ now in amazement,
Lo! the water turns to wine.

Oh how joyful now they taste it,
Tis the best they ever had,
Sweeter far than any other,
Now they're satisfied and glad.

CAN YOU BY FAITH?
Can you see the Saviour hanging,
Bleeding on the cruel tree?
Can you think that all He suffered,
Was in truth for you and me?

Can you think that all He suffered,
Was for you and me?

Can you see Him pale and helpless
Loving hands His form take down?
Can you see them gently lifting
Off that blood stained thorny crown?

Can you think it was for me,
All He suffered silently?

Can you see Him cold and lifeless,
Yielding three dark days to death?
Can you, can you, see him rising,
Draw that first renewing breath?

Can you think it was for me,
He arose triumphantly?

Can you see Him soon descending,
Coming through the starry skies,
Hear the trump of God resounding,
As His own in clouds arise?

Can you think He'll come for me?
Yes, He paid the debt, I'm free.

All His own are quietly waiting,
No man knows the day nor hour,
We shall meet the glorious Bridegroom.
In His own, His risen, power.

Can you think what will it be,
On that day for you and me?

LITTLE FLOWERS
We are little flowers a-growing,
In God's garden here below,
Sometimes pushed aside too harshly
That some showy weed may grow.

We may be like little daisies,
Lowly place below be given,
But when fresh by rain or sunshine,
Lift our little eyes to heaven.

Little flowers like stars a-shining,
Growing fresh amid the dew,
Showing back a ray of sunshine,
Something His in every hue.

Now while little hearts are tender,
Teach us Jesus love to know,
Let us hear of how He blessed us,
When He trod this earth below.

May the Heavenly Father tend us,
Keep us sweet and true and kind,

Helping other ones around us,
Something see of Jesus mind.

[These three poems were extracted from a booklet of poems, entitled "In Praise of The Saviour", by Ellen Jean Bairnson, (1903–1975) of Brakes, Dunrossness, Shetland.]

NOTES

Preface

1. **Brethren/brothers and sisters:** following the custom of the Apostles in the New Testament scriptures, baptised believers in Churches of God refer to each other as brothers and sisters 'in Christ' or 'the Lord'. As saved persons, we are 'children of God', we belong to God's family.

1. Earliest Memories

1. **Translation:** "No-one will be able to say you died of hunger!"
2. **Rector:** The old school name for the Head Master or Head Teacher.

2. Greenock Academy Primary

1. **The 'new' Greenock Academy building:** was demolished in 2015 after several years being used as the film set for the BBC TV programme, 'Waterloo Road'.
2. **'The Belt':** Until 1986 it was common practice in schools for teachers to belt pupils. Corporal punishment was abolished in State schools in 1986.

5. Bentinck Street, Octavia Terrace, Battery Park

1. **Close:** the name given to the communal stairway in a tenement building.
2. **Embassy Regals':** A common brand of cigarettes

8. Halloween and Guy Fawkes Night

1. **Panda Cars:** This was the informal nickname name for the police patrol cars used in Britain during the 1960s. They were so called because the first versions were painted black and white.

13. Dad

1. **Saved:** the term used in evangelical Christian circles, to denote the moment an individual places their personal trust in Jesus Christ for salvation, and has thereby "passed from death into life" (John 5:24)
2. **'The Remembrance'** is the meeting of every Church of God on the first day of each week, when we gather to carry out the request made by the Lord Jesus in the upper room in Jerusalem on the night of His betrayal. First He gave thanks for a loaf of bread and gave it to them saying 'This is my body which is given for you.' Then He gave thanks for a cup of wine, poured it out and gave it to them saying, 'This is the new covenant in my blood, this do in remembrance of me.'

14. Mum

1. **PHSS hymnbook**: PHSS = Psalms, Hymns and Spiritual Songs
2. Grandad's mother: The maiden name of Peter Christison and his siblings, was Jane Dodds.
3. **Saints:** the Greek word translated 'saints' in the New Testament simply means people who have been 'sanctified' or set apart from the rest of the world for the service and worship of God. The original meaning of the word did not confer some special aura of holiness or spiritual privilege in the sense that it has come to be understood by, for example, the Roman Catholic Church, where it is applied to an elite group of people who have died and who are deemed 'holy' enough for people to pray to. This is a completely unscriptural doctrine. We use the term as it was originally used, i.e., to describe the body of people whose names are on the roll of a local Church of God.
4. **Overseer:** The word overseer first occurs in Acts 20, where Paul addresses the elders of the church. Some translations give 'bishops' as an alternative translation. Their primary function is to exercise shepherd care for the local church and to 'feed' them from the Word of God.

15. Friends, Neighbours, Childhood Pranks

1. **'Poke':** the torn off corner of a paper bag.

17. Cedar Hall

1. **Meeting place of the Church:** Contrary to the mistaken idea that the bricks and mortar building is the church, the clear teaching of scripture is that the church (Greek word *ekklesia*) is the collective gathering of people in any locality, on the roll of the Church of God in that place. The building is simply the place where the body of people called the church meets.
2. **The Lord's Day:** This is the name used by the New Testament writers and was the widely used alternative for the first day of the week (Sunday). Saints in the Churches of God along with many other fellow Christians referred to it as such. For example, 'The Lord's Day' was commonly used by Free Church members in the Western Isles and elsewhere.

19. Sunday School and Church Meetings

1. **Have you got the sunshine smile?** Interestingly, when my sister Elisabeth worked at Ardgowan Primary School, she discovered they had a school song called 'have you got the Ardgowan smile?' Elisabeth thinks that a former Greenock Sunday school girl who became a Primary teacher (Carol Reid), may have introduced it when she worked there.

20. Auchenfoyle Camp

1. **Mealtime Camp Hymns:** See the Appendix for the music scores for each of the hymns we sang before and after meals at Camp.

24. Holidays in Scotland

1. **The old book:** *'Sutherland and the Reay Country'* by Rev. Adam Gunn M.A. and John Mackay, published in 1897)

25. More Holiday Memories

1. **Midge, midgie, midges:** The notorious Scottish midge is a tiny flying insect, which is prevalent from late spring to late summer. Female midges typically gather in clouds on warm summer evenings. Their bite is felt as a sharp prick and is extremely irritating, because many of them usually land on any area of exposed skin and bite at the same time.

26. Teenage Years

1. **Sarking:** Long wooden panels, or "sarking boards", nailed on top of the timber roof trusses to provide support for slates or roof tiles. Slates are nailed directly to the sarking boards.

32. Duncan of Jordanstone College of Art

1. **Stovies:** A Scottish dish based on potatoes, usually containing onions and pieces of meat. The potatoes are cooked by slow stewing in a closed pot with fat (lard, beef dripping or butter).

36. Summer Job, Dundee

1. **Loons Road:** The word 'loon' means 'a boy', in the old Scots dialect known as 'the Doric', still spoken in Aberdeenshire.
2. **Swan Vesta:** "Swan Vestas" were a brand of matches that came in boxes of wooden matches for lighting the fire, or in little paper books of thin card matches which you tore off and struck against the abrasive paper part of the 'book', to ignite the phosphorous tip.

37. Adventures in London

1. **'The Fellowship':** this term is widely used throughout the churches of God, to describe the collective body of all the churches. It originally derives from Acts 2:41 & 42, where it means the common bond of social cohesion we share with each other as a Christian community of churches, locally and internationally.

44. From Glasgow to Fife

1. **Scripture reference:** Lamentations 3:27

45. Fife to Dundee

1. **A pithy Scots way of saying:** "the only pleasant thing about Fife is the highway which leads away from it."

46. Kingspark School

1. **forming, storming, norming, and performing:** DEVELOPMENTAL SEQUENCE IN SMALL GROUPS, by B W TUCKMAN, Psychological Bulletin June 1965, p 384-99.

53. The Future Foretold

1. **Freedom march photographs:** Bloggers and journalists who recorded this event, included Simon Elmer for 'ASH' (Architects for Social Housing) and John Goss for the 'Off-Guardian' website.
2. **The Finger of Prophecy:** Available on Amazon or online from Hayes Press. The prophetic chart book which I published jointly with Neville Coomer is also on Amazon and gives a graphic overview of these events. It's a useful aid in piecing together the prophetic timeline revealed in the Word of God.

ACKNOWLEDGMENTS

I owe an unrepayable debt of gratitude to my parents for the great start they gave me in every department of life.

I'm extremely grateful to my dear wife Norma, without whose support and constructive criticism I could not have completed this book.

My brother James supplied several memories which I'd completely forgotten, and my sister Elisabeth did a sterling job of proofreading the manuscript for this book.

Eric Archibald graciously provided his recollections of the legendary poetic duo he forged with Charles Early at Auchenfoyle Camp.

Thanks to James Hunter, columnist and motoring correspondent with The Greenock Telegraph, for generously printing an appeal in 'The 'Tele' for the P1 class photo, which I had lost. In the event, my former classmate Robin Grant kindly emailed me a digital image of his copy.

Greenock photographer, Kenny Ramsay, gave permission for me to use his photograph of the logo on the Greenock Academy school gates in chapter 2.

ABOUT THE AUTHOR

Jo lives in Fife, Scotland, half an hour's drive from St Andrews. With his wife Norma, he divides his time between church, family, writing, tending his allotment and painting.

CATCH UP WITH JO'S LATEST BOOK: jojohnson.uk

SEND JO AN EMAIL: jo@jojohnson.uk

OTHER STUFF: https://sleek.bio/jojohnson

f facebook.com/JoRosebinePress

a amazon.com/author/jojohnson

instagram.com/jojohnsonart